Vietnamese Voices

Northern Illinois University
Monograph Series on Southeast Asia Number 6

Series Editor
Peter Ross

Editorial Assistants
Mishel Filisha
Christopher A. Miller

Other works in this Series

Killing a Buffalo for the Ancestors: A Zhuang
Cosmological Text from Southwest China
(Number 5)
David Holm

The Money Trail: Burmese Currencies in Crisis, 1937-1947
(Number 4)
Marilyn Longmuir

Cambodia Emerges from the Past: Eight Essays
(Number 3)
Judy Ledgerwood, Editor

Southeast Asia: Crossroads of the World
(Number 2)
Clark D. Neher

The Burmese Harp: Its Classical Music, Tunings, and
Modes (Number 1)
Muriel C. Williamson

Vietnamese Voices

Gender and Cultural Identity in the Vietnamese Francophone Novel

Nathalie Huynh Chau Nguyen

Southeast Asia Publications
Center for Southeast Asian Studies
Northern Illinois University
DeKalb, Illinois

Southeast Asia Publications, Center for Southeast Asian Studies
Northern Illinois University, DeKalb IL 60115

Cover art credit: "Young Girl" by Ngoc Dung reproduced from *Nghe
Thuat Viet Nam Hien Dai* [Vietnamese Contemporary Art] ©1962 Saigon:
My Thuat Hoc Vu, Bo Quoc Gia Giao Duc [Directorate of Fine Arts,
Department of National Education]. Reproduction by permission of
Mrs. Ngoc Dung.

Part of Chapter One appeared in "A Classical Heroine and Her Modern
Manifestation: *The Tale of Kieu* and its Modern Parallels in *Printemps
inachevé*" by Nathalie Nguyen. Copyright *The French Review,* 73:3 (2000)
pp. 454-62. Reprinted here by permission.

A shorter version of Chapter Two appeared as "Across Colonial Borders:
Patriarchal Constraints and Vietnamese Women in the Novels of Ly
Thu Ho" in Jane Bradley Winston and Leakthina Chau-Pech Ollier,
eds. (2001) *Of Vietnam: Identities in Dialogue* (New York: Palgrave), pp.
193-210. Reprinted here by permission.

Printed and Bound by Publishers' Graphics, LLC

Library of Congress Cataloging-in-Publication Data

Nguyen, Nathalie Huynh Chau
  Vietnamese voices : gender and cultural identity in the Vietnamese
francophone novel / Nathalie Huynh Chau Nguyen.— 1st ed.
      p. cm. — (Monograph series on Southeast Asia ; no. 6)
  Includes bibliographical references and index.
  ISBN 1-891134-26-4
  1. Vietnamese fiction (French)—History and criticism. 2. Sex role in
literature. 3. National characteristics, Vietnamese, in literature. 4.
Colonies in Literature. 5. Nguyen Du, 1765-1820. The Tale of Kieu—
Criticism and Interpretation. 6. Postcolonialism.
  I. Title. II. Series.
PQ3977.V5 N48 2003
843.009'358—dc21
                                    2003010280

For my parents, brothers, and sister

Contents

Preface and Acknowledgements

Vietnamese Francophone literature is a field demanding increasing recognition and exposure. Rapidly growing postgraduate enrollments in relevant courses; panels at a host of recent conferences including those of the Modern Language Association and the *Conseil International d'Etudes Francophones* (International Council of Francophone Studies); and the first International Conference on Indochinese Francophone Literature in Seattle, May 1999, are among the indicators. As part of a wider resurgence of interest in Indochina and its colonial past which has sparked a vivid re-examination of the work of Marguerite Duras—her 1984 novel *L'Amant* (The Lover) won the prestigious Goncourt Prize[1]—such an environment of lively, scholarly interest provides an ideal setting for the publication of this book.

The situation has changed greatly since completing my studies at Oxford eight years ago. In 1994, the number of dissertations on Vietnamese Francophone literature could be counted on one hand and the only book in the field was Jack A. Yeager's pioneering work, *The Vietnamese Novel in French: A Literary Response to Colonialism*, published by the University Press of New England in 1987 and winner of the University of New Hampshire Book Prize.[2] With comprehensive archival information, and a detailed bibliography, Yeager charts the history of this literature and examines salient themes of cultural confrontation, socio-political reality, and women characters. *The Vietnamese Novel in French* provides a valuable introduction to the entire field, yet serves, as Yeager notes, "as a point of departure for further study."[3]

Slower to recognize the significance of this field, France recently saw the publication of two anthologies: *Littératures francophones d'Asie et du Pacifique* (Francophone Literatures of Asia and the Pacific), by Editions Nathan in 1997; and a substantial volume entitled *Littératures de la péninsule indochinoise* (Literatures of the Indochinese Peninsula) by Editions Karthala in 1999, part of the collection *Universités francophones* (Francophone Universities).[4] The first provides a brief introduction to the literature of each country in the Asia-Pacific region, with biographical information on selected writers and excerpts of their works. The second contains short essays on historical and literary contexts and extracts from Indochinese works spanning a period of 140 years. These publications represent a first step towards mapping and analyzing a literature that France had until then, rather surprisingly, neglected; yet, the most vigorous work continues to take place in North America.

With relatively few works published on the subject to date, then, Vietnamese Francophone literature is a growing field of research, in an area wide open for discussion. The purpose of this book is to provide an effective, original analysis of the Vietnamese Francophone novel and thereby contribute to a deeper, broader appreciation of this newly recognized field. Here, unless otherwise acknowledged, all translations are my own. Since Vietnamese Francophone writers did not use tonal marks on Vietnamese names and terms in their novels, in the interests of verisimilitude and consistency none have been added in this book.[5]

I have many people to thank for arriving at this point. In Oxford, my thanks go to Toby Garfitt of Magdalen College for his patient guidance as a supervisor and his continued interest in my work; to Jennifer Bars, Mary Childs, Rosemary Littlehales, and Julia Briggs; to the Librarian and Staff of the Taylor Institution Library; and to the Director and Staff of the Maison Française d'Oxford. Alison Finch, now of Merton College, Oxford, and Emma Wilson, now of Corpus Christi College, Cambridge, provided insightful comments on my completed dissertation.

In France, I would like to thank my aunt and uncle, Josette and Yves Caussiol, for providing me with a Parisian home on numerous occasions while I carried out research at the Bibliothèque Nationale. Similar thanks go to my great-uncle and great-aunt, Pierre and Simone Thuan, for hosting me in their sixteenth-century house in Arles and for arranging lodgings in Aix-en-Provence while I did a month of research at the Archives d'Outre-Mer. My great-uncle did not live to see the publication of this book, but expressed great pride in my dissertation.

From the first, my meetings with other specialists in Vietnamese Francophone literature have been tremendously enriching. Seattle in 1999 was the first time that I met Jack Yeager, keynote speaker for our first international conference, and a most generous and supportive scholar. I am indebted to him for signaling my work to others and for inviting me to take part, in May 2002, in a double panel on Francophone Asia at the *Conseil International*'s 16th World Congress in Abidjan, Côte d'Ivoire, West Africa where my work was tested before an international audience of Francophone academics and authors. Along the way, Jane Bradley Winston of Northwestern University and Leakthina Chau-Pech Ollier, formerly of Bowdoin College, invited me to contribute to their edited volume *Of Vietnam: Identities in Dialogue*, published by Palgrave in December 2001. *Of Vietnam* allowed me to share in a collected contribution of academics, creative writers, poets, and artists, with "Vietnam" as our common "discursive tableau."[6]

It has been a long journey to convert my original dissertation into book form. In addition to editing and revision, all original French quotations had to be translated into English. In Adelaide, I wish to thank all those who helped me towards the first revised draft in 1998: Vesna Drapac, who told me to "do something" about my book; Katharine Thornton and Michael Lim; Vivien and Brian Greaves, Eva Sallis; Katharine Massam; and Alan Keig of the Barr Smith Library. My thanks also go to Rosemary Greentree.

At Northern Illinois University's Southeast Asia Publications, Edwin Zehner solicited the manuscript, coordinated the peer-review process, and gave detailed comments and suggestions. I am indebted to John C. Schafer of Humboldt State University and Christina Faulk, who have permitted the release of their names as reviewers, as well as to those who remain anonymous. Lisa Wilcox provided a positive and decisive endorsement of the project and gave prompt responses to any queries; Peter Ross assisted in preparing the final manuscript for publication.

Jack Yeager, John Schafer, and Jane Winston kindly agreed to read a final draft of the manuscript. My brother Peter similarly gave a careful reading. I am indebted to Mrs. Ngoc Dung for permission to use Ngoc Dung's 1962 oil painting "Thieu Nu" (Young Girl) for the cover and to Nguyen Ngoc Bich for putting me in touch with her. Friends and relatives in Australia, France, England, and the United States gave their support. Finally, for their loving encouragement and for providing a welcoming home in Melbourne during the Australian summer of 2001/2002, and subsequent semester breaks so that I could work on revising my book, I wish to thank my parents. My father found the cover illustration for this book. He and my mother made helpful suggestions regarding the direction of my work. This is for them, and for my brothers and sister, with much affection.

Nathalie Huynh Chau Nguyen
2003

Introduction

A grain of sand contains all land and sea.
—Zen proverb

Vietnamese Francophone literature is born of two worlds. It illustrates a meeting of East and West; it embodies the interaction of two vastly different cultures and societies. It is, as the proverb says, a grain of sand containing all land and sea. Arising as it did out of eighty years of French colonization in Indochina—a period stretching from the second half of the nineteenth century to the middle of the twentieth—much Vietnamese Francophone literature chronicles the dilemma of writers who were educated within a colonial system they saw disintegrate and disappear. Their novels reveal conflicts of interest, identity, and language. Their work encompasses the encounter of two literary traditions, an encounter that was, moreover, subject to the particular stresses of colonialism. Much of the beauty which surfaces in the images and prose of these novels draws its inspiration from Vietnam and Vietnamese literature, but it is a beauty interlaced with considerable pain. These works deal with the private anguish of individuals caught not only between two cultures and loyalties, but in the grip of a collapsing system of traditional mores, and a country undergoing rapid political and social change.

The majority of Vietnamese Francophone novels were written by men and most were published in Paris in a literary output that peaked in the 1950s and 1960s. These novels vary considerably in style, subject matter, and setting. Many are set in Vietnam during or after the colonial period, whether in an urban or rural environment, while others are set in France, China or Japan. One distinguishing feature that recurs throughout these works is the writers' evocation of alienation from the Vietnamese "mother-culture." Whether through the prism of gender, cultural allegiance, or interracial relationships, the novels examined here all deal with this issue. The colonial and post-colonial worlds that shaped these works and gave voice to the stories of their Vietnamese protagonists also engendered a profound malaise that manifests itself in different ways. The sense of feeling displaced even within one's own culture appears to be a particular product of the colonial experience.[1]

None of these novels contains easy answers. Rather, they reveal "the complex, shifting inheritance of the post-colonial."[2] In *Phantasmatic Indochina*, Panivong Norindr suggests that "'Indochine' is an elaborate fiction, a modern phantasmatic assemblage invented during the heyday of French colonial hegemony in Southeast Asia. It is a myth that has never existed and yet endures in our collective imaginary."[3] Vietnamese Francophone writers expose the reverse side of this coin, expressing the suppressed voices of colonial and post-colonial Vietnamese subjects whose experience stems from within the reality of colonial Indochina. The nature of their insights and the dual heritage they reveal are enriching and enlightening. Their works illustrate the enmeshing of cultures, the encounter of old and new. They display a consciousness that seeks to respond to the vast cultural and literary differences between East and West.

The Impact of French Colonization on Vietnamese Literature

The arrival of the French in Indochina in the late nineteenth century had a significant impact on Vietnamese literature. The French encountered in Vietnam a civilization far older than their own.[4] One thousand years of Chinese rule, from the second century B.C. to the tenth century A.D., had imbued Vietnam with the political, philosophical and literary norms of classical East Asian civilization. Vietnamese literature prized poetry and its "highest and most original manifestation" was the verse romance or *truyen nom*.[5] Texts were written either in Chinese characters or in *chu nom*, the Vietnamese demotic script based on Chinese characters. Literature was considered a moral vehicle and therefore laid great emphasis on the traditional Confucian values of filial piety, conjugal fidelity, loyalty, and honesty: "Required was a complicated plot based on the same general scheme: the hero or heroine, forced to undergo misfortune after misfortune, finds happiness in the end because of a solid moral character."[6]

Vietnamese literature took a radical turn at the beginning of the twentieth century, as the writings of eighteenth-century French philosophers became available and French novels were translated into Vietnamese.[7] This period saw the "introduction and adoption of new literary genres, such as the essay, the short story, the prose novel, and journalism."[8] Journalism first took root in the South of the country, as this was the first region to come under the direct control of the French in 1862.[9] In 1883, Central and North Vietnam became French protectorates and Vietnam was divided into three administrative regions: Tonkin in the North, Annam in the Center, and Cochinchina in the South.[10] It was in Cochinchina that the Vietnamese prose novel first emerged with the appearance of Ho Bieu Chanh's *Ai Lam Duoc* (Who Can Do It) in 1912.[11]

John Schafer and The Uyen relate that the Vietnamese novel "was as much a product of indigenous development in the Sino-Vietnamese tradition as it was the result of Western influence."[12] The new genre developed gradually in the South, with a number of transitional works bridging the gap between the traditional verse narrative and the modern prose novel. The emergence of the novel in the North, however, arrived with "little advance warning" and entailed "a violent disruption of traditional values."[13] Hoang Ngoc Phach's *To Tam* (To Tam being the name of the heroine) was published in Hanoi in 1925 and became a cause célèbre.[14] Its emphasis on individual happiness and its questioning of Confucian morality was both shocking and fascinating to readers accustomed to the traditional belief that the desires of the individual must take second place to the needs of the group. One of the first Vietnamese to have a Francophone novel published was Nguyen Phan Long, a journalist and editor of *L'Echo Annamite* (The Annamite Echo).[15] His novel *Le Roman de Mademoiselle Lys* (Miss Lily's Story) appeared in Hanoi in 1921.[16]

The early decades of the twentieth century were periods of great social change, characterized by an ongoing struggle between "Ancient" and "Modern," between the Confucianists who resisted change and those who wanted Vietnam to modernize and become more Western-oriented. On the political front in 1930, a year that would prove decisive for Vietnamese history and literature, there were several failed uprisings. The revolt of the Yen Bay garrison in February and the bloody repression that followed were symptomatic of the wider failure of nationalist political revolts. The Indochinese Communist Party, later to play such a critical role in internal politics, was founded by Ho Chi Minh. In literature, a new generation of writers and intellectuals shaped by French cultural influences and fired by liberal ideas opted to "wage literary war against what it considered the decrepit institutions of traditional Vietnamese society."[17] The *Tu Luc Van Doan* (Self Reliance Literary Movement), founded in Hanoi in 1933, chose to adopt a clear, concise style and avoid complicated Chinese literary terms and allusions to the classics.[18] Writers dealt with the conflict between the old and the new and questioned the Confucian values of filial piety and adherence to order and hierarchy. Middle-class youth of the period chafed against the constraints of traditional morality and marriage practices. While the scholar class in the past had trained solely to serve in the public service as mandarins, educated people were now working as professional lawyers, doctors, pharmacists, engineers, and journalists. Educational and career opportunities also opened to women. The 1930s signaled change: although the French retained a firm hold on power, the Vietnamese had shown their willingness to stand up and oppose the colonial regime by force. Vietnamese literature urged rebellion against the past and, indirectly, against those in authority, and was instrumental in the movement for social reform.

In concert with these changes, the twentieth century saw the use of Chinese characters and of *chu nom* gradually disappear. *Quoc ngu*, the romanized form of the Vietnamese language, came into use. The examinations for the mandarinate, installed in the country since the eleventh century, had entailed a thorough knowledge of the Chinese classics as well as versifying talents.[19] Candidates were required to write commentaries on the Confucian classics, draft a series of administrative documents, compose poetry and literary essays, and submit a dissertation on a chosen topic. The competition for the doctorate was held once every three years in the capital and only one percent of candidates were successful.[20] These examinations were abolished in 1918.[21]

Writers such as the prominent scholar and educator Pham Quynh (1892–1945) and Nguyen Tien Lang (1909–1976) advocated the use of *quoc ngu* on a national basis. *Quoc ngu* itself had originally been devised in the seventeenth century by Spanish and French missionaries (in particular, the Jesuit Alexandre de Rhodes) to facilitate evangelization. It received a significant boost from the short-lived but influential *Dong Kinh Nghia Thuc* (Dong Kinh Free School) movement, founded by moderates in Hanoi in 1907.[22] The advantage of *quoc ngu* lay in its providing a means to literacy which by-passed the compulsory study of Chinese language and literature and was, in the process, considerably easier to teach and to learn. As a romanized script, the flexibility of *quoc ngu* lay in the ease with which European words and technical terms could be transferred thus providing a vehicle more receptive to the modern world. *Quoc ngu* provided a practical means with which to diffuse literature, news, and political tracts.

The system of education installed by the French allowed a restricted number of Vietnamese students to gain access to French education. Most of these students were from the middle and upper classes and an increasing number of them were sent to do further studies in France. In the late 1920s, the Vietnamese student population in Paris consisted largely of young men from wealthy Southern families.[23] At the *Cité Universitaire* (University City), the *Maison d'Indochine* (Indochina House) was created in 1928 and still exists today.[24] The French-language University of Hanoi was founded under the governorship of Paul Beau in 1907, shut down in 1908 following student unrest, and reopened in 1917. The establishment of the university led Beau's detractors to declare that "an educated native no longer simply meant 'one coolie less' but one rebel more."[25] A policy of assimilation therefore had rather different results from those originally intended. It was said that "the bitterest opponents of the French were the ones who knew the language best."[26] It was inevitable that students should contrast the high minded ideals of Western democracy with their own position as colonial subjects.

Vietnamese Francophone Literature

The earliest Vietnamese Francophone literary texts were a collection of poetry, Nguyen Van Xiem's *Mes Heures perdues* (My Lost Hours), and a collection of tales, Le Van Phat's *Contes et légendes du pays d'Annam* (Tales and Legends from the country of Annam), both published in 1913.[27] A diverse body of material, including novels, novellas, and plays, as well as collections of poetry, short stories, and Vietnamese tales, proceeded to emerge over the following decades. The period between the two world wars saw a significant literary output. Many writers—Pham Quynh, Nguyen Tien Lang, and Pham Duy Khiem—were from the north of the country which had historically enjoyed a stronger intellectual tradition.[28] This situation was to change in later years.

The Second World War, during which Vietnam was under both French and Japanese occupation, culminated in 1945 in the August Revolution, the abdication of the last Nguyen emperor Bao Dai, Ho Chi Minh's Declaration of Independence, and the establishment of the Democratic Republic of Vietnam. The following year marked the start of the Indochina War in which France attempted to restore its control of the country. This ended in 1954 with the defeat of the French at Dien Bien Phu and their withdrawal from Vietnam. Vietnamese Francophone writing peaked in the 1950s and 1960s, in the period immediately following the collapse of French Indochina in 1954.

After Vietnam was partitioned, into two separate states north and south of the seventeenth parallel under the 1954 Geneva Agreement, the number of French teachers in the North declined sharply. Only nine French teachers were left by 1962 while French *lycées* flourished in the South.[29] Francophone literature, however, gradually diminished in the South due to the growing influence of America and the increased use of English. Francophone books and periodicals that did appear in the South were produced solely through the efforts of private individuals and groups and without government assistance. Conversely in the communist North, the production of publications in French was maintained—principally as a means of political propaganda.[30]

Many Vietnamese Francophone writers settled in France during the 1930s and the post-war years.[31] There, perhaps, they felt they could enjoy a greater freedom with which to express themselves or see with clearer eyes away from the polemics and conflicts of their homeland. Thuong Vuong-Riddick writes of exiled writer Pham Van Ky: "Like Joyce, Beckett, Ionesco, and so many others, it is overseas and in exile that he will have to deepen his allegiance and his roots."[32] Lebanese Francophone writer Evelyne Accad notes: "Writing in exile can open horizons, new as yet uncharted pathways. It helps to endure exile. And conversely, exile and the shock created by the clash of different cultures, the pain of separation, the desire to return, sustain the breath of writing."[33] As for those in Vietnam who wrote in French, they may have been motivated by the fact that "colonial legislation showed more tolerance for works in a language whose action, if it was harmful, had its limits."[34]

Vietnamese writers wrote in French for a number of reasons. Pham Duy Khiem likened his writing in French to the use of classical Chinese by Vietnamese scholars for two millennia.[35] As a Vietnamese using French, he felt he was asserting his independence in the same way his ancestors did when they used Chinese. Writers were also aware of the regional limitations of their indigenous language and wanted to broadcast their ideas further afield. Expressing themselves in the language of the colonizer was a means of reaching the French public and through them a wider audience internationally. Nguyen Tien Lang passionately justified his use of French as a writer as ". . . a desire impossible to curb, which resembles love."[36] Vuong-Riddick summarizes in the clearest terms the dilemma confronting Vietnamese Francophone writers: "A symbol of servitude and yet a revolutionary tool, French enjoys an ambiguous status which explains in part the tragedy experienced by Vietnamese Francophone writers."[37] The tangled values and loyalties of these writers are evident in their works: in the subjects, themes, and styles of their novels. To fully grasp these, one must understand the particular pressures experienced by these writers.

Vietnamese Francophone writers are, in Jack Yeager's words, "caught in a literary and cultural anomaly," their works representing "a literature of contradiction and irresolution, one challenging French colonial authority; [and] . . . thus implicitly political."[38] This book sets out to examine the contradictory impulses articulated in the novels of both male and female writers by addressing two central questions: How do these works deal with the post-colonial concerns of place and displacement, self-image, and identity? And, how does the treatment of these concerns differ in the works of male and female writers?

The imprint of classical Vietnamese literature on these modern novels is the first subject of inquiry. Chapter One analyzes the use that individual Vietnamese Francophone writers have made of a highly influential Vietnamese verse classic, *The Tale of Kieu*, as a means with which to interpret the condition of women in Vietnam. Since the main character of the nineteenth-century tale, Kieu, is female, the rewriting of her trials and tribulations within a twentieth-century setting sheds light on modern preoccupations with identity and gender. Four Vietnamese Francophone novels use Kieu's story to interpret the situation of Vietnamese women in the 1930s, 1940s, and beyond: Trinh Thuc Oanh's and Marguerite Triaire's *En s'écartant des ancêtres* (In Distancing Oneself from the Ancestors) (1939), Tran Van Tung's *Bach-Yên ou la fille au cœur fidèle* (Bach-Yên or The Girl with the Faithful Heart) (1946), Ly Thu Ho's *Printemps inachevé* (Unfinished Spring) (1962), and Kim Lefèvre's *Retour à la saison des pluies* (Return to the Rainy Season) (1990).

The exploration of female characters continues in Chapter Two, which examines the work of the writer Ly Thu Ho. Ly explores the constraints experienced by Vietnamese women through war and change in twentieth-century Vietnam. The only Vietnamese woman to write and publish Francophone novels in Paris from the 1960s through to the 1980s, her treatment of the female condition reflects both the changing situation in post-colonial Vietnam and her own exposure to Western cultural and literary movements. She accomplishes this critique through the circumscribed and stifled lives of her middle-class female protagonists in three loosely linked novels that cover the 1930s through to the 1970s: *Printemps inachevé* (Unfinished Spring) (1962), *Au Milieu du carrefour* (In the Middle of the Crossroads) (1969), and *Le Mirage de la paix* (The Mirage of Peace) (1986). Ly reserves the harshest fate for those who most conform to the traditional feminine ideal. Three categories of women appear in slightly altered forms in all three novels: the mother figure prototype (whether mother, grandmother, or nanny), the virtuous daughter or wife, and the prostitute. A fourth category, the servant, is introduced in the last novel.

Following this analysis of female characterization by a woman writer, Chapter Three presents, in contrast, a portrayal of female characters by a male Vietnamese Francophone writer, the most prominent of the 1950s and 1960s. Pham Van Ky's exploration of the female condition differs vastly from Ly Thu Ho's. His early novel *Frères de sang* (Blood Brothers) (1947) contains a violent denunciation of the situation of women in traditional Vietnamese village culture. The later work *Des Femmes assises çà et là* (Women Sitting Here and There) (1964) examines four women who surround the figure of the expatriate male narrator in France; three are French women while the fourth is the haunting figure of his mother in Vietnam. In each of these works, the narrator retains a constant distance from these female figures and remains an outsider to these women's lives.

A sense of cultural alienation in the Vietnamese male protagonist is explored further in Chaper Four in the depiction of erotic relationships between Vietnamese men and French women during the colonial period. Two novels, *Bà-Dâm* (Madam the French woman) (1930) by Truong Dinh Tri and Albert de Teneuille, and *Nam et Sylvie* (Nam and Sylvie) (1957) by Pham Duy Khiem, relate the failure of cross-cultural relationships within a colonial context, in France and Vietnam in the 1920s, and in Paris in the 1930s. Each authors' treatment differs. While the sense of the alien and the strange is underlined in *Bà-Dâm* both by the physical and cultural differences between the protagonists and by the exotic setting of Indochina, this exotica is nearly wholly missing in the post-colonial

Nam et Sylvie, which bears few physical descriptions, and where the differences between the protagonists are minimized. The prejudices and pressures of colonial society contribute nonetheless to the failure of the relationships in each novel.

Four novels, each dramatically charting their male protagonists' gradual alienation from their milieu and culture, form the focus of the last two chapters. In Chapter Five, Nguyen Huu Chau's *Les Reflets de nos jours* (The Reflections of our Days) (1955) and Pham Duy Khiem's *La Place d'un homme: De Hanoï à La Courtine* (A Man's Place: From Hanoi to La Courtine) (1958) reveal a major crisis of identity on the part of the Vietnamese narrator. Both novels appeared in the period immediately following the end of French Indochina and were published in Paris. Both are first-person narratives and convey a sense of immediacy and urgency to the sentiments portrayed. Both present themselves as autobiographical novels since they are purportedly the journals of men who had died in combat. In each case, death provides an end to an unresolved conflict of identity. Chapter Six explores two novels that deal specifically with male protagonists who, on returning to Vietnam from France, find themselves aliens in their own land and, in that most emblematic of Vietnamese social units, their native village. In Pham Van Ky's *Frères de sang* (Blood Brothers) (1947) and Cung Giu Nguyen's *Le Fils de la baleine* (The Whale's Son) (1956), the village, instead of a familiar and welcoming environment, becomes a place of nightmarish and claustrophobic strangeness. Each protagonist discovers that he is a perpetual outsider: a stranger in France, and a stranger at home.

Vietnamese Francophone novels conjure up uncomfortable images and memories of France's colonial past, a phase of history that ended in the crushing French defeat at Dien Bien Phu in 1954. As the later war in Vietnam received massive coverage, the French colonial stage became history, or more pertinently, *un trou de mémoire*—a memory lapse. Yet the effects of this meeting of two cultures live on, in the people and in their literature. In their depiction of alienation, these writers mirror an experience that we can all recognize. In Julia Kristeva's words:

Strangely, the foreigner lives within us: he is the hidden face of our identity, the space that wrecks our abode, the time in which understanding and affinity founder. By recognizing him within ourselves, we are spared detesting him in himself.[39]

Vietnamese Francophone novels expose a complex intermingling of cultures and literatures. In doing so, they reveal both the particular inheritance of the French colonial enterprise in Indochina and the dual awareness of the writers shaped by this encounter.

Francophone *Kieu*

Kieu said: "When one who shines in talent dies,
the body passes on, the soul remains."
—Nguyen Du

The Tale of Kieu is recognized as Vietnamese literature's greatest classic. Composed by the poet Nguyen Du in the early nineteenth century, the *Tale's* main character, Kieu, sacrifices her virtue to save her father and subsequently undergoes trials, forced servitude, and prostitution, before finally being reunited with her first love. In a tribute to its influential place in Vietnamese literature, four Vietnamese Francophone novels draw heavily on the *Tale*. These novels reveal that the dilemmas confronting women remain essentially unchanged, despite the impact of colonization and modernization. Classical themes of fateful beauty and conflict between duty and desire—with its resulting suffering—appear interwoven in all four contexts. At the same time, the novels exhibit a change in values with allusions to the *Tale* highlighting contemporary issues of marital choice, marital roles, and the folly of placing hope of self-fulfillment in marital relationships. Whether the modern female protagonists in these works submit or attempt to rebel, their lives are blighted and tarnished by their struggles. None achieves Kieu's contentment and serenity.

The four novels, *En s'écartant des ancêtres* (In Distancing Oneself from the Ancestors), *Bach-Yên ou la fille au cœur fidèle* (Bach-Yên or the Girl with the Faithful Heart), *Printemps inachevé* (Unfinished Spring) and *Retour à la saison des pluies* (Return to the Rainy Season), are set in Vietnam and with one exception take place in the 1930s and 1940s. *En s'écartant des ancêtres* was written by the female team of Trinh Thuc Oanh and Marguerite Triaire and was published in Hanoi in 1939. *Bach-Yên ou la fille au cœur fidèle*, by the male author Tran Van Tung, was published in Paris in 1946. *Printemps inachevé*, by the female author Ly Thu Ho, was published in Paris in 1962. *Retour à la saison des pluies*, by the half-Vietnamese, half-French female author Kim Lefèvre, was published in Paris in 1990. These novels not only explore women's position in Vietnamese society during the colonial period but also comment on Kieu as a female model. We will examine the *Tale of Kieu* and discuss the key features that emerge in these four works.

The Tale of Kieu

The Tale of Kieu straddles both scholarship and popular culture. As a mark of learning, many Vietnamese have committed its 1,627 couplets to memory and can recite it by heart. As a symbol—of love betrayed and ultimately redeemed, conflicting loyalties, alienation, and fluctuating fortune—Kieu stands out as a character of universal and enduring appeal, a vulnerable individual with whom those most acutely affected by change and misfortune can readily identify. For generations of Vietnamese who have experienced years of turmoil, changing regimes, colonization, post-colonization, war and exile, Kieu's troubles strike a deep emotional chord. While scholars have debated the poem's meaning and symbolism, ordinary people have recognized their own travails in the fate of its central character. Some have called it "the mirror of the Vietnamese soul."[1]

The *Tale* is rich in allusions to Chinese and Vietnamese classical literature and philosophy.[2] In penning the poem, scholar and East Asian classicist Nguyen Du (1765–1820) not only displayed considerable erudition but also superimposed his country's own vernacular and indigenous traditions on an earlier Chinese heritage. Originally entitled "New Plaint of a Broken Heart" (*Doan truong tan thanh*), the poem is known in modern times as "The Tale of Kim, Van and Kieu" (*Truyen Kim-Van-Kieu*), "The Tale of Kieu" (*Truyen Kieu*), or simply *Kieu*. Nguyen Du culled the plot for his poem from an obscure Ch'ing Dynasty prose novel, "The Tale of Chin, Yün and Ch'iao" (*Chin Yün Ch'iao*) set in Ming Dynasty China (1368–1644). The *luc-bat* or "six-eight" verse form which he used to rewrite the Chinese novel is easily recited and commonly used in Vietnamese folk poetry.[3] The *Tale* is held to be the highest form of *truyen nom* or "tale in the Southern script," a long narrative verse form that grew out of a combination of Chinese classical influences and Vietnamese folk traditions. It is, therefore, a distinctly Vietnamese work in the most distinctive genre in Vietnamese classical literature.[4] The language of the *Tale* displays a consummate sensitivity to Vietnamese rhythm, tone, sound, and image,[5] the beauty of which, coupled with its romantic content, has played a significant part in ensuring its enduring popularity among Vietnamese.

The *Tale* is set during the reign of the Chinese Emperor Chia-Ching (1522–1566) of the Ming Dynasty, at a time of peace and prosperity. Descended from a line of scholars, the Vuong family has a modest fortune. Eldest daughter Kieu, beautiful, chaste, obedient, and loyal to her family, is the ideal of Confucian womanhood. Kieu is also intelligent and talented, a gifted poet, musician, and artist, and her younger sister Van similarly virtuous and lovely. Life seems idyllic for these two young women until, in an early premonition of her sad fate, Kieu is particularly affected by the story of a courtesan who dies young and whose tomb is now neglected and forgotten; Kieu reflects that the life of beautiful women is full of vicissitudes. The courtesan then appears to her in a dream informing her that she too is doomed to lead an unhappy life. It is her karma. Kieu finds this so disturbing that even her mother's sensible and consoling words fail to bring comfort.

Soon enough, the courtesan's prophecy comes true. Despite Kieu's blossoming romance with a young scholar Kim, misfortune strikes. Kim is called away because of the sudden death of his uncle and laments having to leave so soon after having met. Before his departure, the two are secretly engaged; Kieu insists, against his wishes, that their relationship remain unconsummated until their marriage. While he is away, the Vuong family's life unexpectedly turns into a nightmare. Kieu's father is unjustly accused of dishonesty and threatened with debtors' prison. Bailiffs go on a rampage, looting the family home. In order to ransom her father, Kieu feels compelled to sell herself into marriage to a stranger, Ma Giam Sinh, sacrificing not only herself, but her love for Kim. She implores her sister Van to honor her engagement to Kim in her stead. She feels that she has betrayed him and bitterly regrets not giving him her virginity.

Kieu leaves her home and mourns the loss of her dreams. It turns out that her situation is even worse than anticipated: the man she married has actually bought her for the owner of a brothel. After an initial suicide attempt, Kieu works for an extended period as a prostitute. She is briefly redeemed as the second wife of a scholar, Thuc Sinh, but this happiness is cut short when she is sold into servitude by the latter's jealous first wife. Seeking refuge in a pagoda, she befriends a nun, before a combination of unfortunate circumstances lead her back into prostitution. Her fortunes take another turn when she is again redeemed and marries, enjoying five years of contentment as the wife of the rebel leader Tu Hai. Yet happiness is once again transient: the hero Tu is killed in battle and she is taken to be the wife of a dignitary.

These circumstances lead Kieu to attempt to drown herself in a nearby river, but she is rescued by the nun she had befriended years earlier. The nun informs her that she has finally expiated the faults of a previous life and after fifteen years of trials and tribulations, her wanderings come to an end. Reunited with her family, at long last, Kieu marries Kim. Yet she does not emerge entirely unscathed. Feeling shamed and sullied by her experiences and unworthy to be a true wife to him, she abjures him to keep their union platonic. Rather than living as man and wife, they will live as friends. Her sister Van will bear Kim's children in her place, hence the poem's title the *Kim-Van-Kieu* following the three main characters.

The existence of such a triangle was not unusual in traditional society where polygamy was accepted, neither was it unusual to have two sisters marry the same man.[6] The arrangement proves successful. Kieu, Kim, and Van all lead contented lives and the *Tale* ends on a felicitous note. Despite their significance for Kieu, Kim, and Van, both play a minor role in the narrative as it is first and foremost the story of Kieu's moral pilgrimage. And though Kieu is finally rewarded with reunion to her one lifelong love after years of misery and degradation, her happiness is qualified.

Like much East Asian literature, Kieu's story can be interpreted as a political allegory.[7] As a scholar, Nguyen Du lived through some turbulent times and changes of dynasty. His lifetime encompassed the fall of the Le Dynasty in 1788, the division of the country under the rule of the Trinh in the North and that of the Nguyen in the South, the Tay Son rebellion (1788–1802), and the establishment of the Nguyen Dynasty under which the country was reunified in 1802. As a mandarin who owed his first allegiance to the Le Dynasty, but eventually worked for the Nguyen Dynasty, he had to deal with conflicting loyalties generated by these various changes. Kieu's story reflects the difficult choices and regrets of his own political life.[8] In recounting a tale set several centuries before in another country, Nguyen Du was also doing what many of his predecessors had done, literature being a conduit for sedition in late traditional Vietnam.[9] Huynh Sanh Thong comments that "beyond its literal meaning, Kieu's prostitution is interpreted as a metaphor for the betrayal of principles under duress, the submission to force of circumstance."[10] As a woman and a victim, Kieu is ideally positioned to embody and symbolize these concepts.

In choosing a woman as the central character of his poem, Nguyen Du was following an established tradition in Vietnam—an apparent propensity among male writers to let female protagonists illustrate and embody the great tragedies and triumphs of life. This issue has not yet been the subject of critical attention. Perhaps, it was more acceptable for a woman than a man to voice personal anguish. The use of a woman protagonist might also have provided, superficially at least, a distancing device to protect a male author from direct accusations of sedition and subversion. However, further insight can be gained from understanding the situation of women in Vietnamese history.

Although Vietnam underwent ten centuries of Chinese domination (from 111 B.C. to A.D. 939), it has always had a more liberal approach to women than China. There were both male and female army leaders during the short-lived rebellion of the Trung sisters against their Chinese overlords in the first century A.D.[11] Footbinding was never practiced in Vietnam.[12] Until the fifteenth century, women were on a par with men in matters of inheritance and marriage.[13] The Code of the Le Dynasty (1428–1788) was far more liberal towards women than the parallel Chinese Codes of the Ming and Ch'ing Dynasties. Women enjoyed a greater degree of protection under criminal law provisions and were entitled to significant property interests that had to be respected by their spouse's family.[14]

Although these rights suffered a setback with the promulgation of the Nguyen Code in the nineteenth century, the relative liberalism of the Le Code continued to influence mores into the twentieth century up to and including the status of women in contemporary Vietnamese law. At the same time, despite this legacy, the tenets of Confucianism—emphasis on male dominance, male heirs, and a woman's observance of The Three Submissions and Four Virtues[15]— were accepted and internalized by Vietnamese society, as reflected in the *Tale of Kieu*. It is perhaps this very conflict of the subordinated position of Vietnamese women in relation to men at the behest of Confucianist tenets that offered writers an analogous situation to the subordinated position of Vietnamese society in relation to Chinese imperial domination. Of all female figures in Vietnamese literature employed by male writers to focus on woman's role in society in this way, it is the nineteenth-century figure of Kieu that provides the most striking example of this.

The *Tale* had its detractors as well as admirers. Nguyen Du, David Marr sums up, "created a scholarly storm for over a century with, among other things, his revisionist interpretation of chastity."[16] For traditional Confucianists, it was clearly unacceptable for a female protagonist to undergo a series of sexual relations with different men. The male scholar Nguyen Cong Tru writes:

From Ma Giam Sinh to Tu Hai
Faded flower sold and resold to pleasure houses
Where is one to trace that famous filial piety
In this shameless commerce of bees and butterflies?[17]

Even though the reason for Kieu's loss of chastity is her filial piety, there is no offsetting the shame of that loss—a view in which Nguyen Cong Tru was not alone.[18] But, Marr continues:

> Nonetheless, the basic tenets of female passivity, of a daughter's piety toward her parents, of fidelity to one's mate were upheld and perhaps even enhanced by the tremendous popularity of this work.[19]

While the *Tale*'s merits were debated by intellectuals, it was embraced by the general public, who saw it as a romance, a book of divination, and a moral fable. Over time, it was made widely available through recitations and cheap printings and became required reading in schools, often used as a collection of maxims, since it covered most of life's eventualities. As Jean Chesneaux and Georges Boudarel observe, "In world literature, there are without doubt few such clear instances of the presence of a great work of the past in the public consciousness of a people, such as the obsession constantly manifested by the Vietnamese towards *Kieu* for a century and a half."[20]

The *Tale* was a particular subject of political controversy through the 1920s and 1930s when arguments erupted between Confucianists, Nationalists, and Marxists over the poem's merits or otherwise. This furor first arose in 1919 when, in his journal *Nam Phong* (Southern Wind), the scholar Pham Quynh endorsed the *Tale* as *quoc hon* (the national soul) and *quoc tuy* (the national essence).[21] "[A]s long as *The Tale of Kieu* lasts," wrote Pham, "our language will last; as long as our language lasts, our country will last."[22] This endorsement politicized the *Tale* in that Pham Quynh was closely identified with the French, having served as Minister of National Education and Interior Minister. As a result, many pro-independence scholars denounced his endorsement.

Although the four Vietnamese Francophone novels discussed here are either wholly or partly set in this period, it is notable that none refer to these political controversies. Instead, it appears the novelists eschewed doctrinal interpretations of the *Tale*, preferring rather to focus on its literary merits and status as the famous work of a great poet. This is a view that has prevailed over time. Although Pham Quynh was executed by the Vietminh in 1942 and the French left Indochina in 1954, the *Tale* has endured beyond the politics of the period and continues to be acknowledged as a masterpiece of Vietnamese literature. Moreover, Kieu continues to be interpreted as a national symbol, a metaphor for Vietnam and its people.

Jacques Baruch notes that there have been seven French translations of the *Kim-Van-Kieu*.[23] Early French translators of the *Tale* were challenged by its complex literary allusions, references, and turns of phrase and felt obliged to provide voluminous explanatory notes to accompany the poem. Abel des Michels was the first of these in 1884.

> In addition to metaphors remarkable for their depth and precision, one has to acknowledge, to be fair, that there are a great many others that are so ambivalent that, without a detailed description, it would be impossible to make them understood by a reader unfamiliar with the language of poetry particular to the Far East.[24]

Detailed notes in Nguyen Van Vinh's 1952 translation include a secondary word-by-word translation with added footnotes.[25] While poetry is notoriously difficult to translate, layers of Chinese and Vietnamese language, culture, and philosophy have clearly increased the burden for these translators. What appears to have been accepted as the definitive French version, a prose translation by Xuan-Phuc and Xuan-Viet, was first published in 1961 in the Gallimard-Unesco *Série vietnamienne* (Vietnamese Series). Xuan-Phuc and Xuan-Viet give no explanation as to why they chose a prose over a verse translation of the poem. Perhaps a prose translation was not only easier to produce but would be more accessible to the French public.

Several key elements of the *Tale* are echoed or adapted in the novels of the Vietnamese Francophone writers we will examine. The first is the beauty and talent of the central female protagonist. From the outset, Nguyen Du establishes a contrast between the quiet charm of Van, the younger sister, and the devastating beauty of Kieu. His use of simile is drawn from classical Chinese literature:

> In quiet grace, Van was beyond compare:
> her face a moon, her eyebrows two full curves;
> her smile a flower, her voice the song of jade;
> her hair the sheen of clouds, her skin white snow.
> Yet Kieu possessed a keener, deeper charm,
> surpassing Van in talents and in looks.
> Her eyes were autumn streams, her brows spring hills.
> Flowers grudged her glamour, willows her fresh hue.
> A glance or two from her, and kingdoms rocked![26]

Kieu is also blessed with talent. "Supreme in looks, she had few peers in gifts/ By Heaven blessed with wit, she knew all skills" (3). Her exceptional looks and wit are evident even in her youth. Nguyen Du writes that she is at the age of pinning up her hair, which in traditional China referred to girls who had reached the age of fifteen.[27]

Beauty and talent are paired with a second element, misfortune. The opening lines of the *Tale* frame this pairing.

> A hundred years—in this life span on earth
> Talent and destiny are apt to feud . . .
> Is it so strange that losses balance gains?
> Blue Heaven's wont to strike a rose from spite. (3)

The Chinese adage that "losses balance gains" implies nothing is perfect and that great gifts have to be paid for by suffering.

A third thematic element drawn on by Vietnamese Francophone writers is the aborted romance between a beautiful girl and a talented scholar, a trope that recurs in one form or another in all four novels. The "beautiful girl and talented scholar" motif has a long history in Chinese literature. It was a feature of Yüan drama (1234–1368) and was prevalent in Chinese novels and plays from the thirteenth century onwards.[28] Talent was traditionally assigned to men, and beauty to women,[29] and Kieu and Kim's love at first sight beckons with this theme: "Beautiful girl and talented young man— /what stirred their hearts their hearts still dared not say" (11). Although betrothed, their love never comes to full fruition. Kieu bemoans Kim's premature departure:

> Why does he hate us so who spins silk threads?
> Before we're joined in joy we part in grief.
> Together we did swear a sacred oath:
> my hair shall gray and wither, not my love. (31)

True to their oath, Kieu and Kim maintain their love for each other through the years of separation that follow.

A fourth element is the female protagonist's strong sense of filial piety. In this, the *Tale* displays the Confucianist philosophy of abiding by family hierarchy and respecting parents and elders. The poem stresses Kieu's clear obligations as a daughter and the overwhelming precedency of these obligations.

> As you must weigh and choose between your love
> and filial duty, which will turn the scale?
> She put aside all vows of love and troth—
> a child first pays the debts of birth and care.
> Resolved on what to do, she said: "Hands off—
> I'll sell myself and Father I'll redeem." (33)

In carrying out this act of filial piety, Kieu as the female protagonist not only sacrifices her love but exchanges her hopes for the life she could have led as a young woman, engaged to a scholar of good family, for a sentence of years of loneliness and unhappiness. Her decision implies that where a woman has a conflict between duty, that is "correct behavior," and desire—of the heart and longing for happiness—she should choose the former.

The fifth element borrowed into Vietnamese Francophone novels is the female protagonist's stress on maintaining her virginity. When Kim is tempted to take untold liberties with Kieu during one of their private trysts, she resists, even though they are already pledged to each other.

> Treat not out love as just a game —
> please stay away from me and let me speak.
> But you've named me your bride — to serve her man
> She must place chastity above all else. (27)

Later, Kieu bitterly regrets her insistence on maintaining her chastity. After being sold to Ma Giam Sinh, she grieves:

> If only I had known I'd sink so low
> I should have let my true love pluck my bud.
> When we're to meet again, what will be left
> of my poor body here to give much hope? (43)

Inseparable from the issue of woman's honor and self-worth, the issue of virginity resurfaces at the end of the *Tale* in the sense of shame and defilement felt by Kieu on her reunion with Kim after her years of prostitution. Kim's reminders of the higher virtue to which she has remained faithful—"True daughter, you upheld a woman's role:/ what dust or dirt could ever sully you?" (161)—fail to sway her. On their wedding night, she reveals:

> What can this cast-off body be good for? . . .
> When you make love and I feel only shame . . . (163)

In speaking repeatedly of her shame, she refers to herself as "a fallen flower," a "wilting flower," a "faded flower," and a "soiled body," and insists on maintaining only a platonic relationship with him. Only after obtaining his reluctant agreement is there some release: "My honor lives again as of tonight" (163). But ultimately, Kieu is trapped by the rules of patriarchy: while embodying female selflessness, she is punished at her marriage bed for her lack of chastity. Though her troubles result from carrying out her filial duty, she is still denied complete self-expression as a result of her transgression.

The sixth element is the issue of fate. The *Tale* illustrates the Buddhist doctrine of karma, or cause and effect, combined with the popular belief in Heaven's will. Every act has consequences and the good or bad deeds of one life play themselves out in the next. In the *Tale*, Kieu must repay the debts of a previous life to break the cycle of suffering.

> [I]n human fortune, Heaven takes a hand.
> If she . . . left her debt unpaid,
> she'd pay with interest in some future life. (53)

This notion of karma left undone recurs throughout the *Tale* as Kieu struggles through adversity, unable to die until her destiny is fulfilled—"A karma of dire woe still weighs on her—/with debts unpaid, how can she die as yet?" (89). Only when the balance is paid in full will she finally find happiness. This element of fatalism in the *Tale* is an aspect that Marxist critics have quarreled over with its implied passive resignation to one's circumstances and reluctance to actively bring about change.[30] From a literary perspective, the motif of pre-ordained fate is a convenient device with which to explain the misfortunes that mark Kieu's life.

Four modern Vietnamese Francophone novels use these key elements to provide an illustration of the condition of women in Vietnam in the 1930s, 1940s, and beyond. In each work, beauty is equated with an unhappy fate, and the woman or women concerned must make a difficult choice between duty and desire. While those who choose duty over desire, like Kieu, have their lives marred and diminished, those who choose to follow their desire not only lose their virtue but suffer much worse punishment. But what differentiates the modern female character from the classical heroine in an overall sense is that her fate is even darker. The modern works therefore paint a harsher picture of social life for women in Vietnam.

En s'écartant des ancêtres (In Distancing Oneself from the Ancestors) is set in Tonkin in the 1920s and 1930s and deals with the lives and fates of three young Vietnamese women from Hanoi's middle class—Mai, the central character, and her friends, Gaby and Dân. All three are caught at a juncture between tradition and modernity. Each, mirroring an aspect of Kieu's story, has her early hopes and dreams blighted in one form or another. The authors, Trinh Thuc Oanh and Marguerite Triaire, use the *Tale of Kieu* to help explain the difficult choices facing the female characters as they attempt to balance the demands of duty with their own desires.

Bach-Yên ou la fille au cœur fidèle (Bach-Yên or the Girl with the Faithful Heart) is set in Tonkin in the 1930s and deals with the tragic love story of Van, a young man from the scholar-gentry, and Bach-Yên, a young woman from a Catholic mercantile family. When Van buckles to family pressure and marries the daughter of a mandarin, Bach-Yên commits suicide. Tran Van Tung uses the *Tale of Kieu* to illustrate the conduct of the entire romance and to highlight Bach-Yên's fate, which despite her faithfulness, is far more tragic than Kieu's.

Printemps inachevé (Unfinished Spring) exhibits significant parallels with the *Tale*. Set in South Vietnam from the 1930s to the 1950s, it relates the story of a beautiful young woman named Tran and her failed romance with a scholar, Châu, from whom she, like Kieu, is separated. Tran experiences trauma—in the form of rape—and hardship, but unlike Kieu, she rejects the possibility of being reunited with her fiancé and dies. Ly Thu Ho rewrites Kieu's story within a twentieth-century setting to comment on modern preoccupations with gender and identity. Her novel criticizes the weight of virtue and honor on the lives of women.

The last of these works, Kim Lefèvre's *Retour à la saison des pluies* (Return to the Rainy Season), is an autobiographical novel detailing the return of the writer and narrator, a Eurasian woman, to Vietnam after an absence of thirty years. In this book, it is the narrator's mother who seeks solace in Kieu's story as a means of explaining the tragedies in her own life, in particular those that she experienced during her youth in Tonkin in the 1930s.

Love and Duty in *Ancêtres*

En s'écartant des ancêtres (In Distancing Oneself from the Ancestors) begins with the childhood and upbringing of the novel's main character, Mai. From the beginning, her capabilities are portentously portrayed as unfeminine. At birth, her father predicts, "[T]his little one will have character like a man; this girl's body houses a masculine spirit." Later, he reiterates, "Did I not say that this little one would have the spirit of a boy in a girl's body?" Even Mai herself determines: "I will dress myself like a boy: I will put on a pair of white trousers and a black tunic and no one will know that I am a girl."[31]

Mai is an intelligent child who yearns to be educated. Like Kieu, she is extremely gifted and consequently will suffer the penalty. In a period when educational opportunities were opening to women, her father sees no harm in letting his daughter learn to read and write and later go to college. Her mother, however, opines that "it is contrary to custom that this little one receive the instruction that is reserved for men" (35). In such a context, "it was the unusual woman indeed who acquired any formal education and came to be respected for her intelligence and initiative."[32] Mai's mother conforms to the conventions of the time—mothers, after all, were held responsible for the socialization of children. Fathers and paternal ancestors, on the other hand, gained credit for the scholarly accomplishments of sons and the approval by in-laws of daughters.[33]

Mai's enthusiasm for her studies and her ambitions for a medical career are assumed to be masculine qualities.[34] Her courage and intelligence are also deemed to be manly attributes. She takes the place of a son in her father's heart, but her mother cannot understand her literate, inquisitive daughter, who fails to conform to a proper womanly mould. Mai is a dutiful enough daughter, however, to refuse the advances of Hùng, a student she loves, when her parents have already arranged a match for her. While Hùng speaks openly of his love for her, she reminds him she is already engaged—to a man whom she has never met—and defends her decision to obey her parents:

- It's not only Corneille's characters who struggle against
their heart. Kieu, the famous heroine of Nguyen Du,
sacrificed her love to filial piety.
- She judged that sacrifice necessary to save her father,
retorted Hùng. But no fatal circumstance forces us to
sacrifice ours; only a ridiculous convention, indeed a local
one. (42)

Protagonists of the seventeenth-century French playwright Corneille
struggle between love and concepts of honor. Like them, and like
Kieu, Mai chooses duty over the desires of her heart. Hùng attempts
in vain to make her see her scruples are needless. Unlike Kieu, she
does not need to sacrifice herself to save her father; she is only
agreeing to this arranged marriage in a conventional effort to please
her parents. But Mai has judged it her filial duty to obey her parents
in this respect. Warning that she will regret her decision, this lost
opportunity for love and freedom, Hùng recites from the *Tale.*

Kieu, with a heavy heart, suffers a thousand torments.
Sad, she dreams and follows thoughtfully with her eyes
The small boats of the old port, at the evening hour
Like wings spreading their great sails. (130 – 1)

In the passage from which Hùng quotes, Kieu is a prostitute far
from home and dreaming wistfully of escape. The sails on the boats
are as fleeting as her dreams; likewise Mai's transitory, potential
relationship with Hùng. When he leaves on a scholarship to finish
his medical studies in France, he offers to take her with him. Though
she agonizes over the decision, she eventually declines, choosing
filial obedience once again. A lecture from her father, whom she
loves deeply, on the intrinsic worth of duty stiffens her resolution:

Towards the end of our life, our only wealth is not to merit
the censure of either our parents or our ancestors: all the rest
is unimportant and the mad ones who pursue their own

satisfaction without any regard for the great rules drawn up by those who possessed wisdom find themselves with empty hands. They have sacrificed, for a selfish and transitory happiness, a delusion, they have sacrificed the true joy, that of accomplishing their duty. (183)

Yet Mai, though she resists the urge to follow him, feels that her joy resides in Hùng. "Hùng! All her love, all her hopes of happiness, all her youth! A mad surge, a surge from her whole soul lifted her towards him. Nevertheless she would not leave" (184).

Mai later realizes that she should have trusted her own feelings. Her dreams of young love, discovery, and escape remain as fleeting as Kieu's sails. Denied even a small measure of "selfish happiness" in her marriage, her husband abandons her while pregnant with their third child, even after she makes a humiliating attempt to win him back. After their divorce, her only consolations are her work and her children, though she is luckier than the majority of women in her generation in having an interesting and challenging career as a doctor. Left to regret not only the lost opportunity for happiness with Hùng but the possibility of living and studying abroad, the conflict between desire and duty she experiences resembles that of the protagonists of Vietnamese novels of the time. Hoang Ngoc Phac's *To Tam* "shocked readers because [the author] allows his characters to dream about individual happiness based on romantic love in a society still dominated by a morality that placed the well-being of the group, especially the family, above that of the individual."[35] This situation is reflected in all three female protagonists in *Ancêtres*.

Mai's friends, Gaby and Dân choose differently. Gaby, the only daughter of a wealthy man, is indulged by her father and leads the life of an emancipated young woman free to determine with whom she keeps company. Allowed to choose her own husband, she makes what she thinks is a love match, only later to discover that her husband has married her for money. Deeply hurt and disillusioned, her marriage becomes a purely superficial arrangement while she entertains a succession of lovers and gradually turns towards opium. While Mai uses divorce to escape her marriage, Gaby refuses to contemplate this option out of respect for her mother's feelings. Trapped too by filial duty, she confides in Mai: "My mother has begged me not to divorce; she is too distressed for me to impose this added sorrow on her" (282).

Dân, having witnessed her friends' disappointments, gives up any hope of romantic happiness and opts for a safe, sober contract with a mandarin, a widower many years her senior. Her choice of the traditional path suggests resignation. She does not love her husband, yet she dutifully bears his children and goes to extraordinary lengths in her effort to fit into a delineated female role, even to wearing turbans and lacquering her teeth in traditional black. Conscious that her choice precludes any great happiness, she finds it preferable in that it obviates disappointment or heartbreak.

As women with dreams that went beyond traditional marriage expectations, all three suffer disappointment. Mai's father reflects, "You suffer because you have progressive views; another, in your place, would consider herself happy. I let you become emancipated, perhaps it is contrary to happiness" (381). Women had traditionally accepted their lot, their happiness or unhappiness being dependent on their husbands. Hopes for a marriage in which a woman would remain in control of her own life and career were still premature. Despite such obstacles, Mai, Gaby, and Dân attempt to carve their own paths. Rather than passively following the path of women before them and embracing, as they see it, the resignation exemplified by their mothers, these three young women attempt to "distance themselves from their ancestors," as the title of the novel suggests, and to shape their own futures. In some ways they succeed; looking back, Gaby weighs their choices—"Is it better to have known our slightly mad dreams, our brief joys, our bitter disappointments? Is the half-sleep of our mothers better?" (431).

Each of the female protagonists illustrates a different aspect of Kieu's story, yet unlike Kieu, none finds happiness or fulfillment. Mai has Kieu's intelligence and talent, the need to atone for these advantages, and strong sense of filial piety reflected in her desire to carry out her parents' plans for an arranged marriage. The weight of duty and tradition is sufficient to stifle her emotional freedom and inhibit her better judgment on loving whom she pleases. Like Kieu, Mai sacrifices her true love in acquiescing to her filial duty. While the results are far less dramatic than for Kieu, Mai bears her punishment in the social and emotional failure of her marriage.

Gaby shares with Kieu the experience of a series of sexual relationships. While for Kieu these relationships bring some relief, none of Gaby's numerous affairs succeed in filling the emotional gap in her life. Bound mid-point by filial duty in acquiescing to her mother's wish not to divorce, she is permanently and tragically trapped in an empty marriage. Thus whether attempting to fulfill her own desires or submit to duty, happiness remains illusive.

Dân, the most subdued of the three, exemplifies the price of conforming. Saddest and most colorless of the three characters, she is, like Kieu, resigned to her fate. While Kieu is rewarded with an ultimate reunion with her love, in return for her dutiful behavior, Dân receives nothing. Simply being a woman is enough to lead to misfortune.

All three women are disappointed in their lives because they are disappointed in their marriages. Despite changing mores and different expectations, despite a colonial situation depicted as conversely opening up educational and career opportunities to Vietnamese women, the condition of women still bears an underlying similarity with that of the society portrayed in the *Tale*. Women's happiness and fulfillment are still linked to their marital status and to the success or failure of their marriage.

Romance and Tragedy in *Bach-Yên*

Although Tran Van Tung's *Bach-Yên ou la fille au cœur fidèle* (Bach-Yên or the Girl with the Faithful Heart) appeared in the year following the August Revolution of 1945, the novel contains no references to the dramatic events of the time. Rather, *Bach-Yên* focuses on the story of a romance between a beautiful young woman and a scholar, much like Kieu and Kim, except that Bach-Yên and Van are from different social classes and both families disapprove of the match. Van finally submits to his filial duty as a promise to his

dying father and marries Hông, a mandarin's daughter. Upon
learning the news, Bach-Yên commits suicide. Such a plot echoes
that of many romantic novels and short stories which appeared in
Vietnam in the 1920s and 1930s: two young people, ill-fated in love,
are forced apart by social restrictions and ultimately either die or
turn to religion. Following the 1925 publication of Hoang Ngoc
Phac's noted romance *To Tam*, "girls disappointed in love
succumbed to the influence of the work and committed suicide by
jumping into Lake Tay or Lake Truc Bach."[36]

In spite of this dramatic twist, *Bach-Yên* is nonetheless a more
stringent critique of social mores than the earlier *En s'écartant des
ancêtres*. The hero Van joins a revolutionary group and the two
young lovers discuss female emancipation and freedom to
determine one's fate. Bach-Yên's suicide after Van's contracted
marriage becomes a symbol for the oppression and coercion of the
young and weak by family, society, and the ancient concepts of filial
duty and obedience. The political implications of Bach-Yên's
suicide—the ultimate message of rebellion and powerlessness—are
absorbed by a large number of young men and women who follow
her funeral procession. The scene is reminiscent of the 1920s and
1930s in China when revolutionaries including Mao enthusiastically
seized on dramatic cases of female suicide, usually just prior to a
forced marriage, to illustrate the destructive effect of patriarchal
authority.[37] Van and Bach-Yên's tragic romance also bears
similarities with the ill-fated love in Hoang Ngoc Phac's novel in
which the male protagonist also agrees to an arranged marriage and
the female protagonist, *To Tam* or "Pure Heart," dies of a broken
heart.[38] Here, Bach-Yên is "The Girl with the Faithful Heart."

Bach-Yên is perhaps partly autobiographical, the author's career
and experiences in some respects paralleling that of his protagonist
Van. Tran Van Tung rebelled against his classical education and an
arranged marriage and left Vietnam for France in the 1930s.[39] His
scholastic heritage is apparent in the significant use of classical
poetry and poetic prose in the novel. This is a unique feature among
Vietnamese Francophone novels, the majority of which are prose
narratives. The distinctive style is reminiscent of *pien wen*, a literary

form that evolved in Han Dynasty China (206 B.C.–A.D. 220) and combined "straight narration with rhymed verses, descriptive prose and allegories."[40]

Tran Van Tung may have rebelled against his Confucian education and upbringing but he is very much a product of a classical literary culture in which the verse romance facilitated display of a writer's erudition through numerous literary and historical allusions. The style in turn harks back to Han poetry, noted for its arcane words and obscure references.[41] *Bach-Yên* is strewn with expressions like "the pink silk thread," "thoughts of Wind and Moon," "the celestial herdsman and weaver," and "the Lake of the Restored Sword," each carrying with it the expectation of studied familiarity with great works of Vietnamese literature (*Lament of a Soldier's Wife, Lament of a Royal Concubine, The Tale of Kieu*) and a legacy of Vietnamese folk literature through which to interpret them. From a stylistic point of view, the work is stilted, the poetry and the prose ornate and exotic, the vocabulary mannered and fanciful. It exemplifies the difficulty of conveying classical Eastern literary conventions through a Western medium. At the same time that it bears such a clear imprint of this literary past, however, in resorting to classical allegory to transmit a modern message of rebellion, *Bach-Yên* subverts these literary traditions and undermines all they represent.

The entire courtship in *Bach-Yên* is articulated largely through the medium of poetry and while conducting their romance, Tran Van Tung has his protagonists quote liberally from the *Tale*. The prose itself is already lyrical and gives a dreamlike setting to Van's first meeting with Bach-Yên as he expresses his admiration for her.

> In a rapturous voice, he spoke the lines of the great poet Nguyen Du:
> *Her face is round like the moon, the lines of her spirit sing*
>   *harmony,*
> *Her lips open perfumed like flower petals, her words are as rare*
>   *and precious as jade,*

The clouds are less beautiful than her hair, snow less white than
*   her divine skin . . .*
Her look undulates like waves in autumn, her brows evoke the
*   beauty of forests in spring;*
The flowers are jealous to see themselves less radiant than she, the
*   willows are sad not to have her ideal freshness,*
Her enchanting smiles overwhelm kingdoms and overthrow
*   citadels,*
Her beauty is unique, her talent incomparable![42]

These stanzas refer to both Kieu and her sister Van. In quoting them, the young man endows Bach-Yên not only with the quieter beauty of the younger sister, but with the more poignant and devastating charm of Kieu. Bach-Yên similarly resorts to poetry, framing the possible outcomes of their relationship through numerous classical allusions.

There did not exist a handsomer couple than Thoi and Truong
But the "Clouds and Rain" had overturned the "Golden stone."
And by dint of embracing each other, "Swallow" ended up by
*   getting tired of "the Oriole." (82)*

While comparing herself and Van to an ideally-matched classical couple, Thoi and Truong, Bach-Yên sounds a warning that, despite their perfect pairing, once sexual relations ("Clouds and Rain") were over (and virginity taken—overturning the "Golden stone"), the restless hero ("Swallow") wearied of his closely held heroine (the brightly colored "Oriole").[43] Later, in trying to persuade Bach-Yên to make love with him, Van counters her argument, again with references to Kieu.

Listen, Bach-Yên, to these plaints of Kieu, when, far from her
beloved, she lost her virginity:
Angels' ornament, between vulgar hands, alas, I am fallen!
I regret having defended myself at such length against the rain and
*   wind of my beloved's desires.*

If only I had sensed my present degeneration beforehand?
O my beloved, you are the first I would have offered my grace to.
Who then stopped the favorable wind of our love?
Near me, he suffered, far from me, he will suffer.
If one day, by some fortunate chance, we find each other again,
From my soiled body, he would have nothing to wait for! (154–5)

Van uses Kieu's laments over her state of prostitution and her regrets over earlier scruples with fiancé Kim to imply that Bach-Yên should agree to become his lover, that if she does not, she will later come to regret it. But Bach-Yên remains unconvinced. To her, the reference appears morbid and ill-omened in its illustration of a tragic episode of Kieu's story. She feels, rather, that she and Van will both be able to defy convention and their families: "I will not have, I hope, a fate as unhappy as that of Kieu. Sooner or later, we will marry and, on that day, we will be as free, as happy as the couples of 'fabulous phoenixes and swallows'" (155). Events reveal, however, a fate far worse than Kieu's. It is Van who ultimately chooses duty over desire and Bach-Yên pays the price.

The match Van's parents have arranged for him is also a tragic figure. The daughter of a mandarin, Hông, falls in love with Van on their first meeting, unaware that he loves another woman. Soon after this encounter, she turns to her copy of the *Tale* in order to predict the course of their love and comes across the prophetic words spoken by Kieu in an early farewell to Kim as he leaves her with great regret to attend to the unexpected death of his uncle.

Religiously, she takes the *Tale of Kieu* (which people treated as a book of divination), kneels on her bed, stammers out a long prayer, opens it with her eyes closed. She falls on these lines which she recites in a low voice:

Why does the God of Marriage set himself against us?
We have barely tasted the joys of meeting when already we drink
   the bitterness of separation
I am linked to you by solemn vows

Even if age changes the color of my hair, my heart will not change
*   masters!*
The months and years of waiting will not frighten me
But my heart tightens at the thought of seeing you beaten by rain
*   and wind on your journey*
Since we have promised each other to forge a "single heart" for our
*   two bodies*
I swear to you, my beloved, to never embark with my guitar on
*   other boats of love during my one hundred years of existence*
As long as these Mountains and these Rivers endure
My love will remain intact until the day of your return.
(61–2)

The episode occurs soon after their having met and exchanged
vows, when Kieu still has hopes of consummating her love match
with Kim. Hông draws immediate potential parallels with her own
fate:

With a desperate gesture, Hông throws away her book and
gives a long sigh: "Great Heaven! Is it possible that all these
clouds are gathering on the horizon of my future? . . . What
mistake have I committed, Great Heaven, to be subjected to
such a sad fate? No! No! Kieu's life is too ugly. I could never
accept such a life! (62)

Hông refuses to accept that, like Kieu, she could be separated from
the man she loves and subjected to long years of loneliness and
hardship. She rejects the prophecy—but her relationship with Van is
to suffer the early separation it foretold. Upon hearing of Bach-Yên's
suicide, Van immediately abandons his newly wed wife, leaves their
house, and eventually the country, never to return. Hông's
relationship with him has barely begun before it has ended. She is
an innocent victim, a good daughter who has simply obeyed her
parents as a good daughter should. Moreover, it was a duty that was
agreeable to her since she found the young scholar attractive. She
had married him in good faith, but dutiful behavior brings her no

more happiness or fulfillment than Bach-Yên's attempted rebellion against these same social mores.

Bach-Yên, however, has at least enjoyed the fleeting experience of loving and being loved before her early death and, like the young women in *En s'écartant des ancêtres*, has attempted to forge her own path, though with tragic consequences. Once again in this novel, the female protagonists are identified with the classical figure of Kieu. Extracts from the *Tale* serve to draw parallels between Kieu's beauty and fate with the beauty and misfortune of its modern women. Although Bach-Yên is indeed "the girl with the faithful heart," unlike Kieu she is not rewarded for her loyalty to the love of her life. Her story, and Hông's, end with no prospect of redemption.

Parallel Lives in *Printemps*

Ly Thu Ho's *Printemps inachevé* (Unfinished Spring) is a straightforward narrative covering the 1930s to the 1950s. Family, society, and the upheavals of war are largely seen through women's eyes. The novel is neatly divided into three parts. Part One introduces the main protagonist, Tran, and her older sister Tuoi, while Part Two—the most substantial section in the novel—consists of the diary of Tran from 1945 to 1947 and narrates her romance with Châu, a scholar, his leaving her to join the Vietnamese revolutionaries and the tragedy that befalls her in 1947: her rape at the hands of a French soldier. Part Three concludes the novel, narrating Châu's return to Tran in 1956, her rejection of his offer of marriage and her death a year later. Her sister Tuoi is left to mourn her premature loss.

Tran's diary opens in February 1945 and ends in July 1947. She is a self-sufficient young woman who works as an embroiderer. Her earnings supplement the household income and assist her widowed mother. She remarks wryly that her mother, "like all mothers who have daughters to marry off, is becoming impatient."[44] Mme Thai reminds Tran reproachfully that her sister Tuoi married at the age of twenty. Tran, on the other hand, enjoys her life, her work, and her freedom, and she is fully aware of the constraints under which her sister Tuoi lives. In her diary, Tran confides: "I have the impression of being a piece of merchandise that one is seeking to sell, an expensive object that one wishes to dispose of at a good price and into good hands. I know that it is unfair on my part so to judge my mother, who, I am sure, only desires my happiness" (59). When Tran meets a young man, Châu, at the house of one of her clients, Mme Sang—the young man's aunt—the two young people fall in love. Tran however, is concerned about the difference in social standing between them: "Who am I? At most a poor orphan, a little bit better off than my neighbor perhaps, but no more. And he, he is an intellectual, a teacher and the sole heir of Madame Sang" (79). Here again, a beautiful girl falls in love with a talented scholar.[45] Châu is Tran's superior in every way—socially, professionally, and intellectually. She has to look up to him. Both families agree to the mismatch, and the couple is engaged in July 1945. Mme Thai has this slightly sour comment to make, despite her daughter's eminently suitable catch: "My second daughter, like my first, has chosen her fiancé, her husband, on her own, without needing either my advice or any go-between" (89), and both daughters realize this: "My sister and I felt that our mother was, despite her joy, hurt in her maternal authority" (90). If Mme Thai feels ineffective in the matter of arranging her daughters' marriages, she is determined to at least inculcate in Tran the classic virtues of a wife. She tells Tran: "A wife must be submissive, gentle, attentive and always smiling. For her, marriage is a source of devotion, sacrifice and principles" (99). In short, marriage means years of unremitting devotion to all except oneself.

In 1946, Tran's fiancé Châu decides to join the revolutionaries struggling against the French occupation of Vietnam. He wishes to consummate the relationship but Tran, like Kieu, refuses to do so before they are formally married. There ensues a painful separation, during which Châu sends occasional lengthy letters informing Tran of the current military and political situation. The last entry in Tran's diary is dated July 1947. She encloses a long letter to Châu. In the letter, Tran informs him of the death of her mother and of an incident in February 1947 when their house was searched by the military and Tran was brutally raped by a French soldier. She begins the letter to Châu with the term "older brother," an appellation of affection between lovers which gradually takes on its literal meaning:

> Farewell, older brother . . . I confide myself to you as an older brother, and not as a fiancée, a brother whose feelings I know. I no longer have the right to your love. I am unworthy. I renounce you forever. If I have neither the happiness nor the chance to become your wife, if I have been condemned to undergo this disgrace, it is perhaps because I have to pay for the misdeeds I have committed in a previous life. (167)

Despite her own modern views, Tran internalizes her elders' philosophy on women's virtue and honor, with tragic consequences. As she had earlier noted in her diary: "traditions, principles, they appall me. But the worst is that, even while I am appalled, I am subject, in spite of myself, to their influence" (138). She blames herself for having been raped. She feels soiled and tarnished and is punishing herself for the wrong that was done to her. At heart, she is conforming to all the lessons instilled in her by her mother and grandmother, and, in so doing, bowing to the wisdom of previous generations. At this point the diary stops.

Two years after the signing of the Geneva Accords in 1954, Châu finally returns. Tran now works as a nurse. Châu pleads with her, blames himself for having left her without any protection and reiterates that he loves her and wishes them to build a life together. She, however, is implacable and refuses to go back on her self-imposed word of renouncing him "forever." Having rejected Châu, despite the pleas of her sister Tuoi, Tran literally works herself to death and dies a year later, in 1957. An independent woman, with a vocation and a profession of her own, she is emotionally crushed by the final, symbolic loss of Châu. After her death, her sister and friend discuss the tragedy of her life:

> Yes, Tuoi, Tran's life was like a rose whose stem was broken at the moment of its blossoming, like a dawn barely golden, soiled by bad weather, like an unfinished spring. (205)

They mourn the death of a young woman whose life was prematurely cut short. Tran is compared to spring or a rose, metaphors evocative of beauty that is fleeting. Her life is indeed an "unfinished spring," as expressed in the novel's title.

Tran's attitude is strongly reminiscent of Kieu's. There are marked parallels between Kieu's and Tran's stories. Both are beautiful and virtuous women who are victims of circumstances: one becomes a prostitute, the other is a victim of rape. Both are engaged before misfortune overtakes them, and refuse to become the lover of the man to whom they are engaged. Both, after many years of separation and misery—ten in Tran's case and fifteen in Kieu's—are finally reunited with their love. Both are offered marriage by their former fiancé and feel soiled and unworthy of love, but while Kieu accepts marriage even though she insists on the relationship remaining platonic, Tran rejects the chance of being married to Châu. Kieu finds a measure of serenity and happiness but Tran dies.

Ly Thu Ho's novel is a dark rewriting of the story of Kieu. In highlighting such clear parallels between her story and that of the most famous of classical heroines, and then twisting the ending, Ly Thu Ho questions and criticizes even more harshly the weight of virtue and honor on the lives of women. Tran's fate has none of the reassuring merit of virtue rewarded (in Kieu's reunion with her first love) and conscience soothed (a platonic marriage between Kieu and Kim), which characterizes the fate of Nguyen Du's Kieu. Furthermore, rather than admiring Tran, as the reader admires the classical heroine, one perceives Tran's insistence on abiding by the social code as needlessly wasteful and pathetic. Tran's torment is self-imposed. Neither her fiancé nor her sister condemn her for what happened to her. And yet she insists that she is "unworthy." Tran's character thereby raises questions about the laudability of Kieu's judgement of her own person as unworthy of the man she loves. Ly

Thu Ho implies that the high value placed on chastity results in the painful and unnecessary destruction of a woman's life.

These differences in the portrayal of the female characters in both works reflect the particular viewpoint of their authors. Although Nguyen Du does give his central character a certain degree of sexual license, he makes her submit in the end to the dictates of traditional morality. She is perceived, moreover, as a noble and heroic figure, a woman who has retained a sense of honor despite her years of prostitution and who insists on a chaste relationship with the man she had first pledged herself to. Ly Thu Ho's characterization of Tran, on the other hand, has quite the opposite effect. Tran's acquiescence to tradition appears tortured and unnecessary. The parallels between her story and that of Kieu serve to reinforce the contrast between the death of Tran in *Printemps inachevé* and the quiet happiness of Kieu's platonic marriage to Kim in the *Tale*. While Kieu is rewarded by her male creator for having conformed to traditional notions of female virtue, Tran is punished by her female creator for the self-same act. Nguyen Du makes a moral tale of the story of Kieu, while Ly Thu Ho, in contrast, gives a bleak account of the consequences of Tran's choice: the loss of a young and gifted life, not through war, but through a desperate adherence to social values. The tragedy of Tran is that she dies not of external causes but because of self-imposed feelings of guilt and worthlessness. Ly Thu Ho suggests that Vietnamese society's traditional notions of morality and virtue also bear responsibility for this death.

Kieu as a Female Model of Endurance in *Retour*

Kim Lefèvre's *Retour à la saison des pluies* (Return to the Rainy Season) was the result of Lefèvre's difficult decision to return to Vietnam in 1990 after an absence of thirty years. Lefèvre's search for herself and the country of her birth are inextricably bound to her search for the woman her mother was and is. Like Kieu, Lefèvre's mother is gifted with beauty, and this brings her great misfortune. She describes her mother (whom she never names) in the following terms:

Her portrait is on the cover of my first book . . . She was then in her forties; she had a perfect oval face and a sovereign yet innocent beauty, a beauty which seemed to ignore its own perfection.

Here you are, my mother, just as I have kept you in my memory, just as you will always be in my thoughts . . . Beauty which you have always carried like the seal of misfortune. (68)

Her mother symbolizes the vulnerability of a woman's existence. As if to make up for long years of silence, her mother sends Lefèvre letter after letter detailing her own life, in particular her youth in Tonkin in the 1930s.

Lefèvre's mother came from a wealthy northern family. Her father, like the father of Mai in *En s'écartant des ancêtres*, was enlightened enough to send her to school. Her mother was his first wife and was respected by the concubines. She would have carried on with further education except that her father called her home to assist him with keeping the family accounts. Her life began to go awry upon the sudden death of her mother in the 1930s. The second wife took over and the father sent his daughter off to relatives in Son Tay, a distant garrison town in Tonkin. There, a number of young French officers came regularly to play cards and to converse with the daughter of the house. This is where Lefèvre's mother met her father, where she fell in love with him and had her first experience of sexual relations: "She was not a prostitute. She was experiencing her first love."[46] In this respect, Lefèvre's mother's story differs considerably from that of the female protagonists of the three earlier novels. In the other novels, first love was an expressed feeling, never a physical art. In fact, like Kieu, neither Mai, Bach-Yên, nor Tran consummate the relationship with their first love. Lefèvre's mother, on the other hand, not only consummated the relationship with her first love, a French officer, but lived with him for several months before he abandoned her. Unlike the protagonists of the earlier novels, she had also fallen in love with a foreigner, not a

Vietnamese. The "beautiful girl and talented scholar" trope has modified into that of "beautiful girl and foreign soldier." Her story is framed by the colonial reality of Vietnam in the 1930s. But like the other romances, this one is also aborted. Lefèvre's mother was twenty years old when her lover abandoned her. Alone and pregnant, she returned to her father, who promptly cast her out. She found refuge with another French officer whom she married and to whom she bore a son (after having given birth to her illegitimate daughter, Kim). It was a short-lived idyll however. In 1938, he was recalled to France and wanted to take her and their son back with him, but not her illegitimate daughter. In other words, he wanted her to abandon her daughter. She chose to stay in Vietnam with Kim, and let her baby son go with his father, one of the most painful decisions of her life.

At this point Lefèvre's mother begins to identify herself with the figure of Kieu. Hers is a voluntary self-identification:

> It is at this moment that there was produced in her an inner metamorphosis which transformed the active young girl that she had been into a broken woman. And as if it would give meaning to her misfortune, she began to identify her fate with that of the beautiful and unfortunate Kieu—the central character in the famous poem by Nguyen Du. She knew hundreds of lines that she recited from memory and that served her in the guise of philosophy and morality. She had adapted one to each circumstance, either to justify the trials she had endured, or to criticize my faults or praise my efforts. My childhood and my youth were nourished, I would even say cradled, by the moving recitation of the misfortunes of the beautiful Kieu. (85)

Lefèvre's mother uses the figure of Kieu as a symbol of individual and universal suffering. She feels that, like Kieu, she is a woman subject to the vagaries of fate. Having experienced great sorrow and loss, she must now accept her lot. She finds a measure of comfort in comparing her fate to Kieu's, an identification that gives her life a sense of nobler purpose. She moves to the South and there, at the age of twenty-two, marries a Chinese man, seven years her senior, a man of cold and severe temperament. It was an unhappy marriage, though it lasted thirty years and produced three more daughters. When one daughter, Oanh, was born blessed with extraordinary beauty, Lefèvre's mother once again turned to Kieu:

> "She is too perfect," she whispered to herself. And she accompanied these reflections with some lines from the famous poem *Kieu*:
>
> > *She evoked*
> > *By her look the water of lakes in autumn*
> > *By her brows the green of woods in spring*
> > *Jealous, the flowers paled not to have her radiance*
> > *The willow despaired of possessing her grace*
> > *Beautiful she was, as the legend says*
> > *To overthrow citadels and cities...*
>
> My mother believed that, following the example of Kieu, her daughter's beauty could only bring her a life of misfortune and suffering. (102)

Lefèvre's mother need not have worried about the sorrows this beauty would cause her daughter. At the age of six Oanh undergoes a horrendous change in looks: "The fine, delicate nose calcified into an unsightly ridge, barring her face. Her eyes became sunken. And at the bottom of those sockets, a lost look. Her eyes seemed to say tirelessly: 'Why?' To that, there was no answer" (102–3). The sixteen-year-old Kim rails against the injustice of fate, but her mother breathes a sigh of relief:

> "At last she is relieved of the weight of her beauty! Now she is like everyone else, she will lead a normal life."
>
> Because my mother knew from experience that beauty is a poisoned gift. (103–4)

For Lefèvre, writing of her mother's dramatic story, "melodrama is the product of traditional societies where each has his or her predetermined place; the one who deviates from that is inevitably cast into degeneration" (88–9). This was her mother's fate. She had glimpsed a different life, had loved and expressed herself in a way that was not acceptable in her milieu and consequently suffered. Lefèvre continues: "You ought not have tasted education, or read those books that spoke of freedom and of happiness" (89). Both freedom and happiness are to prove fleeting. One brief love affair in her youth led to her being ostracized from family and society and to moving far south to seek legal protection for herself and her illegitimate daughter by marrying a man whom she did not love. Unlike the female protagonists of the earlier novels, she gave in to pre-marital sex, but the consequences for her are just as negative.

In contemplating her mother's life, a life which reads like fiction and yet encompasses so much personal tragedy, Lefèvre finally understands, "the passion that you, like the Vietnamese people, bear for that marvelous poet Nguyen Du, who, in narrating the wrecked life of the beautiful Kieu, dignified the misfortunes of ordinary people" (89). Lefèvre's own struggles as an illegitimate female child of mixed background are narrated in an earlier autobiographical novel, *Métisse blanche* (White Métisse), published in 1989 and discussed elsewhere.[47]

Lefèvre's mother chooses desire over duty only once in her life: with her first French lover. His abandonment of her begins her years of unhappiness. But duty also brings her heartbreak. Her first and second marriages, and the decision to let her legitimate son go so as not to abandon her illegitimate daughter, bring no happiness. As in the other novels, the precarious nature of the feminine condition is a parallel between the mother and the figure of Kieu. For her as for many Vietnamese, Kieu's story helps her come to terms with life's reversals. Kieu's mixed message of resignation to one's fate on the one hand, and of fortitude on the other, appears to have a special resonance for those most affected by misfortune, in particular women, since it helps to explain the inevitability of events beyond logical understanding (like great tragedies and losses) and yet simultaneously brings solace and inspiration in the survival of the central character.

Conclusion

The four works present Vietnamese society from the 1930s to the 1950s as a society in which, despite the outward trappings of modernity such as greater freedom for women outside the home, access to education, careers and even financial independence, women continue to be particularly subject to the pressures of traditional morality and continue to pay a high price for it. Their difficulties are made the greater in that they are part of a society in transition between old and new and are uneasy about their place within it. The classical figure of Kieu, although unconventional by the standards of nineteenth-century Vietnam, still has a clear duty as a daughter and as a woman. These works suggest that this situation has not altered despite changed conditions for women in colonial Vietnam of the 1930s and 1940s. Women suffer a worse price because they are unable to reconcile the expectations of traditional morality with the demands of modern life. They are still unable to defy social convention successfully. They are not allowed to choose their sexual partners or to have several lovers for that matter. Worse than this, they suffer a greater punishment than Kieu when they lose their virginity outside of marriage, whether this happens voluntarily or involuntarily. Their happiness is still linked to their marital status. The novels imply that women will continue to be vulnerable if they only link self-fulfillment with the married state.

All four works acknowledge the importance of the *Tale* and of Kieu as a female model. The passages from the *Tale* that recur in the modern works are those dealing with Kieu's beauty, with the enforced separation of Kim and Kieu, and Kieu's loss of chastity. But the novels also allude to the *Tale* in the following ways: All the protagonists, who have in common with Kieu the fact that they are women, that they are beautiful and talented, and that they live in a patriarchal society, are, like her, subject to an unenviable fate, to separation from their loved one, to misery or worse, death. Like Kieu, the main characters suffer for choosing duty over desire, but unlike Kieu, they are not eventually rewarded for it. If they lose their virginity (even when they are the victim of rape) they pay a worse penalty than she does. Tran dies as a result of self-imposed feelings of worthlessness, and Lefèvre's mother suffers social ostracism and a lifetime of unhappiness. Even where they retain their chastity, like Bach-Yên and Mai, their stories end badly. Bach-Yên kills herself after Van betrays her. Mai loses Hùng and is later abandoned by her husband. All these relationships mirror, in their failure, the difficulties and setbacks of Kieu's love relationships, but the result in the modern novels is inevitably starker and the reality portrayed encompasses a greater tragedy. None of the novels end with a neat if somewhat ambiguous "happy ever after" model, in the manner of the serene three-way relationship between Kieu, Kim and Van. Allusions to or parallels with this famous heroine lead to loss, despair, resignation and sometimes death, which raises questions about the significance and symbolism of Kieu. As a model, Kieu appears to epitomize the vulnerability of the female condition in patriarchal society. Her story reinforces the notion that a woman's happiness is conditional with happiness in marriage. It is this aspect that later writers have chosen to focus on. Although these novels use her and her tale as a basis from which to highlight the condition of women in Vietnamese society of the 1930s, 1940s, and beyond, they concentrate on the tragedy of her life without considering its later rewards. The fate of the female protagonists echoes the negative aspects of Kieu's fate but none of its grace. It may be that she is seen to embody a long dead past that has become irrelevant with colonization and Westernization. Or the real message may be that she stands too far apart from ordinary women. Her misfortunes and sorrows find their reflection in the drama experienced by ordinary women, but, as these works relate, her unusual and extraordinary reinstatement remains out of reach to most.

Of all the female protagonists, only the mother in Lefèvre's *Retour à la saison des pluies* makes a conscious self-identification with the fabled figure of Kieu. The reality, as her own life shows, is more somber than the situation depicted in the *Tale*. Her lover abandons her, her father rejects her, she bears a child out of wedlock and struggles to find the only form of protection for her and her child that she believes is effective in the society of the 1930s and 1940s: marriage. Unlike Kieu, she is not rewarded with eventual happiness. The most striking rewriting of the *Tale* is clearly in Ly Thu Ho's *Printemps inachevé*. Ly Thu Ho uses the marked parallels between Tran's story and that of Kieu to provide a compelling commentary on social and gender relations in modern Vietnam. Her novel implies that in a society in which women are still dependent on men for social status and fulfillment, it is they who pay the harshest price by not abiding to the social code.

2

Patriarchal Constraints

Here, yes and no are indistinguishable
Like East and West at the Poles.
Here, truth is a puppet
That doubles in two roles.
—Cheng Min

Ly Thu Ho moved to Paris in the 1950s. For three decades, from the 1960s to the 1980s, she was the only Vietnamese woman to write and publish novels in France. Returning to Vietnam frequently, she became an observer of post-colonial Vietnam. As a writer, she was shaped both by her upbringing and education in colonial Vietnam and her long years of residence in Paris. Ly's work portrays a society destabilized by war and political unrest, a society in transition, with a younger generation looking towards the West, and an older one clinging still to traditional Vietnamese cultural values. Her novels expose the condition of different generations of women in Vietnamese society over a period of six decades, from the 1930s to the 1970s. Rather than attempting to disrupt patriarchal discourse, as some women writers in France did, she examines the actual situation of women under patriarchy.

Ly Thu Ho's treatment of women's lives is subtle and non-aggressive. Rather than show anger or the outward rebellion of robust female characters, she focuses on the bounded and bonded lives of the greater mass of women who conform. A store of residual anger, however, lies just beneath the surface of her works, revealing itself in the self-defeating constraints suffered by her female protagonists and the fate she apportions her most conventional characters. Her mother figures repeatedly stress the traditional patriarchal message: women *will* achieve happiness and fulfillment by conforming to the roles society decrees for them; they *will* receive their just rewards if they behave in a proper manner. But the realities lived by her daughter figures are precisely the inverse: by conforming or attempting to conform to this ideal, a woman loses whatever individuality she possesses, whatever chance of happiness a strong sense of self-respect would allow. Ly's conventional frame does not render her message less relevant: while describing traditional female attributes and interests, she succeeds in presenting a picture of stultified talents and deadened potential.

Ly was a generation older than the angry young women writers of the 1960s in South Vietnam.[1] Like women writers and poets of earlier centuries, she prefers to convey her views indirectly.[2] In Vietnam:

> [a]ssertiveness is often seen as lack of respect. Traditional education advised women to *ngam dang nuot cay* . . . "[to] keep the bitter in one's mouth and swallow the spicy." In other words, repressing one's negative emotions and feelings was considered better than giving vent to them.[3]

This subdued approach has to be understood within the context of her time. A product of her circumstances and cultural background, Ly Thu Ho appears reluctant to express anger outwardly and openly or, for that matter, to have her female characters express it. Indeed, she had few precedents for it; books by women were banned in Vietnam in the late 1920s.

> The political situation of 1929 and 1930, a period of nationalist agitation and Communist activities, made the French very wary of any type of criticism. Women's groups came under suspicion as the authorities were alert to their possible spread of subversive ideas. In Annam, about twenty books on women were banned and five books published by the Go Cong women's press were banned in 1929, its woman editor Phan Thi Bach Van was fined, and the publishing house closed down for "disrupting peace and security in the region by means of literature and ideas."[4]

Ly's approach differs from that of contemporary male Francophone writers such as Pham Van Ky, whose denunciations of an oppressive familial and social system are dramatic and violent. Destruction, death, or escape are the only solutions. In Ly's novels, escape is not usually an option, nor is death—with one notable exception. Instead, they present the slow destruction of women who struggle on, bear children, and endure the ravages of war.

Ly's novels are written in a clear and simple style and deal with gender roles and family relationships within the context of contemporary society. In this, they bear some similarities with the work of French women writing at the time.[5] They are written primarily for a French audience as well as for the expatriate Vietnamese community in France. Her treatment of the female condition reflects a combination of influences: the process of modernization and Westernization in Vietnam that accompanied colonization and de-colonization, and her own exposure, as a Vietnamese woman living in France, to contemporary cultural and literary movements. This chapter will analyze Ly's work from a Western feminist perspective. It will explore three central issues: the representation of women in her novels, their reflection of social reality, and the subversive dimension to her works.

Ly published her first novel, *Printemps inachevé* (Unfinished Spring), in Paris in 1962. This was followed by *Au Milieu du carrefour* (In the Middle of the Crossroads) in 1969 and *Le Mirage de la paix* (The Mirage of Peace) in 1986. *Mirage* won the *Prix littéraire de l'Asie* from the *Association des écrivains de langue française* (Association of Francophone Writers) in 1987. All three novels are set in South Vietnam. They form a loose trilogy and portray the politics and history of Vietnam from the 1930s to 1975. Characters occasionally feature in succeeding novels. Three categories of women reappear in slightly altered form in all three novels: the mother figure (whether mother, grandmother, or nanny), the virtuous daughter or wife, and the prostitute. In the third volume in the series, Ly introduces a fourth category—the servant.

Printemps inachevé stretches from the 1930s to the 1950s. The two virtuous female protagonists are Tuoi and her younger sister Tran.

Close parallels between the story of Tran in *Printemps* and of Kieu in the classical *Tale of Kieu* have been discussed in the previous chapter.[6] Here, I examine the mother-daughter relationship and the generation gap between women. Unlike her more conventional older sister Tuoi, Tran is single, independent, and to all appearances a thoroughly modern young woman. Her story is set within the context of generational differences between herself and her tradition-bound mother. It also reveals the fate of her friend Nam, a prostitute, who dies prematurely during childbirth. Events reveal, however, that Tran's modernity is only superficial.

The second novel, *Au Milieu du carrefour* narrates a young woman's gradual loss of independence and autonomy in Saigon in the 1960s, against a background of war. In the process of being courted, the virtuous female protagonist, Lang, gradually defers to her suitor's wishes and interests, her personality fading as the narrative proceeds. Lang's waning identity contrasts with other minor but more vivid female characters in the novel: Xinh, who falls in love with an American marine, and Thuy, a bar owner. While depicting a conventional romance, the novel tackles issues that are controversial for Ly Thu Ho's generation and milieu—cross-cultural relationships and the bar-girls of Saigon. Ly calls for a greater tolerance in relation to each. Neither the mother figure nor the figure of the prostitute feature strongly. The novel ends with the hope that the war will soon end.

The last of Ly Thu Ho's novels, *Le Mirage de la paix*, takes place between 1970 and 1975. Two virtuous female protagonists, Thu-Thuy and Ngoc-Suong, are set amidst several minor female characters: a mother figure in the form of the nanny, a prostitute, and a servant. Once again, the virtuous female figures experience tragedy and in the end are left bereaved and diminished. Yet, this is the most pessimistic of Ly Thu Ho's works. Constant war had eroded society and the reader is left to surmise that, in such circumstances, it would be selfish for women to look to their own fulfillment. The novel relates the end of the Vietnam War and its immediate aftermath.

Convention and Tragedy in *Printemps*

Ly's first novel, *Printemps inachevé* (Unfinished Spring), relates the story of Tuoi and her sister Tran and consists of three parts. The first of these deals with Tuoi's upbringing, the second with the dramatic events surrounding Tran—her engagement to a young man from a good family and her subsequent rape by a French soldier, and the third, with the aftermath of these events. The first and final parts are related in the third person while the second, Tran's diary, is a first-person narrative. In this novel, the older generation—the grandmother, the mothers Mme Thai (mother of Tuoi and Tran) and Mme Hai, and Vu Gia the Thai's *nourrice* or nanny—conform to the category of mother figure. Models of loveliness and gentleness, Tuoi and Tran conform to the virtuous daughter: "They had inherited from their mother an oval face, a light complexion, a profound gentleness in their expression."[7] The category of prostitute is represented by Tran's friend Nam, the daughter of Mme Hai.

Tuoi is aware from a young age of the defined nature of her parents' marriage. Her father is the undisputed head of the family, something her mother, who even walks behind her husband, does not question. Tuoi's nanny informs her charge of the principles governing woman's position in society: "As a young woman you have to submit to paternal authority, as a married woman, you will be subject to that of your husband, and as a widow you will depend on your eldest son." She finishes with the rejoinder, "Above all, do not forget that you will never be man's equal" (170–1).

Even at school and college, Tuoi cannot escape from the restrictions imposed on her sex. Her grandmother forces her to wear a corset, not—as in the West—to emphasize an artificially small waist and throw into relief the bust and hips, but to flatten the young girl's breasts. Society and fashion in Vietnam at that time decreed that "a generous bosom attracted the disapproval of all." Indeed, "[t]he corset was destined to compress the breasts until they were completely flattened, and so was terribly oppressive" (36). The effect was to desexualize young women by inducing an artificial shapelessness or conversely, to emphasize a hidden sexuality, since female curves were assumed to remain under the flatness.

In a society based on Confucian principles such as Ly depicts, women play a subordinate role to men and girls are groomed for marriage from infancy. Tuoi's ears are pierced in readiness for the traditional engagement gift from the bridegroom. Her grandmother informs her, "Young girls are made to care for the house . . . to serve their husbands and give them many children in order to perpetuate the race" (35). In this matter, there are similarities between Confucian society and Western society. Casey Miller and Kate Swift have noted that:

> Women are said to 'marry into' families and families are said to 'die out' if an all-female generation occurs. The word family, from the Latin *famulus* meaning servant or slave, is itself a reminder that wives and children, along with servants, were historically part of a man's property.[8]

A Vietnamese saying teaches: "One boy and you can inscribe a descendant; ten girls and you can write nil."[9]

Tuoi is a constant witness to her mother's dependence on both husband and mother-in-law. The epitome of the traditional wife, Mme Thai is housebound, submissive, and reliant on higher authority to justify her actions. All three mother figures—mother, grandmother, and nanny—dispense warmth and nurturing in a familiar theme that is repeated in another nanny in the last novel of the trilogy. Yet their primary concern is to exemplify and transmit the roles and duties of women to the young Tuoi, emphasizing the difficulty women face in divorcing themselves from tradition, especially if it is the mother figure who is both victim and perpetuator of this mode of life.[10]

Tuoi's younger sister Tran is also subject to the older generation's views and judgments on issues ranging from marriage to infidelity and divorce. Mme Thai and Mme Hai sum up the female condition: "For us [as] women, our lives, our happiness, depend mostly on the man we marry" (74). Regarding male infidelity in marriage, they relate that "according to ancestral tradition, a teapot can have several cups but one never sees anyone procure for themselves several teapots and only one cup" (74). The metaphor is apt. The teapot, large and bulky, occupies center stage on the tray, while small, delicate, and peripheral teacups surround it: a group of fragile, dependent, delicate vessels waiting to be filled (by a man's seed). This image is of symbolic relevance since traditional society decreed that a man was entitled to several concubines.

Mme Thai continues: "The infidelity of a man can be compared to drops of water on a water-lily leaf, they fall and slide. But the same fault committed by a woman makes one think of a piece of cloth soiled with tannin" (75). Again the imagery is vivid and powerful. There is a striking contrast between the lightness of a man's offence, which leaves no traces, and the severity of a woman's, which leaves an indelible stain, a brand of shame and dishonor, something sullied and corrupted. The double standard of sexuality appears in both East and West. Rousseau writes in *Emile*:

> Doubtless it is not permitted to anyone to violate his faith, and every unfaithful man who deprives his wife of the only reward of the austere duties of her sex is an unjust and barbarous man. But the unfaithful woman does more; she dissolves the family and breaks all the bonds of nature. In giving the man children which are not his, she betrays both. She joins perfidy to infidelity. I have difficulty seeing what disorders and what crimes do not flow from this one.[11]

A poem in the *Classic of Poetry* (edited by Confucius)[12] expresses similar sentiments:

> When a man dallies,
> He will still be excused;
> But when a woman dallies,
> No pardon will she have.[13]

Eva Figes points out that "sexual taboos (or a code of morality) cannot be effective unless they are accepted by society as a whole, and that means both men and women: one of the reasons that a patriarchal society has been able to work for so long is that women are themselves ready to play the roles assigned to them, never having been made aware of any alternative."[14] This system endorses the safeguarding of a man's property, including his wife and children, and the sanctity of patrilineal descent. Mme Thai is fully aware of this.

> Like your father said, the unfaithful wife mixes the blood of the family, because her husband risks raising other men's children. Men view it almost as an honor to take another's wife, but they never forgive wives who are unfaithful to them. You are going to tell me that this is unjust, but since this injustice is inherent in our rules of conduct, why do you rebel? (76)

Divorce, in this view, is not an option, since "a divorced woman is criticized and exposed to public ridicule, even though she is the victim" (75). Moreover, the children have to be thought of. Here, as in all other areas of her life, it is a woman's duty to sacrifice her own interests for the sake of others. In articulating her views, Mme Thai reveals an entire social code of morality, showing not only that the older generation reluctantly accepts that code, but that after its initial misgivings, it transmits that code to the generation of daughters as well.

Although *Printemps'* mother figures, Mme Thai and Mme Hai, are unhappily married, both thus unerringly convey to Tran the duties and responsibilities of married women. In so doing, they reveal the discrepancy between ideal and reality that Susan Stanford Friedman finds characteristic of women: "not recognizing themselves in the reflections of cultural representation, women develop a dual consciousness—the self as culturally defined and the self as different from cultural prescription."[15] Both of these older women are able to recognize the basic injustice of the sexual double standard, but they are incapable of voicing a logical objection to it. Torn between the perceived suitability of marriage for women and the actual distress and humiliation of their own married state, they are somehow unable to take the necessary step that would allow them to reject conventional assumptions concerning woman's role.

Printemps' two generations of Vietnamese women perceive European women quite differently. Tran believes that they are emancipated. They have access to education, professional life, and a public political voice, while Vietnamese women "live cloistered and lead a resigned life, too dependent on their family" (100). Her mother, on the other hand, believes that women who are free are also more open to temptation. In her mind, independence and unconventionality are naturally allied with sexual promiscuity.[16] While women in traditional society may be outwardly submissive, she explains, they wield great power behind the scenes.

> Is it not true, my dear daughter, that the smile of a pretty woman can go to a man's head, and that the tears of an old mother can touch the heart of the most ruthless of judges! Why do you want to become man's equal when, without winning a battle, you can be Madam the General? (101)

Mme Thai may be aware of the inequities in the status quo, but she chooses it over what she perceives as the sole alternative: complete lack of power for women. If her daughter Tran is to challenge this view, she must overcome the inhibitions she grew up with—including the perceptions and judgments by which her parents, her teachers, and her society generally abide. Germaine Greer reminds us:

> It takes a great deal of courage and independence to decide to design your own image instead of the one society rewards, but it gets easier as you go along. Of course, a woman who decides to go her own way will find that her conditioning is ineradicable, but at least she can recognize its operation and choose to counteract it.[17]

Despite her modern views, Tran internalizes her elders' strictures on female virtue and honor with punishing results. In July 1947, her diary ends with a last letter to her fiancé Châu, whom she addresses as "My beloved older brother" (165). Enlisting the traditional form of address, in which a male partner is referred to as *anh* (older brother) and a woman as *em* (younger sister), Tran speaks in the language of the existing social hierarchy. *Anh* connotes seniority, strength, and authority, while *em* connotes youth, deference, and immaturity. These forms of address support a convention in which the woman looks up to the man and he looks after her. While considered affectionate, these terms infantilize the woman and normalize patriarchal hierarchy. As a term for lovers or husband and wife to use, they also desexualize the relationship.

These terms of address take on a symbolic significance when Tran writes to Châu to inform him of her rape at the hands of a French soldier. In her letter, the term "older brother" takes on its literal meaning. Having internalized the guilt that a social code of morality imposes on women who transgress, even though she is the victim, she renounces Châu. "Farewell, older brother . . . I no longer have a right to your love. I am unworthy" (167). Tran's rape is not only a personal tragedy—it can be read as analogous to the rape of her country by its colonizers. Chilean author Isabel Allende writes, "I think rape represents the worst humiliation and the worst transgression against a person, and this theme has become prevalent in the stories, novels . . . that are being [written] nowadays. It is as if in the collective unconscious the rape of a woman has come to symbolize the rape of all of us as a species, continent, and race."[18] Tran's private trauma reflects her country's wider turmoil.

Tran's diary records her relationship with her friend, Nam, who represents the category of prostitute. Nam, a consort to Japanese officers during the war, confides her motivations to her friend:

Why imitate my mother in giving myself a master similar to my father? I prefer to be the lover rather than the legitimate wife. As a lover, I am loved . . . my partner seeks to please me; if he does not satisfy me, I can change to another. The legitimate wife on the other hand, inherits the name and the title, in other words, the official facade, but, in time, she is often abandoned, forgotten or even maltreated. (134)

Nam does not absolve herself from responsibility for her present way of life. She points out wryly to Tran: "It is through girls like me that people can recognize the moral worth of girls like you. But I am seeking neither excuse nor justification with you. The disagreement between my parents certainly affected my adolescence, but it is my own nature that led me towards the life of a demi-mondaine, which pleases me" (134). With these words, Ly Thu Ho lays bare, in a direct and non-judgmental manner, the motivations that shape the consciousness of her category of prostitute. While presenting Nam's actions as a reaction to paternal violence and abuse, she does not have her excuse her life-style but rather explain her decision to lead such a life.

Yet Nam is as much a victim of the system by rebelling against it as she would have been in acquiescing. Rebelling through men, and standing not on her own but on the strength of her sexual attachment to them, she is equally vulnerable and marginalized. Her death in childbirth, rendered by Ly with such irony, is illustrative of this. Having defied society and tradition by asserting her sexual independence, Nam dies in what is considered a natural process and key expression of female sexuality—a process which often proved fatal before the advent of modern medicine.[19] As the women around her reflect, "Nam, who, during her lifetime, in the full youth of a seductive and desirable woman, was surrounded by friends and admirers, could find no man, not even a husband, to weep for her upon her death" (175).

Behind the facade of conformity in the lives of ordinary women, Ly succeeds in conveying the overwhelming and sometimes shocking sadness of these women's lives. Both of her older women, Mme Thai and Mme Hai, have unhappy marriages. Yet while recognizing injustice, they are resigned to it. Both daughters, Tran and Nam, die young. In Tran, Ly presents a heroine who encapsulates all the desired attributes of the feminine ideal: of good birth, gentle, loving, a beautiful and dutiful daughter with sufficient intelligence and independence to love where she chooses. But these talents and gifts are of little use to her in the end, her life marked by distress, unhappiness, and toil. Most vividly in this novel, by way of close parallels between the figures of Tran and the classical heroine Kieu, Ly Thu Ho translates into a modern context the values of virtue and obedience that traditional patriarchal society inculcates in women—a translation that renders an all the more effective criticism as those values result in Tran's early and needless death.

Juxtaposition and Change in *Carrefour*

Au Milieu du carrefour (In the Middle of the Crossroads), Ly's second novel, is set in the mid-1960s. Its main female characters are Lang, a woman in her mid-twenties, and her cousin Xinh. War has been a part of Lang's life since 1945; a sheltered *bourgeoise*, she is being educated about the realities of life in war-troubled Saigon. The figure of Lang, the virtuous woman, is set against that of Xinh, who is of more robust temperament; Thuy, a woman of considerable independence and enterprise; and Liêu, a fleeting figure who works as a bar-girl and falls victim to the casual violence of war. Within the novel, each of the different categories of women inter-relate, sharing their particular views and perceptions. In contrast to the earlier *Printemps*, emphasis is on the younger generation and the novel's mother figure is hardly given voice. Lang's courtship with the surgeon Vân forms the central plot of this third-person narrative.

One of *Carrefour's* few comments on mothers describes a society wedding in Saigon:

> And in the group of ladies what chatterings! The provident mamas were in search of brilliant and highly placed sons-in-law. Fortune and university degrees were no longer enough. They also demanded a certain respectability in their family. And in the absence of honorable titles from the parents themselves, they would take into account those of close relatives, an uncle who was Minister or a cousin who was the wife of a General.[20]

In traditional Vietnamese society, women expended immense energy plotting and scheming advantageous social and political alliances to enhance the family name by bettering the position of its male members, most often achieved by furthering a husband's political career or assuring a son's rise to a prominent position.[21] If a daughter was of marriageable age, then a suitable groom was to be provided. As Ly's character Xinh remarks, "the political barometer of Saigon is so variable, coups d'état so frequent that situation reversals become commonplace" (59).

The archetypal virtuous woman, Lang is a language student. Her more independent cousin, Xinh, works as a sales agent: "She earned her living comfortably, since, as she spoke English and French fluently, she was well paid" (26). Xinh observes with interest Lang's growing love for Vân. The difference in qualifications and age between Vân and Lang recalls that between Châu and Tran in *Printemps*. A brilliant thirty-year-old surgeon, an accomplished sportsman, and a keen appreciator of music, Vân is an extremely personable catch. As tradition dictates, he is older, more mature, and more intellectually gifted than she. Their pairing is yet another example of the "beautiful girl and talented scholar" trope from classical literature.

Paralleling a decision made twenty years earlier by *Printemps'* character, Châu, Vân informs Lang that he has decided to join the *maquis* (Vietnamese guerillas), to work as a doctor and observe for himself at first hand the reality of the tangled state of politics in Vietnam. Naturally distressed since she does not want to see him killed, she reveals: "Oh, I'm afraid, Vân, I tremble for you, my love" (40). Yet at the end of their talk, she dismisses these feelings in a self-deprecating manner: "Well, now that you have made up your mind, I do not want to go counter to your will by reasoning any further, because I risk appearing like a scared and brainless lover, a loving but selfish woman" (43). She later acknowledges her "jealousy" and "feminine pettiness" in her objections to his plans. Her vocabulary stresses the inherent foolishness of the female stereotype.

Vân plans to be away for a few months or a year and does not wish them to be married beforehand. As if embodying the patriarchal roles in which man is the active principle, woman the passive, he declares: "I love you, Lang, and I have chosen you amongst all others" (44).[22] He then continues: "I too am afraid of losing you, but, look, if the worst were to happen to me, you would become a young widow, a twenty-five-year-old widow. A young woman marries more easily than a widow; and what will people say of you?" (44). Like *Printemps'* Tran before her, Lang resigns herself to an anxiety-ridden period of separation, knowing that Vân will be working with the guerillas, even though he does so, not out of political conviction, but out of a desire to observe the human reality behind the propaganda.

In his absence, and fired by his ideas (in this as in every other area, she is led by him), Lang decides to inform herself about the politics of her country: "Vân's ideas roused her. Instead of hiding away at home like before, to keep well out of the way of this war, she decided to take part in it in her way and according to her own methods" (56). Lang frequents the National Library and national information centers; reads books, documents, pamphlets, and newspapers; listens to news bulletins; and observes propaganda methods. Xinh later congratulates her in a tone that the reader is invited to read as ironic: "In any case, I compliment Vân who lost no time in training you as a future doctor's wife" (67).

Despite her firm grasp of current affairs, Lang becomes strangely shy in the company of men. She listens without contributing to a long discussion between men on the political and military situation: "Having no knowledge at all of politics, Lang's only weapon against this war was her love for her torn homeland" (115). Her hours of diligent research and analysis pass unrecognized. Encroaching on an area that is not traditionally acknowledged as a woman's, she feels unqualified to express her views. Her words again capture her supposed ignorance of the political realities of the time and her "feminine," emotive, and, it is implied, powerless response to the situation: her love for her country. There exists a curious demarcation between the world of men and that of women. Men discourse openly on the politics and economics of the country and on the progress of the war. They are instrumental in the running of the country; most are mobilized or in the public service. The world of women is ancillary to and divorced from that of men; women's discussions and assessments of the nation are related in privacy, indulged in with one or two close women friends.

Carrefour's third female character of note stands in some contrast. Thuy is an enterprising woman in her thirties who tries various ways of earning a living before eventually opening a bar. A woman of courage with minimal education, no family connections or husband, she succeeds on her own. While "[s]he remains a good and simple girl . . . she does not hesitate to embark on daring enterprises" (77).

Carrefour's female characters discuss two main topics: the bar-girls of Saigon and interracial relationships. Regarding the bar-girls, Thuy asserts: "Whatever people say about our bar-girls, they are good girls, some of them are even very honest. They often refuse to go out or to spend the night with strangers" (80). Lang counters by pointing to the notorious reputation of the city center as a giant brothel, insisting: "This is a question of women's dignity and national self-respect" (80). Her words provoke a spirited defense of the bar-girls from Thuy, for whom virtue and chastity, essentials of the feminine ideal, are middle-class luxuries:

> When one is hungry and without money, one has to struggle by any means in order to survive. . . . [T]he girls who are here are not all loose girls. Some of them are married women who work to help husbands who have been mobilized as second-class soldiers and earn a miserable salary that does not even cover the rent. Others belong to families who were well-to-do in the past but are nowadays impoverished or ruined by revolution or war. Most of them come from far-off country areas where a rural life is no longer possible. (81)

Thuy comments bitterly that although the bars are reviled by both conservatives and revolutionaries, they are heavily used and taxed. "The people of the *maquis* consider us traitors, while those in Saigon label us prostitutes; everyone throws stones at us and yet no one has forgotten to impose very heavy taxes on our earnings" (85). Lang leaves the encounter in a sober and reflective mood, seeing Thuy and women like her as an entire class bred by continuous war and poverty. Once the situation which gave rise to them disappears, she believes, so will they.[23]

On the topic of interracial relationships, Xinh's relationship with John, the American marine, is the particular focus of debate. If they decide to marry, Xinh believes, it is inevitable that she will have to leave her country and attempt to settle in his. Lang agrees. A Vietnamese woman marrying an American would have fewer difficulties than an American woman married to a Vietnamese, she contends, for while a Western woman would find it very difficult to settle into the constraints of Vietnamese society, "a well-educated Vietnamese woman with progressive ideas will adapt more easily to American society, which is very liberal in its concepts of social life and where women are treated equally to men" (120). Lang is making two assumptions here, the first being that the woman is expected to follow her husband and settle in his country, and the second that a woman in Western society would not be subject to sexual discrimination. In the eyes of a Vietnamese woman in the 1960s, American women enjoyed "equal" rights with men.

Xinh and John's relationship illustrates the concept that opposites attract. "It is the law of opposites, the attraction of novelty. . . . The West is attracted by the East and vice-versa" (139). This notion implies a curiosity regarding "the other side," an acknowledgement of gaps in cultural understanding, and an effort to bridge them. In earlier Francophone novels such as Truong Dinh Tri and Albert de Teneuille's *Bà-Dâm* (Madam the French Woman) (1930) and Ousmane Socé's *Mirages de Paris* (Mirages of Paris) (1937), the man is dark and foreign and the woman, European and fair. Here, in by no means a straightforward analogy, the woman is dark-haired and the man, the foreigner, fair. She represents the homeland while he embodies the outsider, the invader. When John is badly wounded in an engagement with the enemy, his helplessness permits Xinh to take the initiative and propose to him: "If your feelings for me have not changed, this time I'm asking you to marry me" (187). The romance differs further from earlier Francophone narratives in two other ways: set in post-colonial Vietnam, neither partner is French; and, after their wartime relationship in Vietnam, she "rescues" him, only for them to leave her homeland.[25]

The third category of women, the prostitute, is briefly represented in *Carrefour* by Liêu, a bar-girl who is killed by a grenade explosion in the city. She leaves behind a young daughter, one of the many civilian victims of war and terror. Liêu's situation reflects the harsh realities of day-to-day existence for the city's bar-girls and the precarious nature of their livelihood. Xinh acknowledges this when she informs Lang: "Liêu had followed in her mother's footsteps but she was taken in her full youth without having had the time to know, fortunately for her, premature aging in poverty and privation" (71). Indeed, Liêu's mother had also worked as a prostitute and her later years were marked by destitution. Although Liêu died young, Xinh rationalizes, at least her death will spare her the same misery.

In *Carrefour*, as in the earlier *Printemps*, Ly constructs a female protagonist who embodies the traditional attributes of femininity. Although there are many surface parallels between the couples in the two novels, Lang's fate in *Carrefour* is happier than Tran's in *Printemps*. Despite this, Lang's many attributes and her personality fade as the narrative moves along. If she is studying English when she meets Vân, for instance, she soon abandons her studies to accommodate her life to his. Ultimately, she becomes a mere sounding board for the views he expresses through his letters.

Crucially, Lang's conventionality serves to set off the minor but more vivid female characters in the novel: her cousin Xinh, with her more robust and independent personality; and Thuy, the enterprising self-made woman. The novel's conventional heroines relate with the unconventional ones. Thus, as Lang and Xinh discuss prostitution with Thuy, Ly Thu Ho uses Thuy's role as a bar owner to embark on a sympathetic examination of the bar-girls of Saigon. This examination, for Ly Thu Ho as for Thuy, and as in Ly's treatment of interracial relationships, is radical for her generation and culture. For this reason, perhaps, Ly has incorporated these two themes within an orderly account of a young couple's love and eventual marriage at a time of civil war.

Carrefour ends on a more positive note than *Printemps*. Both young couples marry in the end. When Lang is reunited with Vân, he relates his experiences as a doctor in the *maquis* as a long series of human tragedies and decides to return to work in Saigon. The novel ends on a note of hope that the war will end and simply become a memory.

Defeat and Resignation in *Mirage*

Ly Thu Ho's *Le Mirage de la paix* (The Mirage of Peace) elaborates the widest characterization of women. In addition to the mother figure, the virtuous woman, and the good-hearted prostitute, it presents a sturdy servant girl. Set between 1970 and 1975, the novel presents two main female characters, Thu-Thuy, a refugee from the North, and Ngoc-Suong, the daughter of a southern landowner. Both are virtuous women. The traditional mother figure appears in the guise of Ba-Sau, Ngoc-Suong's nanny. Kieu-Lien is a Saigon prostitute; Manh is a peasant girl and servant to Ngoc-Suong. *Mirage* relates the romance between Thu-Thuy and Huu-Lôc, the landowner's son and an Army Captain, and that between Ngoc-Suong and Duy-Sau, the son of the estate manager who is also under Huu-Lôc's orders. A third-person narrative, it ends in tragedy with the fall of South Vietnam.

Quasi-silent in *Carrefour*, the mother figure reappears in this novel in the guise of Ba-Sau, the archetypal nanny. Ba-Sau not only holds forth on the traditional purpose of women—childbearing— she comes out with an ancient saying to illustrate her point that a young woman's unattached and therefore untamed sexuality is dangerous and potentially explosive: "When one has a marriageable daughter at home, it is as if one has to watch a bowl of fermented fish whose lid could possibly blow off any day, letting out a bad odor that dishonors the entire family."[26]

According to Ba-Sau, women are to be promptly married and should quickly bear children. Their sexuality will then be justified and their energies suitably devoted to raising children. Otherwise, they have in them the potential to dishonor their entire family. Ba-Sau iterates the words of generations of women, a message unchanged in forty years since another of Ly's nannies, *Printemps'* Vu Gia, preached it in the 1930s. The voice of generations of mothers before her, she echoes such maxims as, "Dry wood burns better, an ugly husband serves better," and laments, "I would have liked a son-in-law of mature years, a man who already had some experience of life before beginning a family, a solid and sensible man on whom a woman can lean with confidence to travel the long and difficult path of life" (120).

There are no actual mothers in *Mirage*. Both Thu-Thuy and Ngoc-Suong lose their mothers at a tender age. The mother-daughter relationships that had been so fraught with tension in *Printemps* disappear completely here. The effect is an enhanced freedom for the younger women. It is up to Ba-Sau, the nanny, to provide nurturing and a semblance of mother-care. Her beliefs on women's role in society are just as oppressive as those of the mother figure, but because she is not a real mother, the young women can observe her strictures from a greater distance and therefore take them less to heart.

Like Tuoi and Tran in *Printemps* and Lang and Xinh in *Carrefour*, Thu-Thuy and Ngoc-Suong are conceived of as being beautiful. Thu-Thuy's life has been a succession of tragedies. When her father dies she decides to leave Saigon and move to the country where she seeks work on a plantation owned by Mr. Huu-Phuoc. There, well-bred and frail, she is contrasted with the figure of Manh, "a strapping peasant with a slow walk" (65). Thu-Thuy represents the ideal of Vietnamese womanhood as endorsed by patriarchal society—lovely, gentle and biddable—so much so that the middle-aged wife of the plantation mechanic exclaims: "She seems like a good girl and so gentle. What a pity I have no son to marry, otherwise I would willingly have chosen her as my daughter-in-law" (72).

For her part, Ngoc-Suong is a student at the *Couvent des Oiseaux* (The Convent of Birds), a well-known girls' school in Dalat, a legacy of the French colonial education system in which young girls are taught to become perfect housewives. Her education and upbringing have tamed her natural impulses and desires. She is aware that she is repressed and inhibited, but the weight of her upbringing is so ingrained that she has to struggle considerably to show her love and passion for her suitor Duy-Cau. After their first embrace, she swears eternal loyalty to him: "However many months and years of waiting this means, I promise that I will be your wife for the rest of my life and I take Heaven as witness that I will love only you" (83).

Importantly, both Thu-Thuy and Ngoc-Suong are the ones to allow or engineer sexual relations with their men. What was not possible for Tran in 1945 is now possible for these two young women in 1971. Thu-Thuy and Ngoc-Suong are able to express their sexuality while still remaining virtuous women. Their creator imbues them with greater self-affirmation than she did the figure of Tran in *Printemps* or Lang in *Carrefour*. Not surprisingly, their actions entail consequences, but they are at least instrumental in the instigation of events. Thu-Thuy becomes pregnant. Her shocked reaction underscores issues of gender and class. It highlights the importance of external appearance and, for a woman, reputation. While this state of affairs was acceptable for a robust peasant girl like Manh who never made a secret of her attachments, it was not so for a respectable if impoverished young woman like Thu-Thuy.

Thu-Thuy's reasoning reveals the double standard that applies to women and, on another level, to lower classes, servants, and peasants. No matter how impoverished she is, Thu-Thuy has a standard to uphold. The insecurity of her position as an employee on the property adds to this burden. She has no family to call on and no male protector. She is vulnerable because she is a woman, alone. Like Tran in *Printemps* and Lang in *Carrefour*, Thu-Thuy is vividly conscious of the difference in rank and family background between herself and her lover. While she is a penniless refugee from the North with no surviving family, he is the son of a landowner and his father her current employer.[27]

Both Thu-Thuy and Ngoc-Suong fall into the category of virtuous women, later to become faithful and devoted wives. The terms used to describe their physique and general demeanor suggest frail, childlike figures. As such, they are aptly set against their lovers and husbands who are strong, decisive, and both soldiers. A third female character falls into the same category—Dr Vân's wife, Lang from *Carrefour*, whose brief appearance in *Mirage* elicits the following description: "What a simple and tolerant nature, she was always even-tempered and smiling. She only opened her mouth to inquire after her husband's health and to encourage him in his mission" (96).

As a character, Lang has faded into near anonymity as the perfect accessory and helpmate of her husband Vân. Her case represents the purported ideal of a Vietnamese marriage in which "like children to parents, and younger brothers to older brothers, wives . . . [are] expected to be supportive and compliant."[28] The ideal is exemplified by the heroines of classical Western fairy tales. Marcia Lieberman points out: "These stories focus upon courtship, which is magnified into the most important and exciting part of a girl's life, brief though courtship is, because it is the part of her life in which she most counts as a person herself. After marriage she ceases to be wooed, her consent is no longer sought, she derives her status from her husband, and her personal identity is thus snuffed out."[29] For Lang, marriage is literally the end of the story.

In *Mirage*, Ly Thu Ho's category of the good-hearted prostitute is represented by Kieu-Lien, a bar-girl and the recognized mistress of Huu-Lôc (before he meets and loves Thu-Thuy): "All the same, a prostitute like myself does not have the same feelings as other girls. But I too have a soul, a heart, noble and pure sentiments" (114). For her part, Kieu-Lien is just as keen to conform to a socially acceptable role as Thu-Thuy and Ngoc-Suong, but she recognizes that her profession is a means of livelihood that also allows her a measure of independence. Huu-Lôc charitably offers his mistress the use of his studio in Saigon; Kieu-Lien bears an unrequited love for him. Unlike her counterparts, Nam in *Printemps* and Liêu in *Carrefour*, Kieu-Lien is not automatically or visibly punished for rebelling so openly against the feminine ideal. Her fate remains unspecified.

Meanwhile, history inevitably takes its course. Mr. Huu-Phuoc, the novel's patriarch, dies at the beginning of 1975, and is spared the subsequent death of his son Huu-Lôc in combat, the communist takeover of South Vietnam, and his son-in-law Duy-Cau's personality change as a result of guilt and depression. Only the women are left to eke out what living they can on the property. Thu-Thuy turns from a glowing, fulfilled wife and mother into a haggard and prostrate widow. Ngoc-Suong feels herself to be "the widow of a living man" (297). Only Manh, who has lost none of her resourcefulness, holds the household together using her native wit and cunning.

Manh realizes how vulnerable Thu-Thuy is as a young widow. Male military personnel and cadres are already expressing an interest in her. To forestall them, she spreads a rumor that the young widow is suffering from a mysterious woman's illness for which she is receiving treatment. Thu-Thuy is grateful for this and the incident stirs her out of her lethargy. She slowly pieces her health together and sets down to hard physical work in the new conditions. She visits her husband's grave regularly, reporting the latest happenings to him and swearing the following:

> I vow for the rest of my life, and in the hope of better days, to keep my heart intact and pure and to venerate your memory, not to embark on another boat however enchanting it may be, to keep my promise of eternal fidelity to you, and never to leave this land of the South where now your ashes lie, even though this land is enveloped by a veil of suffering and despair. (309)

Of her own volition, Thu-Thuy undertakes to remain eternally faithful to his memory, never to remarry, and never to leave the country. She thus conforms to the Confucian ideal of the perfect, obedient and loyal wife:

> Confucian morality required that the wife remain faithful to her dead husband so as to devote herself to her children. The term which signifies 'widow' (*chung phu*) means 'faithful to the end' . . . Another term more commonly used to designate widows is 'tiet phu,' which means 'virtuous woman.'[30]

Despite the lack of actual mother figures in their lives, the female protagonists in *Mirage* echo ideals espoused by mothers and grandmothers which illustrate the subservient role of women under patriarchy. A woman has neither voice nor presence unless she is attached to a man, and unless she is catering to the needs of other individuals. Although she chooses not to marry, even a robust, capable peasant like Manh devotes her energy to looking after her mistresses and their children. This, Ly's last novel, even more so than her earlier works, depicts female stereotypes that conform to the roles assigned them by society: the virtuous and loving helpmate, the self-sacrificing mother. There are few indications of a woman's independence, free spirit, or outside interests; a woman asserts her will by getting herself a man. In the end, every path returns to catering to husband and child. Her role and her duty are thus perceived, not only by men, but by other women operating under similar constraints. The cycle seems never-ending.

In this last novel, the mother figure, represented by the nanny Ba-Sau, is the upholder of culture and tradition. Kumari Jayawardena observes: "It was claimed that the women of the East were more spiritual; that they were heirs to the wisdom of centuries; that they . . . were still the custodians and transmitters of national culture."[31] Ba-Sau's strictures have the most effect on the two characters that conform most closely to this ideal—Thu-Thuy and Ngoc-Suong. Predictably, both suffer loss and tragedy, but despite a greater measure of assertion (in the sexual sphere) than their earlier counterparts in *Printemps* and *Carrefour*, both embody the traditional feminine attributes that characterized their predecessors. Their personalities stand in marked contrast to the figures of Kieu-Lien, the bar-girl and Manh, the peasant. As in *Carrefour*, it is women on the periphery of society who possess the more colorful and arresting personalities. The passivity and sweetness of the two principal female characters serve to underline their eventual apathy and powerlessness in the face of great loss.

In her earlier novels, Ly invests in her female characters traditionally feminine attributes, providing at the same time an analysis of the hidden tragedies of traditional feminine roles. Carolyn Heilbrun has commented: "Women writers . . . have articulated their pain. But they cannot, or for the most part have not, imagined characters moving, as the authors themselves have moved, beyond that pain."[32] *Mirage* is the most pessimistic of Ly's novels. Constant, unremitting war has eroded society; women have become victims of these circumstances. Neil Jamieson sums up, "By the end of 1968 combat losses of the government's forces exceeded 63,000 dead and 144,000 wounded. In nine years about one of every five soldiers, perhaps one of every twenty adult males, was killed or seriously wounded while fighting for the government."[33] He concludes: "Since virtually every soldier who was killed or wounded had a wife, parents, children, brothers, sisters, and friends who were affected, there were few people in the society whose lives were not blighted by deep personal loss."[34]

This novel permits us to surmise that in such a context, it would be selfish of these women to think of their own fulfillment when so many are suffering and dying. Where would women's intelligence and energy expand? What other avenues exist? Is it not best to conform to traditional notions of womanhood, to give some semblance of sanity and stability to society, to marry and bear children to make up for the losses? From today's vantage point, the prospect of women serving no other purpose but to produce offspring to offset losses is horrifying.

Conclusion

Ly Thu Ho forms part of a minority of female writers in the Vietnamese Francophone tradition. Unlike contemporary Vietnamese male writers such as Pham Van Ky, Nguyen Huu Chau, or Pham Duy Khiem, she does not engage in formal experiments with circular time or splintered perceptions or characterizations. She is not interested in using innovative techniques, nor do the structures of her novels capture the break up of personalities and societies. Easy to read, Ly's narrative progression is orderly and linear. Her characters are drawn without depth and conform to convention: the women are vulnerable, the men, strong. In that her work does not openly challenge the status quo, is not *engagé* (politically engaged), Ly differs from contemporary women writers, both Vietnamese and French.

There exists, as a result, a marked disparity between Ly's experience and that of the women in her novels. Her proficiency in expression as a novelist contrasts with the lack of expression of her main female protagonists. In this way, she shares traits with some of her Western counterparts at the end of the nineteenth century and the early years of the twentieth. Marilyn French has observed:

> It is remarkable that . . . women writers should have set aside their own experience in writing about women. Male writers have not done this, and such a difference must have import. Women writers, on the whole, have tried to write about women on the whole—that is, about the experience of the female sex, rather than that of an extraordinary member of that sex. And the experience of women in general, even those of the middle or upper classes, is one of constriction.[35]

In Ly's writing, then, the paradox is that while female protagonists who belong to the writer's own social class and background are the least articulate on political and military realities of the times, yet these are subjects on which she, as author, discourses at length and with confidence through the letters of her male protagonists. These same, well-brought up women are the most vulnerable to the feminine ideal and suffer correspondingly. Certainly, this does not mean that Ly's novels are not subversive. In fact, their apparent superficiality allows her to express unusual views. The act of writing is in itself a means of assertion. As the Vietnamese theorist Trinh T. Minh-ha suggests, "Power, as unveiled by numerous contemporary writings, has always inscribed itself in language. Speaking, writing, and discoursing are not mere acts of communication, they are above all acts of compulsion."[36]

Using considerable irony, Ly locates the subversive aspect of her work in the fates of its female characters. Her novels convey the restricted boundaries and silenced identities of the truly feminine characters. Virtue and obedience result in stifled lives, or, as in *Printemps*, death. Female traits of filial and wifely deference, beauty, and gentleness go unrewarded. The women who conform to these ideals experience brief happiness, followed by tragedy or anonymity. Her intelligent, attractive, and sensitive female protagonists lose their personalities or, again as is the case in *Printemps*, lose their lives. Her virtuous females are punished, whether by fate or circumstance—by years of torment and an early death for Tran in *Printemps*; by the gradual anonymity of Lang in *Carrefour*; and by the sadness, bereavement, and breakdown of Thu-Thuy and Ngoc-Suong in *Mirage*.

In her most expressive novel, *Printemps*, Ly began by subtly re-appraising the classic tale of Kieu in a modern context, clearly questioning traditional female roles. In her last, *Mirage*, Ly adopts a subdued note of pessimism and resignation, her work reflecting a measure of the vigor of French feminism in the sixties and seventies and its fading visibility in the 1980s.[37] As a Vietnamese Francophone writer, Ly was not only shaped by her life in Paris for nearly half a century, but by the Vietnamese heritage she brought with her. Clearly, Vietnam and the condition of Vietnamese women in particular form a central focus for her work.

It is not surprising, perhaps, that in *Mirage*, more than in the two earlier novels, Ly's women characters stand as a symbol of their country, a country at war. Having borne the cost of the war, experienced loss and despair, still they survive. Beyond the immediate politics of the Vietnam War and the defeat of the South, these women, like the country at large, embody the abused yet still present state of their land. Vietnam has undergone centuries of turmoil, invasion, occupation, rebellion, and lengthy years of war. In the end, despite the reverses in their lives, the women in *Mirage* and their country, will remain and endure.

3

Through Male Eyes

All alone with my shadow
I whisper and murmur to it...
There is no one here I can speak to
Who can understand me.
—Ch'iu Chin

Pham Van Ky is the most prominent Vietnamese Francophone writer of his generation. His body of works includes seven novels, all published in France, as well as plays, collections of poetry, short stories, and Vietnamese tales. Pham won the *Grand Prix du Roman de l'Académie Française* for his novel *Perdre la demeure* (To Lose the Dwelling-place) in 1961. Like Ly Thu Ho, he chose to exile himself in France, but did so at a much earlier stage, in 1938. Pham originated from a landowning family in Central Vietnam. He went on to further his education in Paris where he studied at the Sorbonne and the *Institut des Hautes Etudes Chinoises* (Institute of Higher Chinese Studies).[1] As an expatriate writer, he cast a discerning eye on colonial and post-colonial Vietnam. His work reveals a melding of Eastern and Western influences. Pham's exploration of the female condition in his novels *Frères de sang* (1947) and *Des Femmes assises çà et là* (1964) differs vastly from that of Ly Thu Ho. While Ly's treatment is subdued and characterized by an underlying irony, Pham's two novels are direct and violent criticisms of the social constraints imposed on women.

Set in Vietnam in 1945, *Frères de sang* (Blood Brothers) features an unnamed narrator who returns to his native village to witness the unfolding of a dramatic series of events. The narrator portrays his father, head of the village, as a rigid and intolerant patriarch. It is this rigidity, along with the hypocritical behavior of the all-male village eldership, which leads to one tragedy after another involving his sisters, mother, and the wider village community. The characterization of both patriarch and female relatives and dependents is harsh and unsparing. Pham presents the reader with five categories of women: the bleak mother figure in the form of mother and grandmother, the conformist, the rebel, the servant, and lastly, the adulteress. Throughout the narrative, the narrator remains strangely detached. As if he was watching the drama unfold on a screen, he finds himself unable to interfere or to influence the course of events.

The sense of detachment and distance is even more marked in the later novel, *Des Femmes assises çà et là* (Women Sitting Here and There). This time, the unnamed male narrator is an exiled Vietnamese man living in France in the 1960s. He attempts to ignore messages from his dying mother in Vietnam while helplessly observing both the death of a young French girl he loves and the gradual descent into mental illness of another French woman he once loved. He also narrates the breakdown of his relationship with a third woman. The title of the novel refers to an old German text, *Merseburg Charms*, which deals with women unchaining themselves. In this novel, however, neither the women nor the narrator succeed in escaping their predicaments.

Hypocrisy and Extremes in *Frères de sang*

Frères de sang is set in an unspecified Vietnamese village and contains an unambiguous critique of the patriarchal nature of traditional society. In the introduction to her English translation, Lucy Nguyen Hong Nhiem places the events the novel relates as occurring at the "moment" of the revolution, shortly before the last Emperor's abdication and Vietnam's proclamation of a Republic, all of which took place around August 1945.[2] The novel chronicles the return of the narrator to his native village after years of study in France. Despite—or perhaps because—he feels a stranger in his own land, he is a keen observer of the interlocking relationships and social currents in his family in particular, and the village as a whole.

It is the narrator's father, a tradition-bound patriarch and head of the village, who reintroduces his unnamed son to the family. In his daughter Dinh, we meet the first category of women: the rebel.

The father labels her an "eccentric" character whom married life will "tame." The old patriarch expresses the value he places on his children: "[H]ere, we raise children to protect ourselves against an unproductive old age, in much the same way as we store rice against famine."[3] But Dinh is a young radical and visionary. The narrator says of her:

> Poor sister! This 'eccentric' harbored an immense dream: to emancipate Annamite women, to assure for them a status at least equal to men's. Father had stopped her upper primary education, in a mixed college, because he could not find a girls' only establishment (32).

The narrator is surprised, therefore, and understandably wary when his sister acquiesces to an early marriage. The actual wedding day sees Dinh married to "a slight, sickly man, with a face scarred with chickenpox. . . . [She] has an instant of hesitation, but then rallies quickly" (158–9). As her brother has surmised, however, the acquiescence is deceptive. The entire charade is to allow Dinh, her other brother Hô, and the rebel servant girl Tu, to escape from the village. Their departure signifies the breakdown of traditional divisions of class and hierarchy. The day after the wedding, an abandoned bridegroom presents his father-in-law with the following message from his absent bride:

> I am worth more than one of Confucius' precepts. The "three obediences," I stuff them in my bag. The "four virtues," I chew. . . . I only agreed to "be wed in just nuptials" in order to create a diversion for the escape of my brother Hô . . . and to enable myself to escape. (175–6)

This message, while ostensibly directed towards the bridegroom, is as much a gesture of defiance aimed at the constricting nature of village life and, in particular, at the man who heads it: her father. The Three Obediences involve the submission of a woman to father, husband, and son; the Four Virtues: right occupation, right speech, right appearance, and right conduct.[4] In her critique of Pham's work, Thuong Vuong-Riddick sets Pham's representation of Dinh in its socio-historical context:

> Vietnamese women had remained submissive to men, but their status . . . goes beyond the simplistic image of the Eastern woman-slave. Vietnamese society retains traces of the primitive matriarchal system upon which was subsequently grafted the patriarchal system imported from China. . . . The existence of these two opposites leaves women with a margin for maneuver and allows them to play an important economic role. But in this novel, Pham Van Ky set himself to describe a family regulated by Confucian order.[5]

In this context, each individual's position and role in the hierarchy had to be rigidly delineated and adhered to. Under a Confucian-style code laid out by the nineteenth-century emperor Gia Long, the head of the family had the sole right to discipline family members and to make his children marry.[6] Of the broader social context, Ralph Smith notes:

> The emperor made demands, and it was for the villagers to carry them out. But his guarantee that they would do so rested more on their sense of obligation than on an authoritarian system of coercion. Conversely, when the villagers, who looked to the imperial officials as men who would guarantee their protection and good exactions, found that a local mandarin was corrupt or made unfair exactions, they could not appeal against him to the law: their only defence was either open revolt, or to leave the village and return when the official had gone.[7]

For Dinh and Hô, then, escape was their only recourse. With their father as both head of family and village, they were left with no other option but to flee.

Sharply contrasted with Dinh is another sister, Co, a model of submission and emblematic of the second category of women, the conformist. Co's husband is in prison at the time of the narrator's return and she spends her days writing to her husband. Her letters reveal traditional images of female virtue—diligence and thrift, as well as despair at his absence. Allusions to both classical literature and folksong abound in her letters but the effect in this modern context is mannered and artificial since the sentences do not translate well into French. They illustrate the mode of writing of another culture and era and stand in contrast to the unadorned prose of the novel itself. Excerpts of Vietnamese folksong and poetry throughout the novel mostly relate to women and their general subordination in society. The narrator reveals this sister's first letter to her husband:

> My guts are torn to see us separated from each other, hundreds of *li* away, by the wind and the snow. My tears fall like unstrung pearls and dampen my tunic . . . In the sky, with you, I would like us to be two orioles that fly together. On earth, two roots that crisscross each other. (31)[8]

Co's position as a traditional woman, daughter, sister, and wife is linked with traditional literature, both in its imagery—the hundreds of *li*, the snow, and the orioles—and in its overall tone. She waxes lyrical with numerous references to flora and fauna. In her mournful yearning for an absent husband, she brings to mind a female characterization present in much of traditional Vietnamese poetry. The narrator portrays her as a passive figure, her life held in waiting for the return of her spouse. Instead of having recourse to law or petition, she waits and weeps. In this, she stands in contrast to the dynamic and spirited figure of her younger sister Dinh, whose language, as demonstrated in the letter to her bridegroom, is correspondingly robust and direct. Co indulges in all this elaborate grieving for a husband whom Dinh dismisses as mediocre.

When Co's husband Cung finally reappears on the scene, his arrival, described in classical terms, renders the scene mildly ridiculous. Co has just finished writing another letter, "I harness myself like a dragon to your chariot of jade and ivory . . . a puff of wind suffices to give life to a small light," when Cung suddenly appears "like a puff of wind which gives life to a small light" (111–2). The repetition serves to highlight the melodrama of her husband's unexpected reappearance. Freed from prison by the Vietminh, he had hastened homeward on foot, begging on the way till "At the end of an infinite waiting, he found again his 'little sister,' his 'body' *(minh)*" (112). Here, the narrator mocks his brother-in-law's haste and the appraisal of his wife as both "little sister" and property in these traditional terms of address between husband and wife. After such passionate letters of longing, Co is restrained and demure in her greeting, her response evincing a particularly traditional Vietnamese reserve:

> She was not expansive, as a European spouse would have hoped. But her lowered pupils closed together, one moment, over the wet gleam of her eyes. He had barely touched her that she withdrew gently from him. This sense of modesty was not dictated to her by the presence of her family. It was natural to her. (112)

Despite his record as a prisoner of the French, Cung turns out not to be the hero whom his wife's idealistic younger brother Hô had hoped to emulate. "[H]e soon became aware of his crude mistake: Cung was only a wreck, a live target—for how may shooters?" (113). Yet Co eventually also leaves the village in order to follow her husband.

Perhaps the most discordant figure in the novel, the narrator's mother, illustrates a medley of compromises and adjustments to misfortune:

> Mother wept in fits and starts, her face buried in a red handkerchief—so that it would not be dirtied by betel chews. Her greatest joys were soaked in tears. Her greatest

sorrows provoked a laughter like white-hot, crackling salt.
A nervous person, despite her apparent placidity. (27)

Full of contradictions, these images intimate a woman whose life is
one of unspoken and unacknowledged frustrations and limitations.
The narrator dates his mother's strange laughter from the time of his
father taking a concubine. The concubine has, she informs him, been
sent away for misbehavior and his younger brother Hô has
threatened to kill himself if his father takes another.[9] There is much
to be unhappy about, it seems, and her "laughter like white-hot,
crackling salt" appears periodically throughout the novel. On the
return of her son-in-law, laughter and tears mingle: "Her laughter of
salt dropped off slowly, while the large wet grains of her tears fell
down her tired cheeks" (115). She laughs hysterically during the
preparations for her daughter Dinh's marriage. And her despair is
evident when Co also leaves to follow her husband: "Mother ran to
catch up with them. Her laments were drowned by her crackling salt
laughter. One would have thought it the first cracklings of the start
of a fire" (147).

The mother's laughter is symbolic of a conflagration, not
only in the life of her family, but of the village in general. Towards
the end of the novel, with the loss of three of her children, she is left
empty. "Her nervous laugh had disappeared. . . . her expression had
lost any color and when I bent over to lift her up, I thought of
Grandmother" (173). This, the narrator's last sight of his mother
brings an image of immateriality and impotence with the reminder
of the other mother figure and figure of fate in the family. His
grandmother is slowly dying when he returns to the village. She has
lost her memory and can no longer recognize her grandchildren,
even though she has devoted her entire life to her family. She asks
the narrator: "Who are you?" (63).

Grandmother slumbered in a nirvana-like warmth. Pinned
down in her pearly armchair, following a paralysis of her
legs, she watched herself slowly dying. Events passed her by
as if she were transparent. The only consistent thing she had

was a fibrous cough, which, with each fit, emptied her of
some of her consciousness. Another witness. Another model
of durability! (27–8)

The images are contradictory. Though representing "durability," she
is dying. With neither voice nor opinion, her presence is a symbol of
tradition and family life. She symbolizes continuity, yet
simultaneously death and unawareness. Her passing points to the
end of the society that she knew. Her grandson's arrival coincides
with the winds of change hitting the village. The narrator's inner
conflicts and uncertainties are given public voice in the maelstrom of
events that are soon to shake the village with such violence and
shattering results.

   While unrelated to the narrator's family, the female figure to
whom the narrator gives the most attention is Tu, the cook and
daughter of an old family servant, Ong Chin. Tu represents the
category of servant. She is depicted as attractive and flirtatious,
"beautiful and single," available on several fronts though dis-
advantaged by her youth, sex, and low rank. While her masters and
the other men of the village lust after her, rather than letting herself
be abused by them she succeeds in uncovering their lust, at the same
time depriving them of its gratification. By making clever use of her
father's proprietary attitude towards her, she is able to retain her
autonomy and self-respect, and fend off the unwanted suitors. The
narrator is immediately aware of the effect she has on his own
father:

   Tu, the cook, put away her fan and headed towards
   Grandmother's nook to give her something to drink. Her
   feline body undulated with the lascivious swaying of her
   hips. Under her black tunic, unhooked because of the heat,
   swelled a green bra. Father's glance fastened onto it, burning
   with concupiscence, then switched off like an acetylene
   lamp. (33)

The narrator later realizes that, despite being at the beck and call of her doting father, Tu is able to express her sexuality quite independently. He focuses at length on Tu's physical attributes—a seductive body, a curvaceous shape—and in his short encounters finds himself unsettled by her: "She winked at me, her body brushing mine, her breath as fresh as a slice of watermelon against mine. Perturbed, in spite of myself . . ." (63). In the detailed episode in which Tu outwits her male admirers, the narrator, along with the other men, watches her mesmerized while she bathes:

> Tu was washing her hair, which fell to her ankles, in the pond. . . . A smooth back and tender arms like young shoots of bamboo. All the desires of men seemed to converge on this libidinous creature, above whose head was suspended the threat of the paternal knife and the curse that once again accompanied her mother. . . . It was enough that she was there for the arrival, from all corners of the village, of the pubescents, the libidinous, the dodderers, the canonical. (76)

The Mayor and village notables all find themselves, coincidentally, in the same place. When Tu's father, Ong Chin, also makes his appearance armed with a knife, her erstwhile suitors gradually melt away. The Mayor stays longest in an attempt to hold on to his dignity but finally leaves after a fit of irrepressible laughter from Tu. Hidden behind a tree, the narrator watches these proceedings, realizing that the entire scene has been planned deliberately to cast ridicule on these respectable pillars of society: "What dirty trick had she played on all these overzealous admirers? She had given them a rendezvous at the same time, at the same place, while instructing Ba [her brother], in the meantime, to warn the fierce watchdog so that he could rescue her" (79). In doing so, she not only reveals these men to each other, but does so through the means of a traditional woman's virtue, ostensibly relying on the protection of her father as jealous guardian of his daughter's chastity and honor.

Tu successfully makes the point that she is out of bounds. Though she is poor and single these men have no right to avail themselves of her body. She refuses to be a pure commodity and deftly uses the weapons of traditional society to underline this.

> Tu, triumphant, followed her father like a beaten dog.
> For a long time, she could be heard singing:
> *Ten men are worth three sapèques,*
> *I shut them up in a cage and take them around like birds.*
> *A woman is worth three hundred sapèques,*
> *One has to install her at home on a flowered mat.* (80)[10]

Opposing images are juxtaposed in this passage: the "triumphant" Tu is a "beaten dog." At the same time, she sings that a woman is worth a thousand men. As David Marr writes:

> It would be wrong to assume . . . that Confucian moralists had succeeded entirely in propagandizing pre-modern Vietnamese women into submission. Among the plain people in particular there remained a frankness of expression and diversity of life experience that defied regimentation. Each Confucian platitude, for example, could be turned on its head at the right opportunity. Thus, the saying about a hundred girls not being worth a single testicle was countered by "A hundred boys are not worth a girl's earlobe."[11]

When Tu's brother, Ba, is caught with the wife of the *trùm* or hamlet notable, the reader is introduced to the fate of the fifth category of women, the adulteress. The *trùm*'s wife first appears as a peasant irrigating the fields with Ba. "What a harmonious picture was created by these two peasants who were nearly dancing, rearing up, bracing up, balancing their arms, inclining their chests. They seemed to have gotten used to each other a long time ago, coming together in harmony from the first gesture" (136). The image is one of pastoral bliss. Though they do not know each other, Ba notes her physical attractiveness. Aware, she sings in response, "The world is a spectacle to rejoice at!/ For a fish that swims, so many people to throw it a hook!" (137).

The following scene is violent. "A great commotion in the village: the *trùm* had caught his wife and Ba in the act during the first watch. A gathering had already formed around the couple who were strapped down until they bled" (138). The narrator observes his father's arbitrary censuring. In accordance with a rarely applied law in the Gia Long Code, the adulterers are condemned to a slow death by exposure, tied to a raft that is then set to drift down the river.[12] In exacting this measure, the narrator's father displays an unquestioning obedience to the letter of the law. The woman immediately receives the larger share of the blame in the form of a more severe beating. Even then, the Mayor cannot hide his lust for the accused woman:

> The Mayor, while exposing the facts to Father, glanced furtively at the offender, who had her arms crossed over her breasts. Bronze, firm breasts that looked swollen still with desire. What was left of her clothing, trousers torn in the ... forbidden place by public vindictiveness, hid in vain a troubling shape. (139)

In this context, the Mayor's ill-concealed desire is particularly abhorrent. He judges the woman while lusting after her, and in so doing punishes her for his feelings. The narrator watches as the villagers are carried away by collective hysteria: "A sort of sacred delirium shook them, in which featured a little innate love of justice, a little disdain and a lot of physical excitement" (139). Only Tu, the servant girl raises any objections. "Who shall judge the judges?" (141), she cries. Driven by a desperate wish to save her brother, she continues courageously, exposing the hypocrisy of the male judges who are all village dignitaries: "And if the judge, himself married and a father, had seduced a servant girl delivered defenseless to his pleasure, will he also be accused of adultery and brought before this Court?" (142).

It is Ba's encroachment on another man's territory that is at issue here, and the fact that he was caught doing so by the woman's husband. The novel focuses not on the act itself but on the consequences. Ba and the *trùm*'s wife are both peasants. Neither has any form of redress against those in power. "The Notables made the laws and executed them."[13] The condemned man's own father prepares the raft on which the two will be tied. He knows that crude village justice is inevitable. He does not speak up for his son or remind the head of the village, his master, that he and his children have been lifelong servants of the family.

After an initial stunned moment following Tu's question, order is restored. The narrator's father decrees the death penalty. The sentence is immediately carried out. There are, in the end, three deaths, since Ba's mother joins her son on the raft. Hô, the narrator's younger brother, screams from his cell where his father has imprisoned him for disrespect: "You are monsters! You are devouring each other like monsters! . . . Evacuate the village so that one can set fire to it!" (147). The various states of the bodies of these villagers, Vuong-Riddick summarizes, reflect the village's social hierarchy:

> Through the sole treatment of the body, it has been possible
> for us to retrace the Vietnamese social structure of the time,
> with the empty but sublimated bodies of the governors, the
> present but tortured bodies of the peasants, the cared-for
> bodies of the dead. Such a distribution speaks for itself. . . .[14]

The narrator neither remonstrates with his father nor argues against the savagery and arbitrariness of the sentence and execution. He merely observes. Unable to help his wife or son, Ong Chin follows the raft containing their dying bodies for three days. People in neighboring villages come to observe the drifting raft: "No one took pity on them. . . . Until his last breath, Ba moaned: 'Mother, Mother, why do you cling to me?' And everyone said: 'It is the law'" (144–5). Crows gather around the bodies in a macabre dance to peck:

> There were a dozen of these voracious birds that went at the corpses fiercely, hopping from skull to belly, from belly to thigh. . . . They liked the fleshy parts. They liked young flesh! They pecked at your breasts, pierced your eyes, rummaged about your guts, always replete, always insatiable! One, two, three, four . . . (145)

Ong Chin finally buys two coffins and gives his wife and son a decent burial but his compassion does not extend to the condemned wife of the *trùm*. There is no one to care for her remains. She is damaged goods. Throughout the entire proceedings, she is allowed no space in which to speak. She is beaten, judged, condemned, and executed without a hearing. As in Gayatri Chakravorty Spivak's study on widow sacrifice, "there is no place where the subaltern . . . can speak."[15] In a classic bind of the powerless, she is silenced by the men around her. Ba's distress is recorded, but not hers. "The *trùm's* wife," she is otherwise nameless; not a person, but a body, and in the end dismissed as a body. Ong Chin does not mention her, nor is he concerned about her spirit wandering without rest. Unlike his daughter Tu, he remains servile to the end, acquiescing to society's judgements, society's bias, and his Master's authority. When Tu also leaves, Ong Chin tells the narrator's father:

> My son deserved his punishment . . . As to my daughter Tu, her . . . deposition has turned against her. Truth or false accusation, who cares! What condemns man condemns first of all woman. Your Excellency has turned her out of this house and that is just. Your Excellency will dispose as you see fit of the remaining days of my life! (156)

Old, bereft, and heartbroken, he has nothing left but his lifelong work of serving his Master. He has lost his wife and son and been abandoned by his daughter. He is too tired to start anew, to change his views and the way he lives. It is up to the younger generation to rebel.

The female characters in *Frères de sang* illustrate the common plight of women in traditional society. Their lives are constrained and inhibited, with appreciable emotional and psychological consequences. Dinh and Tu question the status quo but find themselves unable to alter the course of events. They cannot shift the weight of centuries of conformity but can only defy the authority represented by the patriarch and the village notables. In the end, their only recourse is to leave; staying in the village would only result in their lives being stifled in the mould of Dinh's mother and grandmother. Although it seems the village may change, they cannot wait, and they have no assurance that anything fundamental will truly change. As long as the old mandarin lives and the village notables rally behind him, village society and laws will not alter.

The man who notes and records all this is both part of and separate from the fabric of village and family life. The narrator observes the women who live in, bow to, and die under the system and those who question traditional mores and have to flee from the village, and he expresses anger at the constraints imposed on them. As a person who in many ways has become alienated from these roots and traditions, he is more able to empathize with these women.[16] As Marr observes, "Anger at French colonial exploitation of Vietnamese often opened male eyes to other forms of exploitation, including that of women by men."[17]

Pham Van Ky's equating of the female condition with that of colonized men echoes critics of colonialism such as Albert Memmi.[18] Pham's unnamed narrator is in a position to observe the abuse of power by those who uphold authority and the law, even though he does not explicitly allude to the colonial situation. In this, the village becomes a metaphor for the country at large and the village's destruction a reference to the momentous events of 1945. A member of the younger generation and his father's son, the narrator is, like these women, subject to patriarchal authority. Their anger and helplessness are reflections of his own vulnerabilities—but he can only observe. He finds himself unable to act decisively or constructively in the unfolding events, however touched he is by pathos or injustice; he remains on the margin of events, recording them as an onlooker. His lack of effective power echoes that of the women, reinforcing the notion of what Memmi called the colonized's "petrifaction,"[19] and the silencing of the native subject— male or female. Although his presence touches these women's lives, his inability to act increases the sense of alienation. Their only options, he narrates, are to either die, as do his grandmother, the *trùm*'s wife, and Ba's mother, or to leave, as do his sisters and the servant girl Tu. He stands as a foreigner not only to his compatriots, but in respect of the lives and fates of these women.

Pham Van Ky portrays his female characters clearly and categorically. There is little scope for fluidity or depth. Each woman is rigidly confined to a particular group and does not err. Each serves to highlight particular destructive effects of traditional social and family configurations. Pham concentrates on illustrating events and actions that serve to confirm the category into which each female character falls. Radical is therefore consistently radical, conformist excessively conventional, and the traditional, sad and slowly disappearing. The result is a harsh critique of the abuse of power by village elders, the constricting bands of which have a most noxious effect on women and on the younger generation. In this novel, Pham Van Ky expresses indignation at these abuses but is unable to offer a solution. Only three resulting effects are recorded: escape, death, and destruction—of the village, and of the narrator himself.

Standing on the Outside: *Des Femmes assises çà et là*

Published almost twenty years after *Frères de sang*, *Des Femmes assises çà et là* (Women Sitting Here and There) has a markedly different context. Set in France where the unnamed Vietnamese narrator makes a conscious decision to stay, the novel relates the narrator's interactions with his Vietnamese mother and three French women— Eliane, Orla, and Solange. *Des Femmes* is a record of the narrator's experiences and introspective musings which recall, Jack Yeager notes, French feminist Nathalie Sarraute's *sous-conversation* (conversation under the conversation) technique. In a partial return to Eastern sources, Pham Van Ky also draws on classical Chinese philosophy to provide a framework for a Western-style narrative. Eight trigrams which form the basis of the Taoist text *I Ching* (Book of Changes) not only introduce each chapter but impose themselves upon the narrator's thoughts as he obsesses about their meaning.[20]

The narrator's mother is the first female figure to be mentioned in the novel. As in *Frères de sang*, she is a bleak figure. The weight of her presence and of her influence is acknowledged from the outset: "Mother. A word let out, with precise contours, which crushes me but does not entirely cover me" (8). A gulf of mutual incomprehension lies between mother and son. She instigates contact by sending a stark telegram: "*Waiting for you so that I can die. May 26.*"[21] The narrator ruminates:

> Telegrams never explain anything, they say things indirectly and mislead by their color. This one gave me no choice. For Mother to note the date as May 26, Mother's Day in France, when we were at the beginning of December, there would have to have been on her part, not cruelty, but anger, the desire to get at me through the actual means of correspondence even when I lived far from her. (9)

The mother's message, Nguyen Hong Nhiem suggests, can be understood in the literal sense as a call for her son to return home before she dies, as well as a symbolic call for the son to return to his country and discover his roots anew.[22] This second interpretation is significant in the light of the narrator's exile from his homeland. Deeply wary of the West and anything Western, she has warned: "You have given way to a coquetry of science more than to the need for your salvation, *the West* being a place of illness, not one of healing" (11).

The narrator, who like many Vietnamese intellectuals has turned towards the West to understand a civilization that has colonized his own country, responds: "What could I say to her to counter this mistake? That the East is not always to be followed, nor the West to run from, that neither is for our good without being at the same time for our ill?" (11). He sees her as associated with an older world, one which attempts to mould and imprison him within its values and beliefs; he wants to break free from all she represents. Nguyen Hong Nhiem writes: "The Mother . . . incarnates, in descending order, the Far East, the collective 'I' of the Far East, and the derivative 'I' of the narrator/author."[23] Though physically absent, she is ever present in his mind and emotions.

The other three female characters central to the novel are physically as well as emotionally present for the narrator. All three are European, and live, as he does, in Paris. If the mother symbolizes the past, these three figures symbolize different aspects of the present. The neurotic Orla and thirteen-year-old Eliane—the daughter of some friends, she is dying of leukemia—are the first introduced. Throughout the novel they are constantly offset, one against the other. Whenever the phone rings, the narrator wonders, "Orla or Eliane?" and his reluctance to pick up the phone stems from the fact that he wishes to hear from Eliane, but not from Orla. Since Eliane is severely ill, it is urgent that he speak to her whenever she does call. Orla on the other hand, is a constant chore.

In the midst of conjecturing whether to respond to either Orla or Eliane, the figure of the mother again surfaces. Even as he speaks to either Orla or Eliane, he remembers that he is denying his own mother a similar contact: "Would I lend them my aid even when I refused it to Mother?" (22). Both Orla and Eliane are ill. His mother is also ill, but far away. The contrast between the two, perhaps three generations of women is apparent to the narrator: *"Waiting for you so that I can die.* May 26. And Orla-Eliane? Waiting for you so that we do not die" (23).

Death and illness, the "horrible band" which afflicts Orla and Eliane, also symbolize the "band" which the narrator's past loyalties inflict upon him. Despite his determination to step beyond the confines of his upbringing, he is still bound. To him, Orla and Eliane's illnesses are similarly an inescapable weight stifling their lives, visions, and hopes. The narrator identifies with their plight not only because he considers both as friends but also because he can see himself in their sick heads and sick bodies—glimpses of life and the possibility of escaping beyond sickness, just as he is attempting to escape from his own self and the painful image of his mother:

> Ah! To jump out of oneself, into the unknown! . . . Far from space and time: I would escape you, Mother! In a region where all would be possible: therefore impossible for you, Mother! Where imagination would neither undergo restraint nor coordinate anything whatsoever, where a new mythology would direct my actions towards an unknown destination, and would solicit my belief in a radically different way! (34)

One way of expressing these flights of imagination, one that is inaccessible to the Mother, is writing in French. "A difficult operation, this transfer from the shape of ideograms to the sound of the alphabet" (34), he admits. While she remains enveloped in visions of classical ideograms, he has been exposed to this new mentality. While the sounds and images of the language which he can avail himself of take him to new heights, for her they are out of bounds.

Orla represents an aspect of the past that the narrator wishes to distance himself from. Yeager suggests that, because she has lived in China and is both familiar with and appreciative of Asian culture, she is in some sense a "partial counterpart" to the narrator.[24] Just as he is hostile to or incapable of assisting his aged mother, he is hostile to Orla, whose illness is unalterable, and who represents another part of his past: "The simplest reason for my failure, is that I was reticent to attend Orla at the same time that I refused to help Mother. Orla to whom nothing linked me but a very old friendship, dating from our truant years at the Sorbonne" (50). Many of the expressions associated with Orla, the older woman, are images of sterility. Her ravings are set against the innocence and freshness of the young adolescent girl, Eliane. Her "recriminations" are contrasted with Eliane's "marvelous words" (22); "Orla's desert" with "Eliane's oasis" (50). Anything both hurt and aged, it seems, is a reminder of his Mother, with all the guilt and somber reflections associated with it.

The narrator is uneasy with the image of older suffering. But Eliane, in her youth and innocence, is untouched and perfect. His idolization of Eliane persists, perhaps, because part of him knows that she will effectively die untouched. Would he change his mind about her if she grew older, became a woman and lost her "purity"? In *Illness as Metaphor*, Susan Sontag writes of how leukemia has taken up the role in fiction

> once monopolized by TB, as the romantic disease that cuts off a young life . . . Like all really successful metaphors, the metaphor of TB was rich enough to provide for two contradictory applications. It described the death of someone (like a child) thought to be too "good" to be sexual: the assertion of angelic psychology. It was also a way of describing sexual feelings—while lifting the responsibility on libertinism, which is blamed on a state of objective, physiological decadence.[25]

The narrator of *Des Femmes* needs to draw on this youth, a sign of hope and change for the future. If women embody the past, present, and future for him, it is inevitable that he will constantly turn his eyes and hopes towards Eliane, since in her youth, there is little of the past to be associated with her.

> After Orla's desert, Eliane's oasis would bring me freshness, rest and shared nourishment. Adorable Eliane. My idol in the eyes and in the mind. She reigned over my praises, and the perpetual homage I paid her jokes and her discoveries as a child-woman, under which she buried me. (50)

Eliane thus represents the complete opposite of his mother. She embodies all the hopes that have died in his mother. She symbolizes a potential which was never given fruition in the older woman—a woman bound and constrained within her society, culture, and civilization. The narrator turns with relief to the figure of Eliane—young, French, still a child and yet also a woman:

> [I]n the worry that Mother caused me, it seems that I aspired to a counterweight, to a salutary diversion, that I sought in Eliane the image of a child I would have liked to have. . . . Whose? Why not a woman without a navel, as Orla has just wished me? Eliane-fetus would have formed herself in a different way. . . . Eliane-Antigone whom I surrounded myself with, herself wrapped around me, on my summit and branches, easing, with the balm of her soft tendrils, the burning pain that I felt in my roots. (51)

The images are painful and unrealizable. Eliane is not his daughter and he cannot save her. The brief reference to Antigone conjures up the image of her entombment, with its association of asphyxiation and entrapment, echoing the protracted course and hopelessness of Eliane's condition. Although his mother's message, "Waiting for you so that I can die," reverberates in him, the narrator rejects it: "If Eliane mumbled the same sentence to me on the telephone, bringing forward her dried tongue over her lips with a hollow sound of rasping, I would promptly run to her deathbed, while I balked at Mother's" (53).

Eliane calls him "Toitoi" (Youyou), as Yeager notes, "at once one word and two, a repetition of the same term and thus the same—a denial of distance spatially and linguistically."[26] Eliane is the focus of the narrator's attention. Of all the female characters, she is given the most voice and physical presence, since he describes her and allows her to speak at length. The young girl's imagination is presented in a long and hectic series of pictures that she communicates to her parents and to the narrator. Realizing that she may not be able to do so for much longer, she is almost hysterical in her haste to convey this plethora of images that assail her. Among her fantasies appear different women, a cure to her disease, pregnancy, childbirth, and different stages in women's lives that she will never live to experience:

> They played to satiety at being the virgin, the fiancée, the
> wife, the widow, the one who remarried, they played! . . .
> Attention to incest, repeats the other. They become again the
> fetus, I give birth to them, they present well, they deliver
> themselves and me, I nourish them with my shadow of milk,
> I lift them above the bed, I forbid them their cradle, I teach
> them to stand up, to walk, to laugh, to laugh, to laugh. But
> these imbeciles know only how to cry, cry and still cry. (58–
> 9)

"Shadows, shadows," Eliane repeats. She knows that all such images
and fantasies are insubstantial. However vividly she sees them they
will never become realities for her. As an adolescent, between child
and woman, she can briefly glimpse the myriad varieties of women's
experiences, but they are out of bounds to her: "Shadows, shadows:
a sign that something shines elsewhere" (60).

Solange, the fourth female figure in the novel, is the narrator's
lover. She represents sensuality, bodily warmth, and as an artist,
symbolizes creativity. Yet his relationship with her is limited to the
sensual: "It was always slow and hasty, violent and lucid, sad and
joyful, a mixture which broke her. But when all fell back again . . .
there was no longer anything between us" (63). Solange is a well-
read woman with views on a variety of subjects, yet while the
narrator acknowledges this and gives her voice, he cannot appreciate
her as an individual with interests, desires, and an imagination of
her own. Their physical relationship looms largest in his mind.
Indeed, much as his knowledge of the West is new, fragmented, and
incomplete, so his conception of the French female characters around
him is fragmented into distinct categories: neurosis, innocence, and
sensuality.

It seems that the further the narrator attempts to flee from the
figure of the mother, the more he realizes that many roads, in the
end, lead back to her. However attracted he is by the West, and
however Westernized he may have become, he cannot divorce
himself from his past and therefore from the woman who

symbolizes it, his mother. Lisa Lowe writes, "The narrator's ties to his mother become a metaphor for the intense, yet ambivalent longing he feels for traditional Vietnam."[27] Perhaps this acknowledgement will lead to greater acceptance both on his part and hers.

> Now that I am close to losing her for ever, she threatens to restore herself to me entirely and without counterpart, because I have over her the awful advantage of being able to reflect her in a mirror always smaller than what it reflects, and of keeping my cool, while she is no more than anxiety and waiting. (75)

In a reversal of Virginia Woolf's celebrated image of women reflecting men at twice their natural size, the narrator has the ability to reflect his mother in smaller and smaller images. He has, in addition, the leisure to think and ponder on this, while she waits anxiously. His work, his career, "The Novel" as he terms it, takes precedence: "The Novel: the naked sword between Mother and me" (83). It is only through "The Novel" that he will be able to express both his past and his present: "All is there, all will be there or would be: from the live emblems of my childhood to the pomp and achievements of my Westernization" (83). It is through "The Novel" that he will be able to illustrate the whole of himself, his dreams, his imagination, and the reality of the choices he has made for himself.

The narrator is a helpless spectator to Eliane's worsening health. He sees her young life consuming itself: "She aspired, woman-child, to be an orchid that grows without any sun. She had burnt many stages in the interval, compensating for the short life that she had been allocated" (94). The narrator conjectures on the significance of what he terms the "trigram" of Orla, Solange, and Eliane around him. He writes: "In truth, none of them had been given to me nor had consented. I had obtained them at the cost of an unshakeable constancy, after having long pursued them, as a novelist who seeks characters" (99).

This statement reinforces the two-dimensional nature of these female characters. Yeager notes that "the 'real' women, characters on one level, are absorbed and become characters within the interior novel of the narrator. Going beyond the fictionalized 'real' world, they metamorphose into representations of abstracts—symbols and metaphors, aspects of his personality."[28] Although the narrator accords them some say, their representation is largely symbolic. It is as if they were paraded in front of a wall, with the narrator indulging in long monologues detailing his perceptions of them. Even when he lets them speak for themselves, the effect is of him jerking them into life and speaking their set piece before he silences them again and soliloquizes on the many threads of his life.

The narrator refers four times to the title of the book, which forms part of a quotation from "Mersebourg." On the origins of this saying, Nguyen Hong Nhiem writes:

> It is a magical formula, drawn from the first texts of German literature, and dating from the fifth century. Certain witches recited it then, and for a double purpose: 1, to distract the sentinels on duty in front of prisons and 2, to facilitate the escape of the detainee or detainees, on whose behalf they acted.[29]

The title of the book is actually taken from the first of the *Merseburger Zaubersprüche* (Merseburg Charms), one of the most famous Old High German texts, being the only remains from pagan antiquity to have survived in textual form in central continental Europe. Copied in the tenth century into a Latin manuscript, they are now in the cathedral library at Merseburg.[30] As noted by J. Knight Bostock:

> [A]lthough the exact meaning of the words has been much disputed, [the first Charm] may be roughly translated as:
>   Once (the) women were seated on the ground, here and there, one company fastened bonds, one company hindered

the host, one company picked at fetters: 'Leap from the fetters, escape from the foes.'[31]

The Charm is an item of pagan oral tradition that has survived in a single transcription. Nigel Palmer notes that the "idisi" are strange Valkyrie-like women, suggestive of feminine or feminist ideology. It is significant that Pham Van Ky chooses this particular Charm. The lines refer to imprisonment, rebellion, and escape and he relates them to the condition of the women around him. The first and second times the lines are spoken it is in the presence of Orla and Solange: "*Women sitting here and there . . . I read in a maxim of Mersebourg. Women sitting here and there, were fastening chains. . . .*" (140). He does not complete the quotation and does not attempt it while they are there. The quotation is finally expressed fully when he is with Eliane. Again, he has to repeat himself and then finally says:

> In a maxim of Mersebourg: *Women sitting here and there, were fastening chains, others were unfastening them. Leave the chains, escape!* (154)

The irony of *Des Femmes assises çà et là* is that none of the female characters in the novel to whom the impassioned sentence is addressed actually hears it spoken. As he speaks to Eliane, a truck rolls past outside the window and her parents return, so that the sentence and the sentiments fail to reach their mark. The never-ending chains and links are part of the fabric of society, and women are bound to doing and undoing them, imprisoned by their condition as women within patriarchy. The Charm also harks back to an oral tradition. In choosing the saying, Pham Van Ky draws attention to a commonality of experience between European and Asian women. As a Vietnamese, he is cognizant of the bonds enclosing the lives of the women around him, chains that are difficult to undo and indeed few have the opportunity to do so. The narrator wants Eliane to break free of the disease killing her and to achieve her potential as a human being. In the end, she does escape—by dying. Living on, she would have been bound by the same chains that the narrator sees around women—around his mother, Orla, and Solange.

> Outside, I ran to make myself dizzy, so as not to scream at the night: Leave the chains, escape! Leave the chains, Eliane, escape! . . . Leave your fate, Eliane, away from this iron statue, because here Christmas is near, a bitter almond breaking its hard core, a serene healing emerging annually from its shell. (154)

Eliane dies on Christmas Eve. "Eliane was dead. Dead at midnight, at a Christian midnight. O Christmas Eve, Christmas to trample in rage!" (173).

The latter part of the narrative is addressed to Eliane. He carries on an interior monologue with her, asking her where she is, whether she is well looked after, whether she has anything to communicate to him. In the end, the other three women also leave him. His mother dies. She has sent him two further cables after the first. Hearing no response from her son, her second one asks *"Do I need to send you the return money?"* (125). But the narrator is preoccupied by Eliane's condition. He dreams of imaginary dialogues with his mother, of her possible response to him, but he does not do anything tangible to make the dream a reality. His mother's third and last cable, a cryptic *"Tap on the bowl while you sing"* (179) leads to similar digressions before he is brought back to reflect on the meaning of this message. It refers to a Taoist text on the inevitability of the cycle of life and death.[32]

The narrator does not discuss the reference; he feels it is a test of his early education, a reminder of the classical texts he studied in his youth. He does not respond either, lost as he is in his imaginary conversations with Eliane. In any case, it is too late. Eliane is dead. His mother is already dead. Even then she has to die twice over: "Mother so dead that she sent me to search for her in the *I Ching*, a nearly antediluvian book of magic spells!" (184). Whether one woman represented the past, the already dead past, and the other the present, or rather the future, alive with possibilities, the reality is that both are dead. Unable to bring any relief to his dying mother, nor to prevent the death of Eliane, their deaths symbolize the death of his illusions about the East and the West. Solange and Orla also leave him. He is left alone: "Mother and Eliane dead, Solange and Orla removed from my sun for a time or for ever, I found myself alone" (298).

At the end of the novel, the narrator receives a series of letters from Eliane, which she has asked not be sent to him until after her death. These letters, which express her sexual attraction for the narrator, an older man, are shattering to him: "In this new Eliane— probably the most secretive, who had escaped from the chains—who would console me about Eliane, how to place her, before or after her death? But, Lord of Heaven, where is the before and where the after of a same story?" (311). Her letters disturb his categorization of her, his oft-reiterated insistence on her innocence. Her death of leukemia is symbolic. As was the case with tuberculosis, the metaphor is:

> both a way of describing sensuality and promoting the claims of passion and a way of describing repression and advertising the claims of sublimation, the disease inducing both a "numbness of spirit" . . . and a suffusion of higher feelings. Above all, it [is] a way of affirming the value of being more conscious, more complex psychologically.[33]

Eliane's letters are passionate, alive, and angry. *"I kiss the small vein on the edge of your right temple"* (314), *"My God, how thirsty I am. To see you quickly. Quickly! Quickly!!!"* (319). She knows she will lose him and is angry that he does not see her as a woman, that he has reduced her to mere words, that he lives by writing words outside of her—when she herself feels so alive, and knows what it is to be so:

I am a woman.
I am physically a woman!
I am full of semen and of hope.

So much light in the space of a flash of pain and a flash of joy
altogether! . . .
The meaning of life? An addition that I no longer need.
No longer need. No longer need. (321–2)[34]

Repetition emphasizes the urgency of Eliane's sentiments and her despair. She expresses her feelings and gives free vent to her imagination. Her letters follow one upon another, each taking up many pages. Her last letter ends mid-sentence, mid-word, asking him: "be my abode . . . the Flower that arri . . ." (326). Cut off in the middle of a word, the last in the novel, Eliane will live on in the narrator's memory. With this exposure of the woman behind the child, he must accept that she was sexual as well as innocent and imaginative and that this she could not reveal to him while still alive. After the loss of all four women whom he has been close to, the narrator is forced to absorb this revelation and is left, at the end, literally speechless.

Pham Van Ky examines the inner and outer constraints on women's lives. The repeated, impassioned "Leave the chains. Escape!" which none of the women in *Des Femmes assises çà et là* ever hears, is directed towards all four. The narrator wants his mother to escape from unremitting duty; Eliane, from her fatal disease; Orla, from her mental illness; and Solange, from being the purely sensual object he perceives her to be. Yet this imperative to escape is ultimately directed at himself. It is an acknowledgement of his own imprisoning condition as a man caught between two worlds, a stranger in exile.

Conclusion

Des Femmes assises çà et là is a much denser novel than the earlier *Frères de sang*. Both novels are first-person narratives, with an unnamed male narrator. In both cases, the narrator in question is a Vietnamese who has carried out further studies in France. One returns to his native village after many years overseas, the other chooses to remain in metropolitan France.

The earlier novel, *Frères de sang*, contains a greater number of female characters. Its straightforward linear progression of events is not too greatly interrupted by the narrator's inner musings. Female characters, both in the narrator's family and within the immediate village environment, are painted in clear strokes. The narrator cannot remain unaware of the realities and conflicts within their lives. These women's personalities affect everyone around them, whether spouse, sibling, parent, or fellow villager and their actions bear directly on the fabric of their family, village, and society. Their plight serves to highlight the deadening effect that an old and patriarchal system of authority exercises on the people who live within it. The narrator, just returned from study overseas, is particularly aware of these dynamics. The patriarch expects this newly returned eldest son to marry and fulfil his filial duties. The narrator, however, is already engaged to a French woman in France, and refuses to conform to the restrictive limits set by his father.

The physical limits of the village in *Frères de sang* seem to echo the limits imposed by tradition, age, and inertia on the villagers themselves. It is particularly distressing to the narrator that one of the harshest exponents of village and family authority is his own father, a living embodiment of the past. A true patriarch, the father is intent on keeping village and sexual hierarchy in place and power in his hands. He is, therefore, blind to his wife's distress and rejects children who dare rebel openly against him. He *will* stay and perpetuate the life and values he is familiar with, no matter what the consequences. The narrator, his eldest son, is largely ineffectual as he stands by watching while others act.

The narration of *Des Femmes assises çà et là* is ostensibly a linear progression of events, beginning with four female characters and ending with the death of two and the departure of two. The narrative, however, is constantly interrupted by long, digressive passages on the narrator's interior world. Within this lengthy and complex novel, none of the four women emerge as fully developed characters. Even the figure of Eliane only reveals an essential aspect of herself to the narrator after her death. The women in this later novel thus appear largely as symbols of different cultures, stages of life, facets of humanity. As symbols, they cannot be fully realized, nor is it surprising that they fade at the end of the novel. None can tolerate the narrator's single-minded, categorical assessment of them. If he does not consider them individuals in their own right, it seems fitting that they then desert him and fade back into a flat tapestry. If this is the way he sees them, it is the way they will remain, distant and untouchable.

The first novel, *Frères de sang*, begins with the narrator's arrival after many years away and ends with the departure or death of all the female characters. The second novel, *Des Femmes*, begins with the threat of death and ends with the actual death of the mother and Eliane. Whatever actually happens to these women, in each case they end up eluding the narrator. He is an outsider: in the first novel because of his feelings of strangeness upon returning to his homeland after years overseas; in the second novel because he is a foreigner living in Paris and by virtue of his sex, a stranger observing his female characters. As such, he can only perceive and present a partial picture of women. This is particularly poignant in the ending to the second novel, with Eliane's thoughts ending in mid-sentence, mid-thought, mid-life.

From a portrayal of women as recognizable social typecasts in the first work, Pham Van Ky proceeds to a representation of women as symbols of separate human conditions in the second: age, innocence, neurosis, and sensuality. In both instances however, an element of malaise and disorientation remains. The anonymous male narrator is in unknown territory and steers clear of direct interference. He attempts, but does not succeed, in getting to the heart of things, much as he fails to see into the hearts of these women.

Yeager suggests in relation to *Des Femmes* that the women may represent different facets of the narrator's self. The argument could be made for both narratives here. The use of female characters to express aspects of the narrator's personality is a useful distancing device and reinforces the gap in perception and understanding between the narrator and the characters. The narrator, displaced from his native land, is divided between two cultures. His process of identification is ambiguous and difficult. On the one hand, he hears his mother's call, the call of his first culture. On the other, he experiences the pull of the European women of his second. The plight of women in each place serves to underline the pain and conflicts of his own condition.

Pham Van Ky, albeit in a muted version, is repeating a form used by Vietnamese poets and scholars of preceding centuries who chose to let women voice life's vicissitudes. He does not actually place the women in the center of his narratives. In both novels, it is the male narrator who remains the center figure. However, female characters are positioned in such a way as to underline the element of alienation. Trinh T. Minh-ha suggests that, "Trying to find the other by defining otherness or by explaining the other through laws and generalities is, as Zen says, like beating the moon with a pole."[35] The point of view in both novels is that of the perpetual outsider: a stranger to the village, culture, and nation, a stranger as a man writing about women's lives. No matter which other it is, as a writer receptive to both East and West but remaining an outsider wherever he resides, Pham Van Ky illustrates in his novels the difficulty of portraying the other.

4

Colonial Love

They'll lose their way within dark sorrowland,
those passionate fools who go in search of love,
And life will be a desert reft of joy,
and love will tie the knot that binds to grief.
To love is to die a little in the heart.
—Xuan Dieu

The relationships that most vividly illustrate conflicts of identity and understanding are those between a man and a woman of different race. Two novels—Truong Dinh Tri and Albert de Teneuille's *Bà-Dâm* (Madam the French Woman) and Pham Duy Khiem's *Nam et Sylvie* (Nam and Sylvie)—distinguish themselves amongst Vietnamese Francophone novels by dealing explicitly with the relationship between a male colonial subject and a white woman, a subject rarely found in French colonial fiction. Both novels were published in Paris, *Bà-Dâm* in 1930 and *Nam et Sylvie* in 1957. Although the first appeared during the high point of French colonial authority in Indochina and the second in the immediate post-colonial period, both are set in colonial times, both in France and Vietnam. Despite a gap of nearly thirty years between them, both depict the failure of interracial relationships in a colonial context, whether in French Indochina or in France itself.[1]

Bà-Dâm and *Nam et Sylvie* differ markedly from French colonial novels of interracial love which typically illustrate erotic relationships between white males and their indigenous partners. Such a depiction of relationships is devoid of any romance or sentimentality and conveys, in Alain Ruscio's words, "all except tenderness, all except love."[2] "Native marriages" catered to the physical needs of the white partner but exposed the conceptual and social gulf that separated the French man, as a colonizer, from his "native" mistress. Hugh Ridley notes that "French colonial writers followed the flag to all corners of the globe and gave frank and detailed accounts of the lives of French soldiers and administrators with their consorts: the *moresques* of Algeria, the *moussos* of the Sudan, the *congaïs* of Indo-China."[3]

The French male's fascination with the exotic and the strange is illustrated in the works of Pierre Loti: *Aziyadé* (Aziyadé) (1879), *Le Roman d'un Spahi* (A Spahi's Story) (1881), *Madame Chrysanthème* (Madam Chrysanthemum) (1887), *L'Exilée* (The Exile) (1893), and *La Troisième Jeunesse de Madame Prune* (The Third Youth of Madam Plum) (1905). Loti himself believed that East and West were poles apart and "felt a particular antipathy for the Far East."[4] Milton Osborne observes that it is at the end of the nineteenth century "that one comes upon the first extended descriptions of the prolonged French literary fascination with the *con-gai*, the Vietnamese concubine."[5] He writes further that "[n]ot only was the practice of concubinage common, so too were the accounts of it—accounts that were without romanticism but which, instead, were often brutally frank in their details."[6]

The representation of relationships between white women and indigenous men, however, seldom occurred in colonial fiction. Such affairs were usually depicted in a negative light, since the notion of this type of union was deeply repugnant at the time. Indigenous sexuality was either derided (the Asian), presented as unhealthy (the Arab), or exposed with a mixture of fright and envy (the Black).[7] Ridley notes:

> The great majority of serious fiction tackled the problems of inter-racial liaisons from the position of the white *male* partner. It was almost exclusively left to sensationalist popular fiction to chart the murky waters of white women's explorations. (Pierre Mille recalled a certain type of publisher tended to reject novels "because the white woman does not sleep with a native") and serious French colonial fiction took a very negative view of these relationships.[8]

In fiction, love in a colonial context thus generally resulted in failure. Ruscio underlines the fact that "the colonial world postulated that such relationships were impossible."[9] The few positive accounts of such interracial relationships were written by women.[10] It is in this context that the representations of interracial love in *Bà-Dâm* and *Nam et Sylvie* emerge. The two novels do not fall into the category of sensationalist fiction but rather examine the rewards and pitfalls of love across colonial boundaries.

Bà-Dâm is set in Paris and Vietnam in the 1920s and relates the relationship between Sao, a law student in Paris, and Janine, the daughter of his university professor. These two young people marry in France then move to Cochinchina. *Bà-Dâm* charts the gradual corrosion of their marriage and the breakdown of their love and hopeful illusions. Janine does not adjust well to life in Cochinchina while Sao suffers from a feeling of cultural malaise in his own country. As his family becomes more and more hostile towards "Bà-Dâm" or "Madam the French woman," Janine's seeming lack of reserve and indecorous behavior serve to confirm the family's negative assessment. Sao's later illness proves an ideal opportunity for his parents to accuse him of having "sinned" against his family by marrying a foreigner. The collective hostility of the surrounding community underlines the couple's negative reception. As the gulf between husband and wife becomes impossible to bridge, Janine falls in love with a French man and returns to France, while Sao becomes severely depressed and drowns in the river.

The later work, *Nam et Sylvie*, is set largely in Paris in the 1930s. It relates the relationship between Nam, a Vietnamese *agrégation*[11] student in Paris, and Sylvie, a young French woman. Their romance is doomed from the beginning since Nam will return to Vietnam upon finishing his studies and both are aware that the notion of a mixed marriage is inadmissible in the narrow circles of colonial Indochina. Just as the name "Sylvie" is drawn from Gérard de Nerval's protagonist of the same name in *Les Filles du Feu* (Daughters of Fire) (1854) and not the young woman's actual name (Louise Chardonnet), so does Nam and Sylvie's relationship take on the overtones of an illusion, an unrealistic and unrealizable dream. Twenty years later, Nam mourns the failure of their relationship.

Crossed Purposes in *Bà-Dâm*

The appearance of *Bà-Dâm* (Madam the French woman) in Paris in 1930 coincided, in the Indochinese colony, with a year of violence marked by several failed uprisings and savage retribution by the French authorities. In the preface to their novel, the authors assert that they leave history and politics to those more qualified: "Only the domain of psychology has retained our attention."[12] Just as the novel itself is a collaborative effort, they feel that working together is the only way ahead for Indochina—mutual respect and a more liberal approach on both sides. Indochina has yet to reach this state of affairs, a fact evidenced by the attitude and assumptions of the French colonial community towards the colonized and the latter's mixed reaction of suspicion and envy. Colonial power was both coercive and seductive.[13] However, colonialism itself is neither challenged nor questioned by the authors. They evince an idealistic desire to see everyone getting along better without questioning the current order or status quo.

The preface concedes that: "Certain natives, naturalized, raised in metropolitan schools, [and] impregnated by Western civilization, are the equal of many Europeans from the intellectual and moral point of view" (7). European standards, in other words, are perceived to be the cultural and intellectual norm to which natives should aspire and due credit should be given to the few who have reached this norm. Stressing the worth of the natives was important since the novel portrayed the marriage of a young French woman with a native. In concession to French womanhood, the individual in question had to be well-educated and eminently civilized. The preface reads like a justification addressed to what, one presumes, is a largely uninformed and prejudiced French audience. Clearly, *Bà-Dâm* is directed at French readers. Published in Paris, all Vietnamese words and expressions are either followed by French translations or have explanatory footnotes.

In this straightforward third-person narrative, events follow each other in chronological order, beginning in Paris with the announcement of Sao and Janine's marriage and ending in Cochinchina. The novel presents a detailed physical description of the main characters: their height, build, coloring, and facial features. The stress on color and, by extension, racial difference, is underlined by a vivid contrast between light and dark. Each is a stereotypical portrait of their race: Sao has a Far Easterner's slight stature, dark hair and eyes. "Rather short, slender, graceful even, with a sort of nervous fragility which did not exclude elegance, Nguyên-Van-Sao presented all the characteristics of his race, but as if tempered and reduced to an unaccustomed attraction" (22). He is "perfectly courteous" with "a slightly sing-song voice" (20), an apt reminder of the tonality of spoken Vietnamese. His physique is suggestive of the effeminacy ascribed to the Asian male in French colonial fiction. Its darker connotation is that of degeneration and impotence.

Janine, in contrast, is a blue-eyed blonde: "Supple, of medium height, a lover of sports as much as travails of the mind, she displayed a natural and incomparable grace. Her delicate face, with its regular features, was lit by two large and very gentle blue eyes and was haloed by ash blond hair which looked frothy" (19). Janine represents the quintessence of all that is most prized and admired in Europeans: she is exquisitely fair. Like the "Blonde" in French colonial literature, she embodies "the values of Family, Home and France itself."[14] Jennifer Yee suggests that the "Blonde" "is nothing less than the descendant of the heroic Franks themselves, as well as the daughter—more directly—of Imperial France."[15] The stage is set for the alliance of two "ideal" specimens of their race and culture.

In Paris, Sao had appeared a perfectly assimilated young man, a bright and successful student: "His open mind, exceptionally astute, his prodigious faculty of adaptation and assimilation, made him quickly noticed by the professor" (11). Once in Cochinchina, however, his studies appear to have been for naught. There were few opportunities for a member of the colonized in his own country and Sao falls prey to the impotent inertia of the colonial subject. Far more constrained back on his native soil than he was as a foreigner living in Paris, all his ambitions and plans gradually evaporate. Despite his eminent French qualifications, he is still one of the natives. A French man with a simple diploma wields power while Sao is left powerless. As Neil Jamieson notes, "It was one of the firmest principles of French colonialism that 'the lowest-ranked representative of France in Indochina must receive a salary superior to that of the highest Indochinese official employed by the colonial administration.'"[16]

Sao fritters his time away apathetically on the family property while his parents endure the snubs and disapproval of prominent members of the Vietnamese community for having a son married to a French woman. His scheme for a *Société Agricole* (Agricultural Society) results in failure: "From the brilliant Annamite, proud and filled with ambition, there only remained a poor and very weary man, who wept in secret [for] his beautiful destroyed love" (236). *Bà-Dâm* reveals its colonial context in using the term "Annamite" to refer to "Vietnamese"[17] and reflects contemporary Western perceptions of Indochina. In *French Indo-China*, published in 1937, Virginia Thompson writes that "many [Annamites] whose brilliant promise is revealed by their diplomas dissipate their energies in a thousand wild schemes that never come to fruition."[18]

Bà-Dâm exposes the gulf in conceptions of marriage between Sao and Janine. Although attached to his wife, Sao sees her largely as his property and the means to provide him with sons to carry on the family name and traditions. He feels no passion for her and her increasing distance and eventual loss are a blow to his pride and self-esteem. "The French woman believed she had found a total and vibrant communion between two people; the Annamite conceived it as the traditional way of perpetuating the family" (208). In the end, Sao's death by drowning (suicide or accident?) is an admission that he has failed in his ambitions, failed his wife, and failed his family. Such failure was perhaps inevitable considering the nature of colonized society, with its ambivalent mix of desire and rejection. Jack Yeager comments:

The "exile" of Sao's *dépaysement* (disorientation) is his punishment for having crossed the line dividing Vietnamese and French cultures. The message is clear: challenging socially and culturally prescribed roles and places can have fatal consequences. Sao, for reasons only too obvious, is unable to become French but has assimilated French culture to the point that he can no longer be Vietnamese in a traditional sense. He knows too much; caught in an impasse, he cannot survive.[19]

Trapped as he is in his colonized condition, Sao's death provides an end to unresolved problems with self-image and identity.

Critics of colonialism such as Frantz Fanon and Albert Memmi have written on the role of assimilation in relation to interracial relationships. Fanon posits that in linking himself with a white woman, the native absorbs some of the white, dominant culture:

> I wish to be acknowledged not as *black* but as *white*. Now . . . who but a white woman can do this for me? By loving me she proves that I am worthy of white love. I am loved like a white man. I am a white man . . . I marry white culture, white beauty, white whiteness. When my restless hands caress those white breasts, they grasp white civilization and dignity and make them mine.[20]

Memmi, on the other hand, perceived the desire for the other as a reflection of hatred of the self:

> Rejection of self and love of another are common to all candidates for assimilation. Moreover, the two components of this attempt at liberation are closely tied: Love of the colonizer is subtended by a complex of feelings ranging from shame to self-hate. . . . A mixed marriage is the extreme expression of this most audacious leap.[21]

There may be a certain element of both of these interpretations in *Bà-Dâm*, since Sao is disoriented and unsure of his identity, but it does not reflect Sao's and Janine's marriage. If Sao has any illusions of allying himself with European power by marrying Janine (and this is not something that is made explicit in the novel), he soon realizes how futile this gesture is. He and his wife find themselves rejected by both the Vietnamese community and the French expatriate community in Indochina. Grasping the other as a means of absorbing another culture proves illusory, not only for Sao, but also for Janine.

Bà-Dâm operates on three different levels: the first, despite the authors' comments in the preface, is that of politics. Jointly authored by a Vietnamese man and a French man, its collaborative endeavor is evident from its sub-title, "Roman franco-annamite" (Franco-Annamite Novel). The authors' intentions are clearly stated in the novel's epigraph which announces that, "So much harm has been done already by the mutual misunderstanding of the New World and the Old, that one need not apologize for contributing his tithe to the furtherance of a better understanding."[22] The epigraph in *Bà-Dâm* is from *The Book of Tea*, first published in New York in 1906. Its author, Okakura Kakuzo (1862–1913) was an art critic, philosopher, and writer whose works were widely read and were instrumental in shaping Western perceptions of Asian culture.[23] The quotation from a Japanese source is significant; as Amy Ling notes:

Japan . . . had recognized the significance of modernization and had been rapidly importing scientific, military, and technological experts from the west. By the end of the century, she had successfully embarked on a road toward geographic expansion through military aggression and conquest. The victories of this small island nation against the large continental nations of China in 1895 . . . and Russia in 1905 gained her much respect and admiration throughout the world.[24]

Japan was therefore a model for other East Asian countries to emulate. *Bà-Dâm*'s epigraph alludes both to Japan's success and to the importance of following the example she set as a country able to combine elements from both East and West. Truong Dinh Tri and Albert de Teneuille present their novel as an attempt to bridge the gap in comprehension between East and West. *Bà-Dâm* reflects the political concerns of the period, since the 1920s were years "of considerable political activity in Indochina, most of it directed against the reactionary Colonial Administration."[25] André Malraux, co-editor of the journal *L'Indochine* (Indochina), later *L'Indochine enchaînée* (Indochina in Chains), aligned himself with the Vietnamese nationalist movement.[26] He "wanted the French and the Annamites to live together not as masters and slaves, exploiters and exploited, conquerors and conquered, but as equals."[27] To treat the Vietnamese as inferiors was "a betrayal of some of the fundamental tenets of France's liberal intellectual tradition."[28]

This aspect of the colonial situation seems to have particularly troubled Malraux. He did not, however, question colonization as such. As Elizabeth Fallaize observes: "neither in [*La Voie royale*] nor in life did Malraux express the view that French colonial rule in Indo-China should be ended."[29] Walter Langlois writes that Vietnamese intellectuals were not so much opposed to French civilization, as to the French colonial government:[30] "Most of the native leaders *wanted* French citizenship for their people, French schools for their children, representation in the French Chamber of Deputies, and an Indochinese political and legal system organized after French models."[31] *Bà-Dâm* needs therefore to be examined within this general context of "Franco-Annamite" *rapprochement* or bringing together of two peoples.

The second level on which the novel operates is that of culture. *Bà-Dâm* informs and educates the Western reader about Vietnamese mores. The people, the costumes, the houses, furniture and layout, the landscape, the pageantry of traditional celebrations, the food, the heat, and strangeness of Indochina are drawn in vivid colors. Images of exotica abound. Hence Janine "evoked the warm shade of mangroves underneath which she would soon wander arm-in-arm with a husband. She saw herself, dressed all in white, dreaming in the moonlight near the pointed roof of a pagoda. . . . An entire quivering life of unknown beasts swarmed by her side" (34).

To Janine, Indochina is redolent of mystery and the seduction of the unknown and the unfamiliar—and of darkness. Her marriage to Sao is, in a concrete sense, *un cri de défi* (a cry of defiance) to the unknown. Although her parents approve of the match, society does not: "marriages with people of color are still quite rare and are in fact much denigrated" (12). Strong reservations are voiced by her mother's lifelong friends. Yet this only proves an added spur to Janine. She feels a quixotic sense of mission:

> She discovered, in her marriage with Sao, a sort of apostolate, of reparation towards a race often despised and which did not deserve it. She perceived a supreme justice in holding out her hand as a French woman, descendant of conquerors, towards this son of the vanquished, whose submission had not been able to break down their aristocratic mentality. (33)

In a reversal of traditional images of male/female hierarchies of power, it is she who represents the might of a ruling race and he who represents the underdog, the marginalized, the subject race. Janine's French acquaintances bring up in an openly prejudicial manner the status of any children that she and Sao might have: "You know as I do . . . that those of mixed blood have all the defects of the two races and none of their qualities. That is as true for animals as it is for men" (18). The response of the wife of a French colonist in Cochinchina is even more virulent:

> But to marry an Annamite, one of these yellow maggots . . . And then, there are the children . . . Neither Annamite, nor wholly French, they are more than the former and less than the latter. And even more than a real White, they despise their yellow ancestors, whose blood they carry and who belong to an inferior race. (179–80)

Sao's reserve towards Janine becomes proof of the incompatibility of the two races. Her doubts are given voice by the French colonists who tell her that she will never know how Sao really feels about her: "Because with an Annamite you will never know—and it is the worst torture for a woman—you will never know if he loves you!" (184). Although Janine begins by standing loyally by him, his increasing distance, his family's hostility, the disapproval of the French community, and the flattering attentions of a French administrator finally lead her to leave her husband. She runs away from him and all the lost dreams and illusions he had embodied. "She gave up attempting to penetrate the latter's soul. A painful dejection, a sort of moral torpor, the numbness of all her dreams and all her aspirations were pushing her to abandon herself to the progress of events" (190–1). In the end she cannot bear to remain in French Indochina and leaves, even though it means the loss of the French man she loves.

The third level of operation is the fictional representation of the relations between a man and a woman beyond the barriers of nationality, race, and colonization. The plot of *Bà-Dâm* reflects the reality of "mixed unions" between Vietnamese men and French women of the period. According to Virginia Thompson, Vietnamese students had a noted success with French women—the exotic tradition and the courtesy of these young men left an indelible impression: "The poorest Annamite can write a poem or present a flower with aristocratic grace."[32] She adds, however, that although these mixed marriages proved to be relatively unproblematic in France, the reverse applied when the Vietnamese brought his French wife back to the colony:

> The physical adjustment to a totally different way of living, in addition to the psychological adaptation to an anti-individualistic social unit dominated by ritual, would be enough to shatter a more than ordinarily united couple. The Asiatic husband tends to be increasingly absorbed into his milieu, and his French wife isolated in a strange and often hostile environment, which eventually defeats them both.[33]

The cultural gap between Janine and Sao becomes marked in Cochinchina. *Bà-Dâm* includes brief references to Vietnamese literature in the form of extracts of poems, songs and tales. Sao's letters to his fiancée and then wife are replete with classical imagery and written in a flowing, poetic style—missives that, until Janine's loss of illusions, seduced her by the charm of their strangeness:

> United according to our wishes as a well-matched couple who deserve to prance on the Dragon,
> Let us engrave together on our bones the symbol: Union.
> Our love, as immense as the Ocean and the River, will last for a century. (32)

Sao's letter of blame is composed in an equally literary style:

> I blame her who swore fidelity to me on mounts and hills,
> And leaves me for other places of pleasure.
> I blame her whom I carried to Paradise,
> Where, replete with happiness and unaware, she regretted her previous life,
> I pity her who, the first, provoked disunion;
> Who, in the midst of our felicity, plays on the guitar the theme of our separation. (239)

Sao chooses to communicate his anger towards his wife in these terms, rather than to confront her directly. Even then, she only falls on the poem by chance. Ironically, this letter which he had hesitated to show her proves to be the turning point in her decision to leave him. Couched in poetry and metaphor as they are, his recriminations are no less bitter and plaintive and a clear indication to her that he lays the burden of the failure of their relationship solely on her shoulders. For Janine, it is the final straw, the death-knell of their marriage. Significantly, the letter harks back to the classical literary heritage of Vietnam, further distancing husband and wife. Now, instead of perceiving the letter as strange and charming as she had once interpreted his letters of courtship, she sees it as the symbol of the final gulf that separates them.

Bà-Dâm thus illustrates the pitfalls of a cross-cultural marriage in colonial circumstances, even with the best will on both sides. The failure of this marriage, for Sao and for Janine, is perhaps a reflection of the wider failure of political illusions and ideals within the colony. Milton Osborne notes:

> Reality in contrast to illusion was an awareness of the failure of most French cultural justifications for their colonial presence in Viet-Nam and a cynical, even desperate effort to gain economic advantage from a life that if nothing else seemed to offer a better reward, in status as well as in terms of money, than life in France. But the costs were there, in health or rather the lack of it, in personal dissatisfaction, and for some in national disappointment.[34]

Bà-Dâm encapsulates the failure of an attempted synthesis of Vietnamese and French culture and customs through interracial marriage. Its publication in 1930 may have symbolized a last effort to stall the ominous signals of revolt and change in the colony.

Aborted Romance: *Nam et Sylvie*

The color and exotica of *Bà-Dâm* are dramatically absent from Pham Duy Khiem's *Nam et Sylvie* (Nam and Sylvie), published twenty-seven years later under the pseudonym Nam Kim. The bulk of events occur in Paris, with the main characters being, once again, a Vietnamese student in Paris, Nam, and a young French woman, Sylvie. There are, however, no detailed descriptions of their coloring or physique and very little exotica in the novel. The only hint of it is the setting in which Nam first meets Sylvie "in the red and gold party room of our 'Indochina House.'"[35] There are no scenes set in Vietnam and therefore no description of local color, and politics is not overtly mentioned.[36]

The novel's chronology is circular. It begins with the end of Nam and Sylvie's relationship, moves backward in time to the formation of this relationship, and then moves forward, detailing its trajectory. The first scene is therefore Nam's departure from Paris. The action next shifts backwards to Nam and Sylvie's first meeting, forward with the progress of their love, then finally ends on the ship carrying Nam as it approaches Haiphong harbor in Vietnam. The account is a first-person narrative and comprises: firstly, Nam's recollections twenty years later; secondly, numerous letters from Nam to Sylvie and Sylvie to Nam from that period; and thirdly, excerpts from Nam's journal at the time. As Karl Britto observes, the novel evinces a temporal and political shift, since the colonial subject becomes post-colonial.[37] Nam refers to himself as Annamite in his youth, but twenty years later states: "one says: Vietnamese now" (3).

Unlike Sao's missives in *Bà-Dâm*, Nam's letters are written in pure, idiomatic French. There are no expressions or references that would indicate them to be foreign or alien, as Sao's letters evidently are. Both Nam and Sylvie are conscious that "a mixed union" is untenable and Nam refers to "the unlikelihood of such a union at that time" (24). He will thus return to Vietnam once his examinations are over. Sylvie would not be able to cope with life in Vietnam therefore their union cannot be anything but short-lived and ephemeral. Nam relates:

> Even if I had judged it perfect and for ever certain, even if I had envisaged, from that time, to reserve the future . . . and to examine if the general evolution, the attitude of the French from over there and the position that I would have personally acquired made our union possible, I would not have believed I had the right to expose those to her from the beginning. (66)

In the narrow circles of colonial Indochina, the notion of a mixed marriage is inadmissible. The weight of social disapproval and rejection that will ensue from both the Vietnamese host community and the cliquish French expatriate community is more than either Nam or Sylvie can contemplate. Although it may have been possible for them to marry and live in Paris, Nam has family responsibilities and does not even think of staying on in France. Each absorbs, nonetheless and perhaps unconsciously, some of the other's culture:

> Cadot [one of Nam's French friends] exclaims: 'Ah! It amuses me to see Nam so; he is no longer the subtle Oriental.'
>
> So then, add to your list, if you have not already noted it, the European Nam. . . . (75)

> Fifteen years later, in Hanoi, while reading this page (from a letter by Sylvie) in front of friends who had never lived in France or had not lived there for a long time, I was surprised to hear them exclaim:
>
> - But she is Annamite! Only an Annamite woman could have written this letter! It is impossible that it is a French woman! (129)

Both are examples of the preconceptions each race has about the other. Orientals are deemed subtle and mysterious; Westerners are considered thick-skinned and obtuse.

As with Sao and Janine's relationship in *Bà-Dâm*, Nam and Sylvie's relationship is based on illusion. Sylvie is not really "Sylvie." Her name is Louise Chardonnet and she takes on the name of Sylvie, one of Gérard de Nerval's *Filles du Feu* (Daughters of Fire), to please Nam. It is significant that Pham Duy Khiem should have used one of Nerval's works. Gérard de Nerval (1808–1855) was a French Romantic writer. The stories in *Les Filles du Feu* (1854) embody a quest for a lost female figure (whether woman, goddess or saint) and this is what in turn Nam's "Sylvie" comes to symbolize to him: a lost dream and a lost love. The way that the reader is expected to appreciate the significance of this pseudonym, despite the fact that Nerval's work is never explicitly mentioned, is reminiscent of the literary allusions so common in Vietnamese classical literature. The indirect reference to Nerval is relevant for another reason. Nerval had been to the "Orient" (which in this case meant the Near East) and had written a romanticized account of his travels in *Voyage en Orient* (Journey to the Orient) (1851). His quest for a mystical Orient is linked to the quest for a lost woman, as Edward Said has pointed out:

> Theirs [the French] was the Orient of memories, suggestive ruins, forgotten secrets, hidden correspondences, and an almost virtuosic style of being, an Orient whose highest literary forms would be found in Nerval and Flaubert, both of whose work was solidly fixed in an imaginative, unrealizable (except aesthetically) dimension. . . . The Orient symbolizes Nerval's dreamquest and the fugitive woman central to it, both as desire and as loss.[38]

In a reverse trajectory of Nerval's yearning for the Orient, the European figure of "Sylvie" embodies both desire and loss for the Vietnamese protagonist, Nam. Why does Louise Chardonnet take on the name "Sylvie" for him? Is it with the foreknowledge that, like Nerval's "Sylvie," she will come to embody an illusion, a happiness which lies within Nam's grasp but which he then loses? "There perhaps lay happiness, and yet . . ."[39] Nerval's Sylvie is a country girl with serene, classic looks and whose admirer is the Parisian narrator of *Sylvie*. Louise Chardonnet is a Parisian, with a far from placid personality, and the narrator in this instance is a foreigner, a Vietnamese. Like Nerval's Sylvie, Sylvie-Louise Chardonnet comes to embody an untouchable reality. She represents, as Pham Dan Binh suggests, the seduction of the West, and more specifically of French culture.[40] Nam can only accept her for the illusions she represents, rather than the woman she actually is, and in the end loses both. Unlike Nerval's narrator, for whom "the sublime ideal" and "'the gentle reality"[41] are represented by two different women, both are incorporated in the same woman for Nam.

In the end, the pressure of keeping up two selves proves to be too much for Sylvie-Louise Chardonnet. As Nam writes of her: "Wasn't it rather her true nature, that her feelings for me had managed to repress and to tame little by little, and who, for a while now was emerging more freely and imposing itself?" (184). She

gives up her own dreams and destroys his dreams in the process.
The pressures on her are too exacting:

> Deep down I had a presentiment about everything right
> from the start. Upon your contact with me you came some
> way out of yourself, of your accustomed state of mind, but
> you fell back quickly. 'Sylvie' was a straw fire. There really
> is only Louise Chardonnet (203).

Louise Chardonnet does not disappear totally from Nam's life. Her
life carries on, she marries conventionally, and becomes a mother
like Nerval's Sylvie. Twenty years afterwards, however, Nam still
mourns the loss of what might have been. He still thinks of her as
Sylvie rather than Louise Chardonnet and realizes that he has
created a persona in Sylvie. In creating his own perception of the
lover in the other, Nam invests in Sylvie qualities and personality
traits that he wants her to possess. Gradually, he realizes: "At
bottom, was she ever different? It is only when she loved me that she
became comprehending and clear-sighted, willful and submissive at
the same time, voluptuous" (216).

Nam et Sylvie includes a spirited defense of relationships
between Vietnamese men and French women through the critique of
a pseudonymous French novel dealing with the same issue, Eliane
Tournier's *Elle blanche et Lui jaune* (She White and He Yellow), itself
an oblique reference to Christiane Fournier's *Homme jaune et Femme
blanche* (Yellow Man and White Woman) (1933). The earlier novel of
interracial love is alluded to within the later novel, but is viewed
from the perspective of the male colonial subject. Nam speaks out
during a debate:

> *Elle blanche et Lui jaune* . . . was tendentious and unjust
> towards yellow men. In reality, if a union of this type was
> bound to fail, it is largely because it clashed with the
> prejudices and the politics of the French over there; the
> customs of our ancestors and the real or supposed defects of
> our race could only play a secondary role; I demonstrated

that easily, in front of the packed auditorium. But as sure of myself as I was, I did not expect the success that I had, or the lively and spontaneous sympathy expressed by the audience, one of whom, addressing himself to his neighbors, remarked out loud: "For which woman does he speak this evening?" (27)

It is ironic that Nam refers to this novel in order to defend mixed relationships, considering the fact that *Nam et Sylvie* itself chronicles the failure of such a relationship. *Elle blanche et Lui jaune* obviously refers to the failure of a mixed marriage in the setting of colonial Indochina and Nam argues that if such a relationship did fail, it was because of pressures imposed by the community and the politics of the colonizers. The political system is the primary culprit: the French administrators are, after all, the ones who run the country. The weight of indigenous values and traditions plays but a secondary role in the breakdown of their relationships with white women. Nam does not comment on the way the French woman is dealt with in Tournier's novel, whether her particular plight and concerns, her own sensation of alienation in a foreign country also has its part to play in the failure of the relationship. Neither does he touch on the fact that the Vietnamese involved may have proved equally blind to the problems encountered by his partner. Yet therein lies the very different message conveyed by the earlier *Bà-Dâm*. The prejudices and hostility of the host family and community—Sao's parents and his social milieu—are as instrumental as the French colonists in bearing pressure on the breakup of the marriage.

That Nam resorts to a French novel in order to articulate his own strong views regarding colonial power is furthermore incongruous. This play on intertextuality—offsetting his views against Eliane Tournier's—allows him, as an alien, to voice his opinion, but the implication is that as a Vietnamese, he is never a completely autonomous being. Only moving within a French cultural context, only portraying himself in the eyes of the French, he is a projection of the way in which French society views him. It is impossible for him to stand completely alone in the land of his country's rulers.

Though Nam studies and lives in France, he has strong family and filial obligations which lead him to return to Vietnam and there assume the traditional responsibilities expected of the eldest son:

> On the threshold of my country, on the eve of taking my place in this society that was going to close itself over me, I said to myself—because I was still young—that never again would I ever be loved for myself the way Sylvie had loved me as a student. Now, on the sole basis of my diplomas acquired from afar and for the last of which the newspapers were in the middle of seeking a translation into our language, the most handsome parties awaited me, my mother had already been advised, and the most difficult daughters were ready to marry me with their eyes closed. Taking into account our mores, I would not have the opportunity of getting to know them, apart from the one that I had already accepted as my wife. (239)

Nam's years in Paris and his relationship with Sylvie are for him a short experience of freedom away from his country—again ironical since he feels less constrained as a member of the colonized living in metropolitan France than as a Vietnamese living in French-ruled Indochina. In the end, both he and Sylvie return to their own societies and cultures, revert back to their worlds. Sylvie marries a French man and becomes the wife and mother she had always hoped to be while Nam returns to his homeland to obey the dictates of conscience as the eldest son in a Vietnamese family. And since this difference in origin has proved a stumbling block to any future in their relationship, and in the end, defeats them, "the conflict of race," appears, more than the vagaries of the affair itself, the central point of the novel.

In *Nam et Sylvie*, the retrospective account is Nam's. Sylvie is a projection, the projection of his hopes and his desires, and although she is not totally voiceless since her letters to him appear in the novel, the outlook and the representation are essentially his. He is the one to interpret, with hindsight, the way in which their relationship progressed. It is Nam who chooses which of her letters to reproduce. Sylvie, like the Vietnamese under French rule, has a small, distant voice. There is no question as to who is in charge, and who, accordingly, has the power to observe, to note, to judge, and in the end, to regret. The novel illustrates a post-colonial process of mourning—for a lost past and a lost illusion of love.

In this novel, Pham Duy Khiem uses French to convey his perspective as a Vietnamese.[42] One way of confronting the colonizer is to use his weapons—his language, literary models, and his women. Pham consciously avoids his Vietnamese linguistic heritage. There is no poetry here. There are no references to or quotations from Vietnamese poems, proverbs, or songs except at the very end, and the saying there bears an element of fatalism, an acknowledgement of the irreversibility of events. The narrator has undergone an experience that he cannot undo. It is part of his life: "Once you have crossed the river together, an acquaintance is formed; once you have counted a day together, it is a debt and a loyalty" (242).[43]

No Vietnamese words or expressions appear in the novel. The weight of Chinese and classical Vietnamese literary tradition seems to leave Pham untouched—either that, or he made a very great effort to lay it aside and turn instead towards the heritage of French literature. Is this why the novel is in some ways inaccessible? Is it too consciously purged of anything Vietnamese in the way in which it is written? *Nam et Sylvie* may demonstrate that it is impossible to reconcile Vietnamese and French perspectives. If French takes over, Vietnamese is purged and destroyed, and has no voice. Albert Memmi points out that:

> Possession of two languages is not merely a matter of having two tools, but actually means participation in two psychical and cultural realms. Here, the two worlds symbolized and conveyed by the two tongues are in conflict; they are those of the colonizer and the colonized.

Furthermore, the colonized's mother tongue, that which is sustained by his feelings, emotions and dreams, that in which his tenderness and wonder are expressed, thus that which holds the greatest emotional impact, is precisely the one which is the least valued. [44]

In *Nam et Sylvie*, the use of the French language and the resort to French literature convey the sensation of a crippled novel. It is as if, in the way Nam and Sylvie's relationship fails, another outlook, another potential, is briefly glimpsed but in the end, like the child that Sylvie aborts, is never brought to fruition.

Conclusion

Both *Bà-Dầm* and *Nam et Sylvie* deal with the theme of the failure of a cross-cultural relationship, whether through social and family pressure in the setting of colonial Cochinchina in the 1920s, or in the context of Paris in the 1930s. Yeager comments that the consequences are not fatal for Nam as they are for Sao: "Nam, like Sao, has learned the secrets of the West, but Nam is able to adopt and fit them to his individual, that is, cultural, needs."[45] Nonetheless, the result is still a failure in terms of the interracial relationship. There exists, still, a gulf in expectations and understanding, even though in the later novel, the superficial differences of color, customs, costumes, food, and circumstances are not touched on.

Bà-Dầm deals in a straightforward way with the theme of mixed marriage. The intention is to examine the progress of a relationship between two well-educated *bourgeois*, one a Vietnamese with all due credits from Paris University and the other a young French woman from the best academic milieu, qualified with a *Licence-ès-lettres* (Bachelor of Arts). Sao has studied and lived in France and appears to adapt well to his circumstances. He shows himself flexible and accustomed to the manners and customs of the French. Janine, for her part, is intelligent, gifted with imagination, and open-minded and open-hearted enough to accept the offer of marriage from a foreigner introduced to her by her own father as one of his star pupils.

Janine has romanticized yearnings for the exotic and the strange. She thinks that she is fully prepared to deal with whatever Indochina has to offer her. But she assumes somehow that Indochina will simply be a convenient, if colorful, backdrop to her life, that she herself will be able to appreciate the country yet somehow remained untouched and unaffected by it, as if the landscape and the people remain giant projections in front of which she and Sao will carry on with their love and their hopes. Her dream of romance in the darkness of an Oriental jungle is symptomatic: "The young student no longer knew where lay fiction and where reality" (45).

The reality of Indochina proves to be a rude shock. She finds herself physically affected by the heat, the damp, the smells, the food, the people, the colors, and the strangeness of her surroundings. Concrete reality comes to seem dreamlike as she makes the mental and emotional effort to adjust to a vastly foreign atmosphere. Nothing in her childhood and adolescence in France has prepared her for this: "Everything that surrounded her seemed unreal to her. She could not recognize herself in such surroundings. . . . Her soul, unbalanced, floated in full phantasmagoria" (83–4).

Like others who went to Indochina and were confronted with a reality quite unlike their expectations, she is forced to concede the chasm between her dreams and delusions on the one hand, and the actuality of the colony on the other: "Pierre Loti's books had thus not said all, the misery, the corruption, even the crimes of the colonial administration. They had only kept the dream, with its exotic images, its clichés, its obligatory riches."[46] Here is indeed Panivong Norindr's "phantasmatic Indochina," as it existed in the French colonial imaginary. While Janine's responses and perceptions are inevitably tinged by her sensation of dream-like reality, Sao struggles with his own sensation of being torn between two cultures:

Understanding the West without becoming separated from the East . . . Vanquished, he understood the conqueror, cursed at heart the conqueror and imitated him furiously. . . (23–4)

For both of them, the pressures prove to be unbearable. Janine sees him slowly sliding away from her grasp and finds herself left alone among strangers and foreigners: "More than ever she felt herself a stranger that people were forced to tolerate. . . . She was alone in an indifferent and distant crowd, alone with her pain, alone with her regrets" (171).

Sao is to remain the perpetual alien: polite, courteous, cold, and inaccessible. He gives his wife neither support nor encouragement, and nothing with which to offset his family's hostility towards her: "the French woman, a foreigner, daughter of often hated masters" (174). His mother's terrible accusations—"you have offended the ancestors . . . Since you have made yourself French, you should have stayed over there or have become Annamite again upon returning here. You wanted to mix the two bloods. The living and the dead will be against you" (217)—reverberate with drowning effect in his mind because, deep down, Sao finds himself in agreement. He is cut adrift, lost. He has lost sight of all his goals and does not know where he belongs any more. His bright ambitions are ashes. He has alienated his family, community, and finally, his wife. His worst fears, entertained prior to his marriage in Paris, have become a reality: "he became conscious that he was an uprooted man, almost a reprobate" (37).

In *Nam et Sylvie*, Nam, like Sao, meets Sylvie in an academic environment. Like Sao, he is also described as "serious, distinguished . . . of a refined politeness, an exquisite grace" (80). He wryly notes regarding Sylvie's mother: "I found out that she did not like 'Annamites,' until the day she read my diploma" (79). Both are therefore a credit to their race, conversant with French manners and not too excessively foreign in looks. Sylvie describes Nam in the following terms: "Your arm is not even yellow. And your eyes barely slant" (5). The intention to steer away from exoticism explains the tempered foreign looks of the Vietnamese protagonist.

A couple of years later, Marguerite Duras adopted a similar restraint in her depiction of the Japanese protagonist in the East-West love affair portrayed in *Hiroshima mon amour* (Hiroshima My Love) (1960).[47] While Pham Duy Khiem writes of a love affair between a Vietnamese man and a French woman, it is also very much simply that between a man and a woman. André Lebois interprets the novel in this light:

> There is no exoticism here; the author, very rightly, holds the word and the thing in contempt. One cannot even say that the conflict of race is the subject of this analysis, the way it was in the novel by Francis de Miomandre: *The Adventure of Thérèse Beauchamps*. It is not the story of a yellow man and a white woman, but that of a man and a woman.[48]

This last sentence is questionable, since the story, after all, is one between an Asian man and a European woman, and the transitory nature of the relationship is largely due to the fact that he returns to his own country and she remains in hers. However, Pham clearly minimizes the element of exoticism in *Nam et Sylvie*. To a lesser extent, this may also be the case in *Bà-Dâm*, although there is a full measure of the exotic and the strange in the description of Indochina itself. Yet Sao is not too utterly "foreign" in looks and there appears to be a conscious intention to distance the text from the sensationalism of bizarre and exotic descriptions, such as that which surfaces in Pierre Loti's works on Japan and China.[49] In both *Bà-Dâm* and *Nam et Sylvie*, it is the human, rather than the freakish element that is focused on. Both Nam and Sao are unable to divorce themselves from their families or to avoid internalizing their families' judgments. For both as well, the relationship with a French woman has the cadence of a dream about it, the fleeting sensation of a short-lived, ephemeral experience: "A few dreams, a few hours of enchantment, but reality kept watch" (131).

The major difference between the two novels lies in their form. While *Bà-Dâm* describes, in an orderly manner, the growing mutual alienation of the main characters and the slow collapse of their relationship, *Nam et Sylvie* illustrates this fragmentation in a complex structure of discordant extracts from narrator, diary, and letter. It is at first unclear what is recollection and what is contemporary recording, a narrative device that underlines the unreliability of memory and the process of continuous recreation it entails. In order to follow the events and feelings depicted within, the reader has to make constant adjustments.

All of these elements form a whole illustrative of splintered perceptions. Not only is the narrator, Nam, split between past and present. The woman he loves is split into two personae. In her letters, she refers to herself as both "I" and "she" or "Sylvie." The insertion of a novel within a novel, Eliane Tournier's *Elle blanche et Lui jaune*, provides a further layer of complexity. For the narrator of *Nam et Sylvie*, self-knowledge takes the form of an attempted synthesis of various pieces of his life, in particular his intense and troubling relationship with "Sylvie." He attempts to purge himself of all the outward trappings of his culture so that his use of the colonizer's language is pure and uncluttered, but his feelings are anything but. The bare prose leaves little to the imagination. Instead, a complicated juxtaposition of various literary forms combines to make an uneasy whole—difficult to read and difficult to follow.

The thirty years that separate the two novels bring no acknowledgement of a greater understanding. The strange has not become familiar; the foreigner is still a foreigner. While *Bà-Dâm* exposes, in a measured way, the plight of an individual torn between two cultures and two states of mind, *Nam et Sylvie* illustrates in a broader way the collapse of an entire system and the individuals enmeshed within. *Bà-Dâm* was written at a time when colonialism was a political reality, when the French were secure in their hold over Indochina. Then, there existed a set and stable order of society, or at least the perception of it. The colonizers ruled and arbitrated and the colonized, with some inner reservations, deferred to and even strove to emulate them.

Nam et Sylvie was published only three years after the collapse of this order, the end of French Indochina. Whatever the author's political leanings, he was educated under that regime and beholden to it. At the same time this colonial system cheated him of his cultural heritage, it made him what he now was. It opened up avenues—the language and literature of the colonizer, and cut off others—his rightful inheritance. It released and constrained; was reward and punishment. The result is a work expressive of loss and alienation. Madeleine Rebérioux summarizes:

> [C]olonization corrupts all, true feelings as much as hoped-for achievements in the field of human rights . . . It cruelly exposes the most diverse forms of domination and denigrates, in literature as well as in real life, good intentions.[50]

Bà-Dâm and *Nam et Sylvie* both demonstrate the failure of interracial relationships in a colonial context. Love, it appears, cannot in itself overcome the pressures and stresses of colonization.

5

Divided Loyalties

So many, stricken by a thousand blows
still walk the earth as bodies with dead souls.
—Nguyen Gia Thieu

The destructive effect of colonization on the Vietnamese male subject is the focus of two novels which appeared in Paris soon after the fall of French Indochina. Nguyen Huu Chau's *Les Reflets de nos jours* (Reflections of our Days), published in 1955, and Pham Duy Khiem's *La Place d'un homme: De Hanoï à la Courtine* (A Man's Place: From Hanoi to La Courtine), published in 1958, each feature as their chief protagonist a French-educated Vietnamese man. Where does identity lie for such a man? Where does self-respect take hold? Is it with the colonizers to whom he is indebted for his formal education and qualifications, or the colonized to whom he is indebted for his cultural roots and literary traditions? The choice is painful—perhaps ultimately there is no real choice. The protagonist identifies partly with each, but as a Vietnamese, no matter how well educated, he remains forcibly a member of the colonized.

Both novels open with the statement that the enclosed journal or collected papers are the writings of a man now deceased.[1] Neither novel is autobiographical in the sense of presenting a traditional chronicle of progress in an individual's life: the development of a personality through childhood, adolescence and adulthood. Neither charts the onward progression of the protagonist towards the present narrator. They are, however, explorations and analyses of the narrator's inner self, with each being culturally indebted to the autobiographical writing tradition of the Far East and the West.[2] The influence of the confessional literature of sixteenth and seventeenth-century China as well as the modern Western tradition of autobiography exemplified by Jean-Jacques Rousseau's eighteenth-century *Confessions* are both in evidence.[3] On the autobiographical genre in Vietnamese literature, Nguyen The Anh notes:

> The autobiographic discourse is up to a recent date widely believed to be a particular product of the West, a form of expression belonging specifically to Occidental culture: if it ever occurred to some Oriental individuals to relate the story of their life, it is because they have been affected by contagion from Western culture, because they have been "annexed into a mentality which is not theirs." Challenging this opinion nevertheless, some authors have demonstrated that writing about the self did thrive in the non-Western civilization of China, where such procedures available to autobiography as historical self-explanation, philosophical self-scrutiny, poetic self-expression and self-invention, had been put in practice for a long time.[4]

In Vietnam, exposure of the self was largely conveyed through the medium of poetry. The first confession of a Vietnamese man's private thoughts through his writing was Cao Ba Nha, a relative of the dissident scholar Cao Ba Quat who was imprisoned after the latter's execution in 1854.[5] During his incarceration, Cao Ba Nha composed an "Exposé of his feelings" (*Tran tinh van*) in classical Chinese and a "Confession" (*Tu tinh khuc*) in Vietnamese *nom* script, asking for justice and clemency from the court.[6]

Cao's poems are an early example of what became a tradition of prison poetry in modern Vietnam, where the writing of autobiography is linked with the individual in captivity and becomes "a mode of justification, an act of self-defense."[7] Both *Les Reflets de nos jours* and *La Place d'un homme* can be similarly described. As autobiographical novels, they each seek to present, explain, and justify Vietnamese mentality to a Western audience. In that they are written in the language of the colonizer but expose the perception of the colonized, they are, at least metaphorically "prison literature"—having been produced by individuals who felt in their situation, virtually imprisoned. The implication is that they are boxed into a colonial framework and that they are only free to express themselves through the voice and thoughts of men now gone. These "posthumous" journals or letters are the most effective means for them to convey their sense of incarceration. Like the writings of Vietnamese political prisoners and poets of the nineteenth century, the novels are "a mode of justification, an act of self-defence."

Nguyen Huu Chau's *Les Reflets de nos jours* (1955) is set in Vietnam in an unspecified time period and depicts a male protagonist whose personality fragments as a result of an overload of linguistic, literary, and cultural input from both East and West. The narrator is overwhelmed by a crushing sense of aloneness and mourns the loss of a woman he had loved. His only recourse is a violent death in guerrilla warfare after which his journal is "discovered" and "published" by a friend.

Pham Duy Khiem's *La Place d'un homme* (1958), set in France in 1939 and 1940, is purportedly the journal of a Vietnamese man who joined the French Army and died in the battle of the Loire in June of the second of these years. This journal takes the form of a series of letters explaining and justifying the narrator's decision to enlist to both Vietnamese and French correspondents. His brief sojourn in the army is the only way for him to gain a spurious sense of "freedom" from his condition, as a Vietnamese intellectual and a member of the colonized.

Analysis of a Breakdown: *Les Reflets de nos jours*

Les Reflets de nos jours (Reflections of our Days) begins with a preface which states: "The Vietnamese [man], author of this journal, was my friend. Alive, he would not have published this himself."[8] The author of the preface then goes on to identify himself with respect to the author of the journal: "In this book I am referred to under the initial Ph . . . Our friendship led us both to that region of 'forest and marshes' from which he did not return" (9). Guerilla warfare and the death of the journal's author in combat are suggested in these lines but there are neither dates nor place names and nothing to inform the reader whether publication of the purported journal is to be understood as taking place soon after its author's death or years later. Such a lack of concrete detail, while possibly due to discretion necessitated by the *maquis,* also fits neatly with the complete absence of dates or indeed any sort of discernible chronology in the journal itself. The preface warns the reader that the journal's format and contents may be difficult to decipher and appear as strange as a Chinese painting of the Sung dynasty set against a work by Renoir. To counter the reader's *dépaysement* (disorientation), the preface even includes excerpts from other writings by the author, in order to "acclimatize" the reader to the text itself.

In its foreignness, the journal presents an Eastern sensibility to the eyes and judgment of a Western reader. Yeager reveals that the novel is a response to André Malraux's *La Tentation de l'Occident* (Temptation of the West) (1926).[9] In this work, Malraux attempts to illustrate the crisis in Western civilization by presenting both European and Eastern approaches to life.[10] One of his characters, the Eastern observer Ling, takes special note of Western concepts of power and individual action.[11] Yet for this young Chinese correspondent of *La Tentation,* "at the center of European man, dominating the great movements of his life, lies an essential absurdity."[12] *Les Reflets de nos jours,* in a similar vein, records a specifically Vietnamese response to Europe, its art, and literature. The results of this encounter are deeply disturbing to the Vietnamese protagonist. His attempt to absorb European thought and art while struggling with his own dilemma as a colonial subject proves too demanding and stressful and ends in his self-destruction.

Les Reflets de nos jours is a first-person narrative and the two strands of thought which permeate it are solitude and death. "[T]he power of art lies in what it makes of life . . . But the human condition is essentially one of solitude" (10–1) philosophizes the anonymous narrator. In its focus on aloneness and pain, the novel is reminiscent of Malraux's *La Condition humaine* (Man's Estate) (1933).[13] The narrator is bereft after a separation from his wife "M," to whom the first part of the journal is addressed, and his family. Instead of explanations for this state of affairs, it is the resulting engrossing pain that is conveyed. His loss of her is all-encompassing; no other grief is comparable. He mourns: "Why say to a woman: 'Have I lost you?' What has she really given you that she is now taking away? Has one ever truly possessed her to lose her?" (26). Paradoxically, while he suffers from this intense loneliness, he yearns to be free and alone. When he meets the second woman in his life, Thuy Vân, he continues to stress: "There is such a solitude in me" (159).

Allied to the sense of solitude is a yearning for death—a violent, agonizing death—as if the notion of dying in pain is the only means of alleviating his pain in life: "To die like beasts in the desert, to find in death an even more profound exhaustion, to die in stunning pain, and assure myself that each drop of my blood is charged with all the pain in the world" (16). The narrator cannot wean himself away from such thoughts. The novel conveys images of decay and loss, of things that have been beautiful once, like his love for his wife: "One would think that each moment has its weight in dead matter, the weight that we feel before the stones of ruins or before a trampled flower, in a street bathed in sunlight" (29). Even in the latter part of the journal where he addresses Thuy Vân, his love for her is so tinged. He had first been drawn to the young widow by the sadness of her smile and their shared suffering. When this relationship also ends in separation, he concludes: "True pain is not to lose a being in death but in life" (151). Fighting with the *maquis* provides him with a means of escaping his situation and escaping a life that was neither free nor independent. His was "a life that asked to be freed" (107).

The conflict between East and West is a constant part of the narrator's life. He writes of Western conceptions of the East:

> They think they can understand us under the guise of Confucianism, in other words of constraint. But what characterizes our soul and the feelings that adorn it, that we name grace and modesty, is in reality our way of struggling. Our rebellion is inner and we refuse it all violent or unorganized expression. (112)

According to the narrator, the conflict that characterizes Easterners is internal rather than the outward demonstration of the West. Yet, the

Easterner's feelings are still strong, perhaps even stronger by virtue of the fact they are kept hidden and not displayed. The narrator's father epitomizes this approach. Referring to a recent visit by his father, he notes: "He had in effect taught me that one does not make a life from the passions . . . that a soul draws its truth from contemplation" (45). A more concrete example of this outlook is illustrated when the narrator recounts the advice of an old teacher: "When one is already in a decline like myself, one becomes aware that the only truth is that of principles" (111). Upon his pupil challenging this, the teacher details his own experience: "There has been one woman in my life, one only, and whom after our second encounter I decided not to see again . . . For our feelings, we do not require real object" (111–2). Nonetheless, this Eastern notion of detachment is one that the narrator has difficulty accepting and putting into practice.

Although there is no indication of day, month, or year, a rough chronological order emerges. Paragraphs and sentences are short and phrases occasionally appear without verbs as if the narrator has chosen to set down whatever random thought strikes him at a particular moment of time. This haphazardness reinforces a sense of a split self. The narrator is unable to reconcile the Oriental inside with the Western-educated man on the surface. *Les Reflets* conveys immediacy in the sense that any moments of self-discovery or insight are experienced by the reader at the same time as the narrator. The structure of the novel displays the disorder and intensity of the narrator's emotions.

Les Reflets portrays a protagonist in a society in flux. During the 1940s and 1950s Vietnam was in a state of continuous military and political upheaval. While colonial power was being eroded, no independent government clearly emerged.[14] From 1940 to 1945, Vietnam was subject to both French and Japanese occupation. The war of independence begun in 1945 ended with the 1954 Geneva Accords that divided the country into two politically opposed halves. In a society that had operated under colonial authority for the past eighty years, political controversy and economic hardship were accompanied by a questioning of values and beliefs. In this disorder, the narrator attempts to find a fixed point, a measure of stability.

Where will he find this center of calm and with whom or what can he identify? A Vietnamese educated in the language and literature of his colonial masters, is he perhaps a "traitor" to his country because he has absorbed the culture and values of the West? Yet he feels deeply Vietnamese underneath; the Orient in him is too deeply a part of him to be submerged by his Western education. This dichotomy is a source of conflict and anguish for him and ends by destroying him. Death is an escape route: "It is in the self that all source of life falls back. When one has decided to leave the world, one has to climb up" (170). Perhaps symbolically, his death is a violent one, a microcosm of the toll in human bloodshed that was the price Vietnam paid for de-colonization.

Yeager suggests that the narrator's relationships with women in this novel reflect contemporary social and political circumstances "in which the lover lost is also the country lost—its heritage, traditions and culture."[15] The narrator desires to blend into humanity and into time; the notion of transcendence is underlined by the narrator's disappearance at the end of the novel.[16] This analysis can be extended to show that not only the external facets of the narrator's relationships with these women illustrate the political climate of the time, but the contradictions and conflicting demands of the period reveal themselves in the breakdown of the narrator and in the format of the text itself.

The nameless protagonist of *Les Reflets* is in constant and visible torment, a state of mind that is reflected in the writing of the journal. Images of the East are constantly juxtaposed with images of the West—study, travel, literature, and art. The ensuing fragmentation is clear in the journal's narrative construction, with its intrusion of thoughts, images, memories, and sudden reflections. Rather than forming a coherent whole, these pieces of experience illustrate a despairing, broken-up consciousness. The torrent of allusions, to Eastern upbringing and philosophy, to Western art and interpretations, appear to have overwhelmed the narrator. He has been exposed to so much that he cannot choose what to absorb and what to reject. As a result, he tries to encompass all of both cultures then comes apart at the seams because of the strain. *Les Reflets* is not wholly successful as a novel: its confused and meandering exposure of the narrator's dilemma detracts from its appeal. It does expose, however, the strength of the protagonist's despair—a despair that reflects the conflicts tearing a country apart.

Traitor or Hero: *La Place d'un homme*

Published under the pseudonym Nam Kim, Pham Duy Khiem's *La Place d'un homme: De Hanoï à La Courtine* (A Man's Place: From Hanoi to La Courtine) consists of a collection of letters compiled by an anonymous individual. The novel contains neither preface nor introduction but simply begins with a statement: "Nam Liên disappeared in June 1940, during the course of combat in the Loire valley, a few days after having written the note which ends this collection. He was thirty-two years old."[17] The author of these letters, his age, and where and when he died are thus identified. His background, the uniqueness of his recruitment, and the portent of his letters are then established:

> A teacher in Hanoi, he had been the only native from Indochina to ask, in September 1939, to go to France as a volunteer recruit. Why, this done, was he severely judged by his contemporaries? Why had he not hesitated . . . ? How did he live his last experience? It is what his own letters will tell us—simply, if not without poetry, at least without literature. (1)

Pham Duy Khiem served as a volunteer for the French Army when the war broke out in 1939.[18] The work thus contains a strong autobiographical element. Significantly, Nam Liên is a volunteer; France had extracted a heavy toll on the Indochinese colony during the previous war.[19] The direction of as well as the justification for this compilation of notes and papers are exposed from the outset. In contrast to *Les Reflets*, what follows is a clear, chronological progression of events beginning in Hanoi, following the long sea journey to France and ending finally at the last military encampment attended by Nam Liên: La Courtine in June 1940.

A major difference between *Les Reflets* and this collection is that while it is claimed that the author of the former would not have wanted his writing published in his lifetime, the latter consists of short notes addressed to an entire circle of friends and acquaintances. There are antecedents in the European tradition of the letter-autobiography for this: while a journal is written for none other than the individual himself, notes and letters, while still private, are written for others, whether close friends or simply acquaintances and correspondents. Here, the variety of correspondents allows Nam Liên to explain his unorthodox actions to a spectrum of both Vietnamese and French friends and acquaintances. Again unlike the anonymous narrator of *Les Reflets*, he does this succinctly and comprehensively.

Conflict within the individual in Pham's *Place d'un homme*, in comparison to *Les Reflets*, is portrayed in a less vehement way, even though the outcome is similar: the protagonist dies in violent circumstances, disappearing anonymously in the shambles of war. Further, the actual details of the war do not feature in this account. Rather, war forms a perpetual background which provides an external impetus for the protagonist's significant act of volunteering, as a member of the colonized, to fight for the colonizer against what he perceives to be the greater threat Germany. This threat is not spoken of in concrete terms but remains implicit.

Nam Liên's volunteering is heavily ironical: fighting for the oppressor against another oppressor. More than two decades later, the Francophone theorists Aimé Césaire and Frantz Fanon put forward the interpretation that Fascism was not a unique aberration but "simply . . . European colonialism brought home to Europe by a country that had been deprived of its overseas empire by World War I."[20] This colonial greed of one European nation for another does not, however, strike Nam Liên. For him, the war is too vast a struggle to query the "rights" or "wrongs" of his own decision. The situation is an emergency and needs urgent action. It is a matter of fighting together against a greater threat and he has acted in response.

Nam Liên does not think of himself as "Vietnamese" or "French" nor as owing particular loyalty to the French. He cannot, however, escape from the political consequences of his act. Vietnamese nationalists, patriots, and revolutionaries disapprove of his actions. Why should he lay his life on the line for the colonizers? What had the war in Europe to do with him as a Vietnamese? Should he not struggle for his country's independence instead of acting quixotically as the sole native volunteer for the French Army and travel half-way around the world to act out this impulse?

Nam Liên is not immune to criticism even from the French for his signing up. It is the rare acquaintance, whether French or Vietnamese, who accepts his choice. As he writes to Mr. T... in the first note dated September 1939, "In the midst of unkindly commentaries that rise on every side, it is sweet to read your: 'I understand you'" (5). Nam Liên himself becomes gradually becomes aware of the meaning of what he has done. Yeager writes of *La Place d'un homme* that the novel is:

> "à peine romancée" (scarcely romanticized) according to André Rousseaux—and Khiem's own statements elsewhere serve to confirm his own fidelity to France, his gratitude toward French culture, and his hope for a lasting relationship between Viet Nam and France.[21]

Nam Liên's actions, however, can be interpreted in another light, namely an act of independence and self-determination in a colonial subject.

La Place d'un homme charts the gradual unfolding of the protagonist's feelings and emotions and the entire train of events which follows his request to volunteer in France. As he informs his correspondent Mr. T... :

> Today, I would only like to confide in you first, what I feel above all, is an unexpected transformation. It seems that I am discovering, at the moment when I expect to give up on it, the exact dimensions and value of things. There is nothing

that does not appear under a new aspect, as if bathed at last by real light. It is an infinite freshness, certainty and lightness. (5)

This sentiment of "a certainty" permeates his account. It is as if the rest of his life has lain in wait for this decision and that nothing afterwards really matters. Whether he lives or dies, he feels at peace with himself because he has made the right decision and has acted on it. He writes that he was physically frail as a child and that this undertaking will also be a physical challenge for him: "I want to see if I can endure everything, resist until the end" (8).

What is Nam Liên setting out to prove to himself and others? That a member of the colonized can show proof of enterprise, courage, and resilience? That he alone has undertaken to carry out his resolutions? He is coerced into acting thus by neither the colonial authorities nor his peers. It is a decision that he makes independently. He is not carrying out a family or patriotic duty but simply responding as an individual to a particular situation. Ironically, it is also something that he can only undertake in metropolitan France. As a "native," he does not have the right to bear arms in his own country.

Nam Liên points to the difference, as he sees it, between his own upbringing and that of young European men. "The young French man, the young German, expect to fight and to die one day. They grow up with that thought, and then afterwards they are trained for it" (9). He observes with admiration as well as some trepidation the militaristic tradition of European manhood as opposed to the relatively impotent upbringing of Vietnamese youth, an impotence imposed on the colonized. He feels that they are permitted to die only by illness—illness itself suggesting weakness and helplessness as opposed to the virile choice of marching out and dying on the battlefield.

One may wonder why anyone would yearn for this sort of fate, but for a member of the colonized the crux of the question is choice. He has no choice and no power in his own country. He cannot assert himself in his native environment, both because of an oppressive colonial system and because of familial and social pressures. Neil Jamieson observes,

> Contradictory demands and expectations exacted a heavy toll from many Vietnamese, especially young educated males from "good" families in urban areas. Socialization within the family had systematically stunted the psychological independence required for efficacious performance within the individualistic culture of the West. At the same time immersion in Western culture . . . had eroded the capacity for dependence and nurturance required for efficacious performance in family life . . . Thus were the best and the brightest of a generation of Vietnamese to some degree rendered ineffectual.[22]

Nam Liên is not master of his fate in his own land. He can only assert his will by leaving. His enlisting conveys rebellion against both imposed bonds and inertia. He struggles to express himself as an individual, to act in defiance of the colonizers. In a note addressed to "A French man from Indochina," he writes: "You are not the only French man to do a complete about-face regarding me. . . . People had to know that there were honest and worthy Annamites who were nevertheless ready to offer themselves to France's defense" (10–1). His action thus counters the colonizers' opinion that no native is honest or worthy. The novel's colonial context is clear from Nam Liên's reference to "Annamites" rather than "Vietnamese."

To Nam Liên, others' concerns and queries about his motivations are baseless: "There is a peril, a man stands up—why ask him his reasons? It is rather those who remain silent who should give their reasons for abstaining" (12). He should not have to justify his actions. It is the others, who have not acted, who ought to justify theirs. He acknowledges his appreciation to those who let him go his own way, even though they may, for political reasons, disapprove. He writes to an old Vietnamese nationalist, Mr. Trân Trong (to whom France, naturally, is the enemy): "I acted alone, not wanting to drag in anyone else, nor lose time. I will thank you to let me follow my destiny, after having first disapproved of me" (17).

Nam Liên does not expect a reward for his actions, whether for himself individually, or for his countrymen politically. As he writes to the old nationalist, "Whoever makes calculations risks disappointment. Nobility, especially, expects no salary. When the neighbor's house catches fire, even if this neighbor did not like you, you do not ask him: 'I will bring you a bucket of water, what will you give me in exchange?'" (18). He is not seeking rank or glory but goes with a sense of fatalism: "What is most difficult is not to give up the present and the future, but to separate oneself from the past" (24).

In a reversal indicative of the perverse nature of colonialism, Nam Liên can thus only assert his self-will by volunteering to fight for the colonizer. He rationalizes that the fight against oppression is a worthy one and that the threat and the emergency are real, but he is not overly concerned about the actual nature of this threat. His letters are empty of references to Nazism, Fascism, domination, annexation, or the master race. Perhaps such discussions are an uncomfortable reminder of the reality of colonialism so he omits them. Safely absorbed in a wider struggle he can turn away from the uncomfortably close reality of French Indochina, escape from the claustrophobia and constraints he has experienced as a member of the colonized in his native country and move towards a measure of freedom. Unfortunately, his escape is largely illusory. In reality, his constraints and his relative freedom both lie within the domain of control of the colonizers.

Nam Liên writes of the reality of soldiering: the repetitive nature of army chores, the tough and Spartan conditions. Certain aspects of army life affect him more than others. As a Vietnamese coming from a warm, near-tropical climate he is particularly vulnerable to the misery of winter in France and the sheer physical pain of coldness often surfaces in his notes. At first glance he is an unlikely recruit. An intellectual, university graduate and high school teacher in Indochina, he enlists as a private, and resents the lack of quiet and privacy. At the same time, he notes with some wonderment: "What a strange and rich life! . . . They are there, it does not smell good, one hears banalities and stupid remarks, one is embarrassed—suddenly one forgets all for this camaraderie, these seconds of purity that I have known nowhere else" (42).

Nam Liên appreciates the anonymity provided by a soldier's uniform. This is something new and alien to him. No longer is he "Monsieur Liên" or a "native" from the colonies but a soldier in the uniform of the French Army. The anonymity allows him to surrender himself, his individuality, his aspirations, and his fears. He blends into a general mass and in this way finds happiness:

> In one word, despite the cold (it has been freezing for three days), despite the discipline, the fatigue, the sergeants, despite the dust, the earth, the cold water, I am happy. Precisely because I have wanted this deprivation, to be a soldier and nothing else, no expectation, no calculation, no hope. (45)

In his "deprivation" he finds the freedom to put away his burdens and leave behind his obligations. By the same token, this state of readiness means that he is resigned to any eventuality: "to expect everything, at any moment" (49). His friends, he feels, misunderstand his state of mind. No one, it seems, can comprehend that he could feel contentment or happiness in his chosen path: "Even those who understood my departure are completely mistaken about my actual state. One writes to me that I must feel lonely and unhappy, the other hopes that my life will not be empty" (50). His friends mistakenly pity him, while he, on the other hand, feels a deep sense of satisfaction and purpose because this is his decision and he is abiding by his choice. What this reveals is the scarcity of choices left open to him. If the only way for a man to achieve happiness and self-respect is by becoming an anonymous soldier in barracks, it is a dispiriting comment on the paucity of options left to him.

Nam Liên does not glorify or idealize army life. He comments wryly: "Intelligence is rare, in the army as elsewhere" (51). Tasks are boring and yet he dances: "It's a slow waltz, it is sunny, and it is the first time I am dancing alone." (57) Along with this external and internal dance, the notes bear many descriptions of the beauty of nature, and the surrounds of the army camp. Nam Liên observes this grace with surprise and delicacy:

> I must tell you that we can see Mount Saint-Clair, and the slopes that come to die at the foot of the barracks spread their bouquets of pines, their pink and green houses, their gardens and their orchards. The sun that hides and uncovers in turn caresses the dog lying in the alley. Over there, towards the town, delicate peach trees are pink in color, a pink that is almost white. (63)

The war seems very far away. There are neither news bulletins nor comments on the progress of the war, and only a brief mention towards the end that there exists a threat from Italy. Despite his solitary recruitment from Indochina, thirteen "Annamites," most of them established permanently in France and married to French women, are in Nam Liên's unit. Yet he feels troubled by this:

> I have always thought that the efforts of men of good will are ridiculously vain. But one has to justify one's presence on this earth . . . It is unfortunately true that I was the only one who could come, that we were only a few to want to come. I am deeply saddened by this, both for France, and for Annam. (69)

Despite his claims of a measure of pride in acting voluntarily and alone, he wishes that more of his countrymen had responded to a similar impulse. He does not want to think of the future and his response to friends who write and inquire as to his plans "afterwards" is: "You have to believe me, I am not thinking about any future" (66). Absorbed in the daily minutiae and concerns of army life, his thoughts do not stretch any further. It is useless to conjecture a "future" when he may not come back at all.

Having passed the army recruits' test, he is now, along with the others, in intensive training. There is no purpose in his friends lamenting his situation when he himself is too busy to do so: "[I]f I do not return, or if I return without an arm or a leg, or gassed, it does not matter in the least to me. I do not see why people would take pity on me" (68). Although occasionally reminiscing about his past life, his childhood and early education in Indochina, his later university education in France, his German friends, most of his notes discuss the current concerns of his unit. Occasional reminders of another "peace-time" existence, such as an impromptu evening of music at a friend's house, are painful: "Why are you tearing me away from the reality where I have to live? I have already forgotten everything. Why remind me that there exists a world of beauty and of gentleness?" (75).

Nam Liên is constantly rationalizing his decision for old friends and acquaintances, clarifying his reasons for himself, and attempting to communicate to others the measure of serenity he is experiencing—something they have obvious difficulty accepting: "It was not an élan. Neither was it 'a gesture,' as a journalist wrote. But a natural act, which needed no preparation or prior reflection, any more that it demanded the whip of enthusiasm or the tension of effort" (76). As his expectations of army life turn out to be worse than the reality, in the end he is rather agreeably surprised; he expected to serve under lesser men. In a sense, his temporary abdication of concern for the future or anything other than the immediate present is a means of escape. It is easier for him to absorb himself in the minutiae of a soldier's daily life, in the plethora of images, impressions and colors around him, than to think of his own condition and the deeper (and unresolved) concerns arising from it.

Nam Liên writes often to women, especially a Mrs. B... towards the end of this writing. Images of gentleness, care and comfort are associated with them. As he is transferred to different military camps and gradually gets closer to the fighting, the war, and the possibility of being killed in combat, he writes note after note describing his immediate impressions of his surroundings and the people in it. To another woman, Mrs. D..., he communicates his guilt over his mother:

> I have just translated your letter for my mother, and she will regret not knowing you, never knowing you. For my part, I appreciate the fact that a French woman expressed this idea to me: that my mother must suffer more than a French mother, because she could not have expected to see her son suddenly go to war. But I am especially moved because you said it. (106)

As the time to face the enemy head on draws closer, Nam Liên evinces a mixture of anticipation, apprehension, and indifference: "I discover in myself a perfect indifference to what is my own security. All day, I sew calmly or I write, wondering whether my letters will go" (116). If he is indifferent to his physical fate, however, he is keen to communicate his feelings to the utmost of his capacity and by the same token, receives with joy any letters that reach him. To Mrs. B... he writes, "When a letter reaches me, it's a miracle! If you knew! Ah! The awful disorder!" (118).

Nam Liên continues to justify himself in defense of those who disapprove of his volunteering. To a French man he writes, "I don't like war, I don't like military life, but we are at war, and I would not know where else to be. It is not a matter of making a choice between France and Annam. It is only a matter of knowing the place of an Annamite like myself, at this point in time. It is here" (120). He pities the men who are fathers of young families: "Their letters; those poor envelopes, those addresses written in pencil, the badly formed writing. . . ." (129). He questions the sensation of unnatural quiet before the storm: "Why this tranquility? Why?" (131). Finally, his last few notes mention major battles and visible results of war: "the refugees with their appalling distress (neither photos, nor newspapers, nor books will tell all)" (133). His closing note, extremely brief, is dated 12 June and addressed to Mrs. B...: "We are leaving. God keep you!" (136).

Unlike *Les Reflets*, *La Place d'un homme* contains no afterword or epilogue, though the presence of whoever compiles the collection is pervasive throughout in the short explanations which describe the recipients of these notes: "old nationalist", "Mr. R... a French man who had not approved of Nam Liên's commitment" (119). The variety of correspondents stretching over two continents provides a wide array of political and personal views which in turn allow the narrator to respond and comment on the politics and personal reasons for his actions, as well as to convey his private feelings. The work is a path to self-justification, a plea for understanding before all his correspondents, whether male or female, French or Vietnamese, revolutionary or conservative.

Nam Liên is in a category apart, belonging to no discernible group. He stands as a lonely and isolated figure, yet finds a measure of relief and happiness in shedding the doubts and uncertainties surrounding his life in French Indochina. Plunging into his daily existence as a private in the French Army, into the largely anonymous, dull, and repetitive nature of such a life, he finds a measure of freedom. Nonetheless, his sense of liberation, of casting all previous worries aside, is deceptive. Still uncertain of his identity and confused about his loyalties, his many notes and letters try, somewhat desperately, to convey the reasons for his decisions. They indicate the fragmentation of his identity for which, as for the narrator of *Les Reflets*, there is no relief in sight. While war provides a temporary distraction and death in combat is a fitting end to his dilemma, again like the narrator of *Les Reflets*, Nam Liên is a prisoner of his condition. He tries, through his correspondence, to communicate to the many "outsiders," but remains and dies within his own prison. His escape and happiness as a soldier are illustrative of the underlying entrapment. In the end they are illusory.

Nam Liên behaves, even if he denies it, in the manner of a patriotic French man volunteering to go to the defense of his homeland. But Nam Liên is, of course, not French and France is not his homeland. His action reveals much, not only about the nature of the colonized, but also about that of the colonizer. As Robert Young suggests in *White Mythologies*:

Mimicry at once enables power and produces the loss of agency. If control slips away from the colonizer, the requirement of mimicry means that the colonized, while complicit in the process, remains the unwitting and unconscious agent of menace—with a resulting paranoia on the part of the colonizer as he tries to guess the native's sinister intentions. Though of course the native may well have violent thoughts of forms of resistance, we are not here, it should be stressed, talking about such orthodox forms of resistance, but a process which simultaneously stabilizes and destabilizes the position of the colonizer.[23]

It is because he could not deal with the conflicting demands and restrictions imposed upon him as a member of the colonized in Indochina that Nam Liên turns with such eagerness towards this method of escape. His action, while on the surface a subject of self-congratulation on the part of the colonizer (the ultimate act of native gratitude towards the colonizer) bears on the reverse side a negative critique of colonialism—in that it has the power to reduce the native to such means in order to assert an individuality submerged under a greater system.

Conclusion

Unlike *Les Reflets de nos jours,* which charts the disintegration of a personality, *La Place d'un homme* charts the gradual formation and affirmation of the narrator's thoughts and feelings. The notes portray an unfolding consciousness as the protagonist clarifies, both for his correspondents and himself, the motivations that lie behind his decision to enlist and the positive assertion of self which ensues. This way of reaching for and achieving a measure of happiness—the greatest sensation of happiness he has ever experienced in any circumstances in his thirty-two years—leads also, however, to the eventual destruction of his self. As with the anonymous narrator of *Les Reflets,* his decision leads to physical death. While *La Place d'un homme* is far less gloomy and pessimistic than the earlier novel, in the end the narrator similarly disappears in combat. Both deaths appear to serve a definite purpose, providing an end to the insoluble problem of identity and of identification.

In Indochina, colonization afforded the colonized a glimpse of freedom and potential in the form of education and a few brief years of university studies in a foreign metropolis, but at the same time slammed the lid down on any hopes or ambitions.[24] Once back home, the newly-educated Vietnamese intellectual had to reconcile himself to the true nature of his condition as a colonial subject. As a native, the language in which he communicated, his gaining access to European thought, and any consequent privileges, all he owed to the magnanimity of his colonizer. By the same token, he was debarred from exerting any autonomy. He was, in large measure, denied his power.

The tangled vein of loyalty and resentment that resulted manifests itself in different ways in *Les Reflets* and *La Place d'un homme*. Both narratives reveal a crisis of self-questioning on the part of the narrator. In *Les Reflets*, the gradual disintegration of the self is manifested in the style of the novel itself: a mass of disparate impressions, emotions, perceptions, and illustrations of the corroding despair of the narrator. In the case of *La Place d'un homme*, splintered perceptions appear in more orderly form as a collection of letters addressed to different correspondents. These letters nonetheless attempt to communicate a sense of loss and the lack of a firm base; they signify a search for identity that *Les Reflets* displays in more violent form. For the protagonists of both novels, the end result is death, the only means of resolving their conflict of identity. Neither novel is either a denunciation or exposition of the virtues and vices of colonized and colonizer. Instead, they portray the simultaneously enriching and destructive effects of the enmeshing of two cultures when the balance of power is heavily skewed.

The fate of the two protagonists can be read as a metaphor for the ensuing fate of the colonial system. Inevitably, it would destroy itself. The system, like these two protagonists, carries within itself the impetus for its own disintegration, but the damage is of course the greater and more costly, in individual terms, for the weaker and more vulnerable participants: the colonized. For those Vietnamese who stayed on in France after their studies and settled down with French wives, adjustment was generally less stressful. The French metropolis recognized their educational qualifications and competence. If prejudice did exist—inevitably—it was less marked than that evinced by the colonial administration in French Indochina.[25]

Both *Les Reflets* and *La Place d'un homme* portray the fate of Vietnamese intellectuals educated at university level in France and later returning to Indochina. Each protagonist comes from the more privileged classes and has the opportunity not only to study but to travel in Europe and mingle with European intellectuals. For both the narrator of *Les Reflets* and Nam Liên, the memories of these formative student days are poignant, but the discovery and freedom of those years proves transitory and deceptive. It can now only be looked on with nostalgia.

For many Vietnamese during this period, their years in France would be their only experience of freedom, of laying down, if not putting away for good, the ties which linked them to family, the burdens of duty and obligation, and the constraints exerted by both society and the colonial administration. In these novels, this transitory illusion of freedom, of letting worldly burdens fall away, is briefly experienced again by each protagonist towards the end of his life. Involvement in guerrilla or army life allows each a brief surrender of self. Each sacrifices himself to a greater cause, setting aside the concerns of his existence for a greater emergency. In both cases, however, their actions only serve to underline the destructive and hypnotic nature of the colonial system to which they are subject and from which they attempt, in the end, to free themselves. For both of these two protagonists, writing is a way of exorcising the contradictions of their situation. In this, their dilemma echoes that of other Francophone writers. Evelyne Accad elucidates her own experience:

> Writing as refuge, as quest, and as expression of the division of the self . . . Writing helped to heal certain wounds. It reconciled me to my past. In expressing what overwhelmed

me, I exorcised the anger, the pain and the suffering of insurmountable situations and I could go ahead.[26]

Les Reflets and *La Place d'un homme* are a metaphorical reflection of the prison literature which has characterized autobiographical narratives in Vietnam.[27] They do not detail the physical incarceration of the narrator-protagonist, but instead expose his condition as an individual caught in an inescapable bind between two cultures and two conflicting loyalties.

6

Strangers

The self must hide from wind and dust—
the door is always tightly shut.
—Cao Ba Quat

The sensation of being a stranger in one's land is a powerful and disturbing experience, all the more so if it occurs after a period of exile. For some, the return to their native village proves the ultimate experience of alienation: from one's roots, family, and society. The village—small, contained and familiar, the place of one's birth and family memories—becomes in this context a place of nightmarish unfamiliarity. The traveler, instead of returning home, finds himself an alien in his own land.

Pham Van Ky's *Frères de sang* (Blood Brothers), published in Paris in 1947, and Cung Giu Nguyen's *Le Fils de la baleine* (The Whale's Son), published in Paris in 1956, are indictments of village life and of the narrowness of perspectives within a restricted environment. The village in Vietnam has historically maintained a fierce independence from royal and bureaucratic authority: "The old proverb *'Phep vua thua le lang'* (The laws of the emperor yield to the customs of the village) is known by all Vietnamese."[1] In the north of the country, each village was surrounded and protected by a thick hedge of bamboo, a physical and symbolic barrier which, while it protected, also cut the villagers off from the outside world.[2] As a self-contained unit, "the village directed its own affairs, supervised by a Council of Notables recruited from the village oligarchy."[3] In many ways, it remained impervious to the changes brought about by the French administration of the country:

> Whereas the French began to reform the Cochinchinese
> village system in 1904, they did not make similar changes in

Tongking until 1921, and in Annam the village system
appears to have remained largely unchanged down to 1940
... Both in Cochinchina and in Tongking-Annam, the French
impact on peasant life in the villages came very slowly, and
the cultural assimilation which made fairly rapid headway
in the metropolis of Saigon or Hanoi never completely
embraced the countryside.[4]

In both *Frères de sang* and *Le Fils de la baleine*, the village is
particularly resistant to change. In the end, in whole or in part, it is
destroyed. Meanwhile its inhabitants, embodying an entrenched and
outmoded mentality, are capable of acts of petty and occasionally
intense cruelty. In both novels, the villagers' way of life is threatened
by the arrival of an outsider, a spark that eventually leads to a series
of changes and questionings that shakes the village's foundations. In
each case, the village becomes a symbol of the individual's alienation
from tradition and, by extension, from his cultural identity.

Pham Van Ky's *Frères de sang* (1947) portrays the return of a
prodigal son to his native village after ten years in France. The
unnamed narrator's inability to aid his female relatives has already
been explored (Chapter Three). Alienation from his native culture
and his problematic relationship with his two brothers—his younger
brother Hô and blood brother Lê Tâm—form the focus here. The
narrator gradually distances himself from his brothers and in the
end loses both. Cung Giu Nguyen's *Le Fils de la baleine* (1956) relates
the arrival of a total stranger in a Vietnamese village. The sole
survivor of a shipwreck, a man named Mô has lost his memory and
becomes trapped in a village that is isolated and lost in time. This
novel charts the growing hostility of the villagers towards Mô until
he finally makes his escape out to sea.

Each protagonist in these narratives provides the initial
momentum for change in the village but the portrayal of this
protagonist, the circumstances of his arrival, and his response to the
village are different in each case. One, the traveling son returns to
his native village; the other, the traveling stranger has lost his way.
While the first realizes himself he has become a stranger in his own

land, the second, already suffering from amnesia and having from the outset no sense of belonging, is made to feel a stranger as a result of his reception by the villagers. The first, in other words, is fully aware that he returns a changed man. The second, in attempting to adapt to village life, is steadily rejected, and eventually recognizes and accepts his condition as an outsider.

The Prodigal Son: *Frères de sang*

In a brief note at the end of *Frères de sang* (Blood Brothers), Pham Van Ky indicates that the novel was written in 1946.[5] The period between August 1945 and December 1946 in which it is set is judged "one of the most important periods in Vietnamese history from the fact that it sees the end of the last emperor, the victory of the Viet-Minh Communist Party and the start of the Indochina War."[6] The contrast between tradition and revolution that characterizes the novel has its historical counterpart in the events of this time. Although the novel does not allude overtly to the contemporary political situation, its historical setting is undeniable. Nguyen Hong Nhiem comments:

> The action is set in the charnel-house of bipartition. Or, what is more full of imagery, at the [17]th parallel, which will cut Vietnam into two. In this case, in a village, in a pure expanse which, in Sino-Vietnamese geopolitics, represents the totality of the country.[7]

As an exile, Pham Van Ky had a greater degree of freedom with which to express the political tensions of the time. He was less subject to the ideological pressures both North and South exerted on their writers and intellectuals.[8] Yeager notes that "[t]he character of the narrator reflects the psychological background of the larger socio-political landscape."[9] Similarly, tensions within family and village reflect, in a microcosm, the wider events of the country, though this recognition is implicit rather than explicit. Pham Van Ky mentions the "League for the Independence of Vietnam," for example, but he does not elaborate on it. The "League" serves instead to offset the intensely reactionary nature of his father and the village over which the latter presides:

> No change of dynasty, no political upheaval could have modified the structure of my family. . . . Had the "League for the Independence of Vietnam," for a year now, broken the social triangle, changed the name of the country, denied the king, discredited the mandarin, Father continued to hold sway, endowed with absolute power. The Court's ordinances giving way to communal law, according to a maxim, tradition was his scepter. (25)

Looking beyond the social and political meanings which other critics have already acknowledged,[10] the most striking elements in *Frères de sang* are the twin motifs of alienation and duality which appear throughout the novel. Molded first by the East then by the West, the returning prodigal is a personality split between two cultures. He is contrasted with his blood brother Lê Tâm and younger brother Hô; a particular difficulty he experiences is that he bears aspects of both brothers within his self. This dilemma has a paralyzing effect on him as he finds himself alienated not only from those around him but also from a firm sense of self. Throughout the novel, objects or people with distorted mirror reflections of themselves illustrate this dichotomy in the narrator's background, formation, and identity. Nguyen Hong Nhiem sees the narrator's use of *Je* (I) as the foreign, Europeanized part of his personality, while his *Moi* (I/Me) remembers and recognizes his roots and traditions.[11]

The first image of duality to greet the narrator on the night of his return is one of reflection and contrast: "Two moons seemed to mark its height: one on the dish of the sky like a cake for the mid-autumn festival, the other drowned in the bowl of the pond" (13). In this striking image of duality, one moon is triumphant in the sky, the other drowned in water. The first, shedding its light on all living things below, can be construed as a vivid metaphor for the colonizing power as it imposes education, "civilization," and paternalistic control over a subject country. The drowned moon can be interpreted as a metaphor for the submerged voice and literature of the colonized; a symbol of lost values, cultural norms, and practices. The moon, reflecting the sun's light, has a long cultural association with the feminine.[12] This gender coding is an added indicator of other meanings which lay behind the surface. It is fitting that the first sight to greet the traveler returning from faraway lands is this shining and submerged duality, two possible markers of the reception he will receive in his native village.

What emerges in *Frères de sang* is a partial and in some sense crippled perception of the village and its people. The narrator returns to his village, but has changed, while the village, or rather those who run the village, have not. The moon and the water, whether indicative of a hierarchy of power within the country or within a Vietnamese village and family, embody two concepts. The first is the dominant image and its distorted reflection on a shifting, uneven surface. The second is the difficulty of seeing and adequately representing this reflected image. The narrator of *Frères de sang* is in a position to observe both—as a member of the colonized, but having lived and studied in the French metropolis. He is a product of his family, his village, and society but has detached himself from them by going overseas and exposing himself to a different society with different values. Vuong-Riddick writes:

> This body modified by its contacts with Western culture, how is it perceived in its native milieu? What are the signs of change which betray the process of acculturation? From the approach to the village, this body presents with its particular smell, not recognized by the village dog and uniquely perceptible by the blind friend. [13]

The narrator reflects the values of both East and West. Like the shifting and reflected moon, his is a difficult and uneasy personality.

The second image of duality emerges as the narrator meets his blood brother after ten years of separation: "There are two kinds of wells: drinking water and brackish water. . . . What brutal frankness under so many metaphorical precautions. Would I be a bitter well?"

(18). These two wells illustrate the possibilities and dilemmas confronting this man. They encapsulate, concisely, the options that lie in front of him. "Drinking water" indicates a palatable medium, the narrator's acceptance of his status in the family, the village, and in his country as a member of the colonized. "Brackish water" suggests bitterness and rebellion against his situation. Water however, is also a sign of regeneration, as it provides life. In this context, the water in the well has an ambiguous significance. The narrator is returning to his homeland, his village, his "source," but rather than providing him with sustenance, the native village contains elements which are potentially destructive.

Upon first arriving, the narrator does not know which it will be. A well can provide life in the form of drinking water or can poison in the form of brackish water; he must either resign himself to the situation or struggle against it. The dilemmas facing him are overwhelming: "Ten years of European education had taught me to define, to outline, but had not untaught me to give to things dimensions relative to my worries" (13). Both the narrator and his blood brother Lê Tâm must make a concerted effort to understand each other across a gap of years, experience, and cultural separation. It is an immense task for the two to rediscover each other: "Blood brothers! A parable with what it contained of truth and error" (19). The image of the well in this context is quite apt, for just as it takes effort to bend over and draw water out of the well, so an effort of will is needed to see into another's personality and motivations, to look beyond the surface reflection—of an individual or for that matter a country or a culture. "I contented myself with relearning what I had unlearned, to prepare my real return among my people" (20). The narrator's reflection takes place on his first night back in his native village after an absence of ten years. His arrival is unexpected and although he enters his family compound, he leaves it again without being seen by anyone. (He leaves because he has a sudden desire to be anywhere but back at the family compound). The first person in the village with whom he speaks is Lê Tâm. It is only after conversing with his friend that he makes his "official" return to the village. Having left his family, society, and culture far behind in

order to adapt to life overseas, the narrator must now unlearn all he
has learned during that time.

Lê Tâm appears as an antithesis to the narrator: two blood
brothers like the two sides of a coin. Both are Vietnamese from the
same village but one is Westernized, the other imbued with the
philosophies of the Far East. One has been educated in Europe; the
other "condemns all initiatives as futile."[14] One is a symbol of a
changing Vietnam facing an uncertain future, the other of tradition
and a certain past. While Lê Tâm is at peace with the traditions of his
country, he is not necessarily at peace with the values of the society
he lives in. He regrets the old ways of learning and the
dismantlement of Vietnam's ancient mandarinal system of
education. The narrator records his friend's "disappointment at not
being able to sit for the Triennial Examination, due to the
establishment of French-Vietnamese schools" (19). Lê Tâm is firmly
turned towards the past. Even the narrator's father, head of the
village, traditionalist, autocratic, and conservative as he is, has his
veneer of Western education. Lê Tâm's values, on the other hand,
pre-date the Europeanization of Vietnam. While the society around
him cannot help being affected by changes engendered by the West,
Lê Tâm stands out as an anomaly. Vuong-Riddick observes:

> All the mystery, the paradoxes, the subtleties of Taoism
> showed through in the person of the strange Lê Tâm who
> incarnates here one of the greatest spiritual forces of the
> East, one of the most opposed to all systems in place, since it
> refuses any definition. But if Taoism can constitute a source
> of absolutely fecund inspiration from the poetic, mystical
> and philosophical point of view, on the daily and the social
> level, in the urgency of choices and confrontations, it only
> offers (as it is presented here) the denial of the world, the
> withdrawal into the self, the search for annihilation, in short
> an escape inside. [15]

Lê Tâm, himself, is a dual image, a "scholar-goldsmith" (21). He is
skillful with his mind and skillful with his hands; two images that fit

into the mould of traditional society. The way in which he works reflects the slow workings of the East: "Stamping is done cold, contrary to Western practice. For if hot, pure gold, which is very malleable, would risk cracking during the process, because of the tightening of the grains" (41). Symbolically, the slower way is in the end less likely to cause damage. Changes may occur slowly in the East, but they may need to be slow to have a firmer base in the end. By contrast, the fast-moving changes that the narrator has experienced can lead to the fragmentation of the individual as resulting stresses take their toll. Lê Tâm is not pulled in two ways like the narrator, but, in standing apart from his contemporaries, he is similar to the narrator.

The split between East and West is evident in the gap in perception that exists between the narrator and his father, illustrated in the father's advice to his son: "Confucius never said 'I think' but 'Yao thinks'" (49). Yao, a mythical ruler of ancient China, was greatly revered by Confucius.[16] In response, the son points out the mixed nature of his father's education:

> Always this logic which unbalanced me! Aggravated in Father's case by that hybrid state which he held from his Confucian education and a veneer of French culture acquired during his contacts with the occupiers in the province. And how should we take this man who sometimes expressed himself like me and other times preached to me humility in front of Yao? (49)

The father uses "I think" and "Yao thinks" for his own convenience, either to assert himself or to point at humility in front of his son. There exists, however, a world of difference between the two, between what is acceptable behavior to the son and to the father. While the father makes a drama out of the return of his son: "The West has returned my son. A thousand blessings to the West!" (24); for him, as for the son, the reunion proves illusory.

It is through his brother Hô, the revolutionary, that the narrator is presented with a particularly vivid image of escape: "I want a door to the East, a door to the West, a door for dawn, a door for noon, a door amid violence, a door amid madness, a door amid what never happens . . . I want . . ." (84). The images, this time, are not dual, but multiple. Doors potentially symbolize many things, since they can lead in divergent directions and to different ways of thinking. Hô speaks of many possible destinations and these in turn suggest a multiplicity of meanings behind the image of "doors." A door can mean access to another being or country. Doors are a means of making a space completely enclosed, a barrier with which to lock oneself in and lock others out, much as the village itself shuts its inhabitants in and strangers out. The door is an actual, physical barrier to freedom for Hô. Kept in a cell, his revolt against a physical barrier is echoed by a revolt against the constrictions of the village and the old traditions around him:

> "We are suffocating in this cell. Not a single window. And all these stale ideas! . . . All this dead literature in a dead language! All this hotchpotch of 'Confucianisms'!"
>
> The young man who yesterday had taken Lê Tâm's part, that most ardent depository of "Confucianisms," now flung curses at his peers! It was imperative, at all costs, that that rebel find obstacles against which to try his gratuitous force. (84)

Hô's rebellion, his physical and mental attempt to escape from prison and the imprisoning effect of customs and traditions is something that the narrator admires but cannot act on for himself. With the narrator's help, Hô escapes in more ways than one, but it remains otherwise for the narrator. Having opened one door, he finds himself unable to step through it. Doors, with a number of openings suggested by Hô indicate a number of options available to the narrator. Although he recognizes them, he cannot avail himself of any. A man in a room of many doors, he has neither the will nor the energy to use any of them. His situation reflects the setting described by late eighth and early ninth century poet Han-shan in his *Cold Mountain* poems:

Cold Mountain is a house
Without beams or walls
The six doors left and right are open
The hall is blue sky
The rooms are all vacant and vague
The east wall beats on the west wall
At the centre nothing.[17]

Rather than pointing to freedom, doors serve to reinforce the narrator's inertia and paralysis.

A vivid image, literally of black and white, underlines the narrator's alienation from the village community when he attends a village burial: "Dressed all in black, to fit in, I realized that white was the color of mourning, that white which reminded me of the brilliance of Olympic stadiums, the candor of wedding gowns" (90). In his response to the colors of mourning, the narrator reveals the extent of his *dépaysement* (disorientation). To him, white is the color of life indicating movement, vitality, and potential and opposed to black, the color of death, stillness, and finality. As Frantz Fanon writes of black and white: "Blackness, darkness, shadow, shades, night, the labyrinths of the earth, abysmal depths, blacken someone's reputation; and, on the other side, the bright look of innocence, the white dove of peace, magical, heavenly light."[18] White is the light of the West, of the colonizers, black of the East, opaque and mysterious. In Vietnam, however, white is the traditional color of mourning, not black as in the West.[19]

Lê Tâm makes a significant sacrifice for the sake of his blood brother. Having practiced a doctrine of detachment for ten years, he interrupts it with the arrival of the narrator: "I have spoken to you as to a blood brother . . . I have guessed it; you broke off the cotton bracelet that linked us. And you rushed to my rescue. And I, to yours, each according to his means, each according to his truth. Why?" (94). Each of them comes to the rescue of his own blood brother. Each has his own truth, his own abilities, his own concept of the significance of blood brotherhood and the responsibility this entails. The contrasting notions are of bonds and freedom. For each brother it is a sacrifice to give up the normal patterns of life to go towards the other.

For the narrator, the capacity and the ability to love and to accept his roots are encapsulated in his feelings for Lê Tâm, his opposite. His country, culture, and traditions are embodied in the person of his blood brother. The bracelets of cotton and gold, which were used to formalize the bond between the narrator and Lê Tâm, reinforce the notion of reversion to native culture. The bracelets are circles, with neither end nor beginning, just as the brothers' responsibilities towards each other have neither end nor beginning; they are inevitable and inescapable. Each man is dependent on the other.

The image of the circle also bears an element of destructiveness. Lê Tâm refers to a gold circle as a dragon trying to swallow its tail. Will each consume the other? The issue of Lê Tâm obsesses the narrator: "To love Lê Tâm or to reject him, that is where the game should be played. From the red or the black camp, who would carry it off?" (101). It is a clear dichotomy, to love or to reject Lê Tâm as a metaphor for loving or rejecting an entire culture. In reasoning this way, the narrator gives his past the power to maim the present and potentially, the future. His failure to resolve this issue is borne out by his failure to act in any way later on in the novel. Sunk in apathy or detachment, trapped in his past, in the limitations and constraints of his culture and milieu, he observes events passing him by. His passivity, in the end, signifies the failure of his "I think" as opposed to his father's "Yao thinks."

The live game of chess that takes place in the village provides a symbol of a society abiding by the rules of a game. All players in the chess game are individuals. "What are we if not a sum of numerical, physical or moral relations? What are we, in the last resort, if not the value of a prop?" (102). The narrator stresses that what individuals make of themselves is surely more important than what the past has made of them. Events in the village reflect the political realities of the country around it. Nguyen Hong Nhiem writes: "The chessboard of *co nguoi* (live chess pieces) . . . thus assumes the totality of conflicts in the village and by extension of all of Vietnam, two years after the

August Revolution of 1945."[20] It is one game in which the narrator voluntarily plays a part, but the game, unlike the village itself, is artificial. It is not a prelude to the narrator participating fully in village life.

The narrator acknowledges his debt to both his blood brother Lê Tâm and to his younger brother Hô. To Hô he says, "Lê Tâm was a part of my truth, if not its totality. . . . You are also a part of my truth, I don't dare say the totality. But such an actual, undying part" (165). But when Hô leaves, the narrator does lose his brother. Admitting his failure, he laments: "I did not know how to get to the end of myself. That is why I got lost on the way" (167–8). Hô escapes from prison, while Lê Tâm dies in a fire. The fire and the wind conspire to destroy all that is left of Lê Tâm, his house and his body. The fire consumes all the currents running through the village, the good as well as the bad:

> A flame for good, one for evil, one for right, one for wrong, one for advantage, one for inconvenience. The seventh for reason! Reason crackled, smelling of rancid grease. Good smoked, smelling of calcified bones. Evil whistled, smelling of cooked viscera. Right sniggered, smelling of smoked skin. Wrong sputtered, smelling of charred hair . . . (199–200)

Lê Tâm's grisly immolation marks the final stages of the village's disintegration. The silence that falls after his death is brooding rather than peaceful: "The weather darkened" (200). For Nguyen Hong Nhiem, the *Je* (I) of the narrator empowers him to help Hô escape while the *Moi* (I/Me) stands paralyzed as Lê Tâm dies.[21] The novel ends: "I am a poor little thing, without reality, without homeland, without truth: a small chance to live, black matrix over the fine grain of gold that I had been! And Lê Tâm tells me. . . And Hô tells me. . . " (205).

The narrator is left alone with the voices of both brothers, chiming in his ears, pulling him one way then the other. Brother Hô, symbol of rebellion and of high ideals, is gone. Blood brother Lê Tâm, the resigned, acquiescent embodiment of the ancient traditions of his culture, is dead. Left to himself, the narrator is no longer confined to one race or one continent. Yet instead of experiencing freedom, he finds himself adrift with no country, no self, no truth. His inability to reconcile past with present leads to total inertia. Like a puppet which has swung back and forth too far, his strings have finally broken, leaving him a crumpled, helpless mass with no volition of his own. He can do nothing but judge himself in self-explanation: "I had committed no evil deed. I had committed no good ones. I was superfluous!" (202).

Frères de sang records the alienation of a man within his family and village, and most of all within his self. Having returned unwillingly, the narrator finds himself a stranger in a setting that should have been familiar. The fact that he can neither reconcile the changes in his personality to this new situation nor activate any changes within the community reflects his isolation, not only with regard to others, but also with regard to his own desires. He does not take up the traditional responsibilities that his father expects him to shoulder. Neither does he rebel against the abuses of power he sees perpetrated in the village. He loses his brother Hô through imprisonment, then escape, and his blood brother Lê Tâm through punishment, then death. Lê Tâm's death by fire is reflected in the village's own death by fire. Unable to reconcile the separate halves of his self—thinking and active, conservative and rebel, East and West—the narrator finds himself in the grip of a crippling paralysis during which he watches the unfolding destruction around him. He remains nameless, and an outsider from the first to the last.

The Nightmare Village: *Le Fils de la baleine*

The dramatic impact of a stranger's arrival in a Vietnamese village is the focus of Cung Giu Nguyen's *Le Fils de la baleine* (The Whale's Son). In this third-person narrative, published nine years after *Frères de sang*, the arrival of a very real outsider is described in the following manner: "Two fishermen had dragged onto the sand a body wrapped in algae and kelp. The battered face was unrecognizable. They washed away the blood and mud stains that covered him. It was not someone from the village."[22]

The stress on the arrival's being "not of the village" is symptomatic. The villagers realize that the man is still alive and are afraid of possible repercussions. While the women, in concern for his well being, try to revive him, the Mayor has one overriding concern: "This stranger must not die in the village. It would cause too much of an outcry. We would be accused of having killed him. Take him quickly [to the county hospital], while he still breathes" (22). The stranger is removed. The village and its reputation remain uppermost in the Mayor's mind, contrasting with the attitude of the women and the demands of common humanity. The Mayor is one of a group of male notables who preside over village activities and are responsible for implementing local policy. They are distressed when the unknown man is returned to them.

> —But it is not one of our men, said the mayor. It is not a village citizen. We don't have anything in common with him.
> —Yet you were the ones who sent him to hospital. Anyway, I have my orders. I am only carrying them out. Here are the papers. Give me the full discharge.
> —Ah, it's the drowned man. But we cannot sign this. We have to send him back to his native village. (27)

The drowned man, who comes to be known as Mô, is suffering from amnesia. "Each time that Mô tried to reflect, to wonder what life he had lived, he ran into a brick wall. . . . Mô supposed that the now healed fracture had been the origin of his misfortune, of his life being broken into two universes, one plunged in darkness, the other still to be discovered" (35). For the villagers, Mô is a veritable source of pain and anxiety. Since none of the villagers show much sympathy or understanding of his plight—they feel that his loss of memory is a convenient ploy to mask an unsavory past—Mô tries to seek understanding and compassion from those outside the village. As it is, only four people evince good will towards him, and all four, like himself, are outsiders to the village. The first is an old man, a self-imposed exile. The second is a young girl, an adopted orphan. The third is a thief, a total outsider. The last is an old coral merchant.

Mô is unable to identify himself or his own village. Although he is a fellow countryman, he is not a native from the village and is considered a stranger as a result. The village is ostensibly an aspect of "home." After all, the same language is spoken, and the same race and nationality of people inhabit it. But Mô finds himself completely adrift within this setting. He is doubly an alien here, an alien in the village, and an alien to himself through his loss of identity. He does not recognize himself, nor do the villagers recognize him. Yeager writes:

> Mo's single voice, like the novelistic "voice" outside Vietnamese tradition, contrasts sharply with that of the Vietnamese community, an opposition that plainly shows that in traditional Vietnamese society collective concerns outweigh those of the individual, that the public surpasses the private.[23]

Beyond the social dimensions of the novel lies a further level of meaning: the private dimensions of an individual's anguish in an environment which not only should have been familiar but is not, and is actually hostile. Memory of a past identity returns slowly to Mô. Glimpses are fleeting, triggered by momentary contacts, sights, and sounds. He tells a young village girl, "I had just discovered a scrap of myself and wanted to offer it to you in exchange for a square of cloth. The screen which had been lit has darkened again" (49). The dearth of any positive response to what he does recall only serves to reinforce his already existing doubts about the validity of his "memory." Handicapped by the general perception he is mad, he must continually struggle to establish that his recollections are true recollections and not the results of an active imagination: "I am not mad. I have gaps in my memory. Do you understand? It's an accident that can happen to anyone. To you too" (55).

The significance of the title *Le Fils de la baleine* is explained when Mô inadvertently discovers the body of a dead whale on the beach.

When the villagers rush to view the remains, the *maître des cultes* (the master of cult) tells him: "Mô, you will be the whale's son" (64). Though Mô remains an unwilling recipient of the honor, an elaborate rite is undertaken to officially confirm his new identity. The importance of creating a shrine to the whale is an integral part of village tradition. The whale "as protector of Vietnamese fishermen, is celebrated and enshrined in every fishing village as a guarantee of safety. The whale cult is one of the oldest and most respected of traditions."[24] Ralph Smith notes: "Whilst each family or clan in the village had its own ancestral altars, a more important temple was the *dinh* which contained a shrine to the protective deity of the village."[25]

Like its honorary "son," the whale portends the breaking rather than the protection of traditions and customs. The whale thus becomes a symbol of invasion, the invader in this case represented by Mô, bereft of memory and identity.[26] Mô's journey is charged not only with Eastern symbolism, but also with Western significance. Jung recounts the following legend:

> A hero is devoured by a water-monster in the West (*devouring*). The animal travels with him to the East (*sea journey*). Meanwhile, the hero lights a fire in the belly of the sea-monster (*fire-lightning*), and feeling hungry, cuts himself a piece of the heart (*cutting off of heart*). Soon afterwards, he notices that the fish has glided on to dry land (*landing*); he immediately begins to cut open the animal from within (*opening*); then he slips out (*slipping out*). It was so hot in the fish's belly that all his hair had fallen out (*heat and hair*). The hero may at the same time free all those who were previously devoured by the monster.[27]

This legend contains a number of similarities with Mô's story. Mô and the whale are both beached within the domain of the village (although separately). The water-monster in the legend is from the West. Mô also comes from the West. He is on his way home from studies, when a mishap at sea causes him to be washed up unconscious on the beach of the village. Both he and the whale "glided on to dry land." Instead of being deprived of hair, Mô is deprived of his memory. Mô has been "devoured" by the West during the extent of his years of study overseas. A combination of circumstances lands him on this shore, with a privileged and foreign education behind him, but handicapped with a temporary loss of memory.

Mô's effect on the village, however, is dramatic and it is in a fruitless attempt to nullify the risk he poses that the villagers baptize him "the whale's son." The beached whale, in this instance, does not bring luck or fortune to the village. The familiar emblem becomes instead a portent of disruption and later destruction. The sea, symbol of life and of regeneration, and the source of the fishermen's livelihood, this time brings in strangers. These changes signify renewal, in the sense of the questioning of ossified values and customs, but also bear the reverse effect of undermining and eventually destroying the village that has harbored these values. Both these potentially positive images, the whale and the sea, thus herald negative events for the villagers and for the village itself.

The stranger, however handicapped on the surface because of his lack of memory, comes to threaten not only the mores and values of the village but also the village itself. The honor of being "the whale's son" does not gain Mô greater acceptance amongst the villagers and he is no closer to finding his own identity: "If your gods are powerful, ask them to give me back my memory, to tell me who I am, who I was, to bring down this curtain of ignorance which separates me from my entire past, from all I have acquired in terms of knowledge. I would like to be a man like other men" (71). His one desire is to be treated like a normal human being: "I want people to treat me in a proper manner" (74).

Mô thus seeks acceptance from the village, since he must belong somewhere. He is willing to work and to learn. Apart from the still unresolved question of his identity, he is young, fit, and able and can see no reason why he should not play a part in village life. Constantly, however, he runs up against a wall of obfuscation, a succession of bureaucratic and administrative obstacles:

—I don't exist in the eyes of the village, and I ask to be something.
—One must not ask too much of men. Besides, no one has ever asked you anything, not even to come and vegetate in our village which does not need your presence.
—That's the point, Mister Teacher! But I am no longer allowed to leave this land, since I don't have any identity papers. When I ask for an I.D., I am told that I am not known, that I need three witnesses, which naturally I cannot find. You who hold the records of the Communal Council, tell me what I have to do to become a citizen like the others. (102)

His problems are circular in that he cannot have recourse to the law or civil rights until he is identified and he cannot identify himself since he has lost his memory and has no one to vouch for him. What is he to do? The village teacher is unmoved. His response is revealing.

—Especially, we will not modify them to satisfy the desires of a single …
The teacher hesitated on the choice of a suitable word. . .
He wondered whether he should use the word "person."
Was Mô a person? He could not say "of a single man" . . .
However, Mô whispered the word "creature," and finding this word suitable because it also applied to birds, mammals and fish, he repeated:
—Yes . . . of a single creature. (103)

If the laws have "always" existed, it stands to pass that they are not going to be changed for the sake of a "creature" who doesn't conform to an accepted mold. The instructor elaborates: "To belong to the village, you would need to have been born here, or to have five years of uninterrupted residence, or to marry, legally of course, a local girl. Be patient" (103–4). What these laws approximate to are in effect immigration and citizenship laws for modern nation states. The village here is truly a microcosm of society and of the country at large where citizenship is obtained either by birth or via marriage to a citizen.[28] Sadly for him, Mô's desperate yearning to form part of the fabric of the village and his willingness to work do not lead him any closer to acceptance by the villagers. Yeager suggests that:

> The outsider who unmasks the real concerns and motivations of the villagers behind their posture of piety and respect is perceived as a threat and imprisoned. His fresh perspective, uncluttered by acquired cultural baggage, enables him to cut through the veneer of civility and "ultimate truth" of the traditional Vietnamese hierarchy.[29]

The sense of isolation Mô experiences does not dissipate or ease with the passing of time. The return of his memory, a momentous event, does not change the situation. The proof of the massive indifference of the villagers, or for that matter, society, is that they remain ignorant of his condition. In a curious way, Mô is like the only man moving in a static tableau, giving the novel a surreal effect. Mô is changing, discovering, and noticing things while the rest of the villagers appear unmoving, unchanging, static and indifferent. He is battling against obstacles that no one notices. The only figures who remain separate from the symbolic inertia of the villagers are those who stand apart from the village. In effect no one, and certainly none of the notables, believes him. To compound his problems, Mô has forgotten how to write; an attempted written request is undecipherable. The realization that he cannot write comes as a shock: "The ground had disappeared under his feet; he had found himself at the bottom of the abyss" (131). He begins to doubt his own memories, feeling a possible multitude of personalities within. How will he uncover the truth? How will he sift imagination from reality?

> He was often seized by doubt. Men showed the same hostility or the same indifference towards him. Everyone,

from the youngest to the oldest, had never wanted to believe
what he said. Were they in possession of the truth? Wasn't
everything that he found in his head just vivid illusions? The
past to which he thought he belonged was perhaps linked to
no reality. A hundred characters could live in him. Which
one corresponded to his real self? (131)

It is difficult to divorce oneself from one's past. Mô is obsessed with
the idea of repossessing his, yet it is something he feels is constantly
eluding him. He wants to give meaning and structure to his
existence but cannot do so when his own past self remains vague
and unacknowledged by either his fellow men or the authorities. He
has no status to speak of. It is not enough that he is a person. He
needs to be given a civic identity. Nonetheless, the village authorities
and society at large refuse to grant him this identity unless he can
give civic proof of it.[30] An old man advises him, "Let go the
moorings and let the boat drift. You will have fewer troubles" (139).
But Mô finds it impossible to heed his counsel. He cannot let things
go. He wants his situation to be resolved. Events are precipitated
when he discovers his boat vandalized and destroyed. It is the final
indication that whatever he attempts, however hard he tries, the
villagers will never accept him as one of their own. Mô has to make
a decision on his life and destiny. He cannot wait any longer. The
wanton destruction of his boat, the only real means of livelihood in a
coastal fishing village, becomes symbolic of his ultimate rejection on
the part of the villagers.

> He could be the first or the last man to feel, in the middle of
> a deserted land, close to the wreck of his boat, the terrible
> choice that was imposed upon him, to perish or to survive.
> He was not necessary to the world; the whole of humanity
> that he represented could disappear forever without the sea
> changing the rhythm of its tides or the sun extinguishing its
> light to mourn. (174–5)

Marc Laurent writes that Mô "symbolizes the drama of the one whom the gregarious instinct rejects."[31] The village authorities will only tolerate those who abide by their rules and laws. Anyone with the temerity to defy village conventions is ostracized. Respect and good will are only extended to those who bow to the village bureaucracy and uncomplainingly accept the notables' judgement on right and wrong. Charity is selective since the village goes to enormous lengths and expense to bury the carcass of a dead whale but refuses to give an old man a simple burial.[32] Mô is once again imprisoned. As is the case with the village in *Frères de sang*, an ill wind blows. This "wind of the common people," is vividly illustrated in the early Chinese *fu* entitled *The Wind*:

> The wind of the common people
> Comes whirling from the lanes and alleys . . .
> When this wind blows on a man
> At once he feels confused and downcast
> Pounded by heat, smothered in dampness,
> His heart grows sick and heavy,
> And he falls ill and breaks out in a fever . . .
> He stammers and cries out,
> Not knowing if he is dead or alive.
> This is what is called the lowly wind of the common people.[33]

A wind blows up against village injustice and misguided beliefs. When a fishing boat is lost at sea, Mô has to escape before the villagers vent their superstitious wrath upon him. Before leaving, he desecrates the temple of the whale and pays his respects to the coral merchant. The old man tells him: "There is nothing in this village, neither justice nor injustice. Your acts are quite useless if you do not find within yourself your own justification" (213). So Mô leaves the village engulfed in flames in a fire powerful and symbolic enough that it destroys not only the village but all that the village represents, sweeps all away, the good and the bad, "justice, injustice." Mô, having left Europe and returned to his homeland, finally finds himself heading out to sea for an unknown destination. West and East have provided their choices. He has refused and has been refused.

Conclusion

The destructive effect of the outsider's arrival in the village is more marked in *Le Fils de la baleine* than in *Frères de sang*. In *Frères de sang*, the narrator undergoes a drastic reexamination of his personality and motives within the context of the disintegration of his native village—a disintegration that is further symptomatic of the times. The more distant authorial voice in *Le Fils de la baleine* describes the upheaval of an entire village community. The arrival of the "whale's son" is traumatic for the villagers. Much village xenophobia becomes evident in the confusion arising out of clarifying Mô's civil status and his place within village life. While in *Frères de sang* the narrator's arrival initiates the changes that sweep through the village, he is the catalyst rather than the instrument for change. In *Le Fils de la baleine* Mô is both, and the resulting impact on the village is all the greater. Mô escapes from a village that is burning and consuming having already been subject to a steady undermining of its values, rules, and practices.

The village, especially in *Le Fils de la baleine*, has an anachronistic feel. The fishermen, the huts, and the sea are conveyed as a timeless and unchanging scene into which is thrust the disturbing body of a young man and the beached carcass of a whale. The village appears as if disconnected from the twentieth century. No mention whatsoever is made of the colonial presence, the French authorities, or the impact of French civilization. Like villages long past in Vietnamese history, it remains impervious to central bureaucratic authority. The village is isolated temporally and spatially, an impression conveyed by the stranger's lack of mobility, imprisoned within its confines until his dramatic escape by sea. Walking to a nearby village is not even an option.

The same sensation of constriction is conveyed in *Frères de sang*. The male protagonists of both novels seek an escape from the village, whether physically or symbolically. As cultural and linguistic hybrids, these men are clearly misfits in the context of the Vietnamese village. They do not wholly fit into French society, hence their return to their native land, but then neither do they fit into traditional Vietnamese society. Isolated in a world of their own, just as the villagers are isolated, in the end they find themselves adrift, either in madness, a form of escape, or at sea, another form of escape. Writing from exile in Paris, Pham Van Ky portrays the return of the protagonist to his native village as an unsettling experience that "ends with the disintegration of the village, the family and the narrator, leaving a great void of history to fill."[34] Writing in Vietnam, Cung Giu Nguyen presents, through the image of his protagonist Mô heading out to sea, a vision of the wider possibilities awaiting Vietnam beyond the shambles of division and war, a vision that hauntingly presages the Vietnamese diaspora.

Conclusion

Of old and now, the world has tales to tell,
Strange stories making plain the universe.
—Anonymous (*Tre Coc*)

Vietnamese Francophone novels feature an interplay of thoughts and words across cultures. Inspired and influenced by both East and West, they provide a rich field for detailed study and analysis. Vietnamese classical literature influences the structure, language, and themes of work by a number of authors, enlightening their discussion of gender and cultural identity. In the work of Pham Van Ky, for example, the philosophical heritage of the Far East provides a narrative framework. In his novel *Bach-Yên*, Tran Van Tung attempts to convey the language, imagery, and form of classical Vietnamese poetry. European and modern Asian influences are also in evidence. Pham Van Ky draws the title of one of his novels from an Old High German source while Truong Dinh Tri and Albert de Teneuille quote the Japanese writer Okakura Kakuzo in the opening of their novel *Bà-Dâm*. These works convey the difficulties and rewards of their writers' exposure to conflicting traditions and cultures. When that conflict becomes overwhelming, withdrawal and a desire to lose oneself in external causes can result, as the protagonists in the works of Nguyen Huu Chau and Pham Duy Khiem demonstrate.

The central post-colonial concern with vision and identity expresses itself in contrasting ways in the novels of male and female writers. Works of male writers indicate a much greater level of despair and fragmentation, perhaps because they, and their male protagonists, identify to a greater extent with the dominant colonial culture. Their writing echoes the disintegration of the colonial system that had educated and shaped them. Female writers, given their minority status, unsurprisingly appear less affected by the destruction or emasculation of the colonial structure. In general, the works of women are accounts of survival against a background of oppression and war. A notable exception is Ly Thu Ho's *Printemps inachevé*, whose female protagonist symbolizes the destructive effect of traditional mores on women. Like the fabled heroine of the *Tale of Kieu*, this protagonist also represents her country in the midst of conflict and change. Works of female writers reveal a closer identification with the Vietnamese "mother-culture" and are less fraught with underlying questions of self-image and place in the face of colonization and post-colonization.

Female characterization provided a connecting link between the first three chapters of this study. Women either symbolize the resilience of traditional beliefs and practices or the rapid changes and modifications to these beliefs in twentieth-century Vietnam. They are represented variously as victims, sufferers, instigators, and agents of change. In a number of works, writers transpose the classical figure of Kieu to a modern setting as a means of both asserting the centrality of Vietnamese identity and culture and simultaneously questioning many of the assumptions carried within the symbolic persona of this acme of Vietnamese female protagonists. While the portrayal of female characters by women writers reveals an appraisal of the condition of women in modern Vietnam, and a wider symbolic conflation of their trials and tribulations with that of the Vietnamese nation, male writers offer blunter indictments of the restraints imposed on women by patriarchal society. The male handling of this issue differs radically from that of female writers such as Ly Thu Ho, whose use of irony and subtle condemnation is perhaps less obvious, but in the end no less effective. The post-colonial mirror reflects an image of transition and change for the Vietnamese female subject, an image that is superimposed on a background of continuing social and political upheaval.

In Trinh Thuc Oanh's and Marguerite Triaire's *En s'écartant des ancêtres* (1939), three female protagonists attempt to assert a new modern identity in Vietnam in the 1920s and 1930s amidst a society in transition between old and new. In contrast, Tran Van Tung's female protagonist in *Bach-Yên* (1946), set in roughly the same era, falls victim to the tyranny of traditional family pressure and patriarchal authority. Ly Thu Ho's central protagonist in *Printemps inachevé* (1962) is likewise a victim of the social system, though Ly's indictment of the pressures experienced by women in Vietnamese society of the 1940s and 1950s is indirect. The figure of Kim Lefèvre's mother in *Retour à la saison des pluies* (1990) again exemplifies the hardships confronting women in an age of colonization and instability. This figure draws comfort from the heroine Kieu, symbol of the suffering but also the resilience of the Vietnamese people. Ly Thu Ho's female characterization throughout her trilogy, *Printemps inachevé* (1962), *Au Milieu du carrefour* (1969) and *Le Mirage de la paix* (1986), exposes the constraints experienced by middle-class women in Vietnamese society over a period of four decades from the 1930s to the 1970s. Considerable use of irony underlines her point that women's lives are often tragically wasted within the context of patriarchy, colonization, post-colonization, and war. When Phan Van Ky situates women within traditional village culture in the 1940s in his novel *Frères de sang* (1947) or as opposing symbols of East and West in the later *Des Femmes assises çà et là* (1964) he explicitly denounces the shackles placed on women by patriarchal society in both East and West.

The common thread in the novels of male writers is the feeling of disorientation experienced by the Vietnamese male protagonist. Whether he is mourning a lost love, a lost cultural identity, or a lost sense of purpose, he is alluding to a past that is long gone or has never truly existed, except in his imagination. This past may be a metaphor for the vanishing French colony of Indochina and the spurious and impermanent structure that it engendered during its brief existence. Male writers may have felt that they were an accident of history, one that would not survive beyond the end of colonization and the immediate post-colonial era. This might explain why the only way out for their protagonists is either death or exile. To the Vietnamese male subject, the post-colonial mirror reflects either broken glass or emptiness.

Male protagonists of Truong Dinh Tri's and Albert de Teneuille's *Bà-Dâm* (1930) and Pham Duy Khiem's *Nam et Sylvie* (1957) experience a feeling of cultural malaise, not only in relation to their own society, but also to that of Europe through their failed relationship with French women within the colonial setting of the 1920s and the 1930s. Failure to understand their female companions reflects a deeper failure to understand themselves and assume a stable sense of identity and belonging. This breakdown in identity is emphasized in Nguyen Huu Chau's *Les Reflets de nos jours* (1955), Pham Duy Khiem's *La Place d'un homme* (1958), Pham Van Ky's *Frères de sang* (1947) and Cung Giu Nguyen's *Le Fils de la baleine* (1956). In the first two of these novels, the crisis of identity experienced by the male narrator is so acute that the only way of exorcising it is to seek to die in combat. The first narrator does so by joining the Vietnamese revolutionaries, the second by volunteering for the French Army at the onset of World War II. In the last two, the Vietnamese village becomes the setting for the protagonist's final severance from his cultural roots. In a symbolic representation of the violence of this parting, the village is destroyed by tragedy and fire and the protagonists left adrift to face an unknown future.

The Lebanese Francophone writer, Evelyne Accad, questions the negative emphasis in the portrayal of those caught between cultures. She sees instead the positive and enriching effect of such perspectives:

> Numerous North African writers, such as Driss Chraïbi, Albert Memmi, Abdel Kebir-Khalibi and Marguerite Taos-Amrouche, to name those who have spoken of their being split between two cultures, their heartache, and finally their misfortune, use words such as "bastard of history," "cultural alienation," "between two stools," "malaise." As to myself, I share the vision of Andrée Chedid who insists on what there is that is positive in this mix, that she terms hybridity, underlining cosmopolitanism, enrichment, tolerance and the broadening of the mind that it brings.[1]

Her sentiments are echoed by Kim Lefèvre, who expresses a similarly positive outlook:

The older we grow, the more our primary personality, our childhood, comes to the fore and becomes present in our consciousness. I have noticed that there are great cultural differences in this respect between those who are French natives and those who have been adopted by French culture, because the latter carry another culture within themselves, but to me this difference is a difference that is enriching and not at all reductive.[2]

Vietnamese Francophone writers express their conditions as cultural and literary hybrids. They are the inheritors of a literary legacy of both Far East and West. Their works highlight the difficulty and also the complexity of combining the two traditions. As Elisabeth Mudimbe-Boyi notes: "The characters' quest for identity and history goes against the grain of totalization and of an invariable, fixed identity."[3] Although they write in French and use the modern mode of the novel, the sensibilities and philosophies which permeate their works are largely Eastern in inspiration. In some novels this leads to a manner of synthesis, in others to fragmentation. Although they are all shaped by the colonial experience, each writer responds in his or her own way to this condition. The fact of the novels' existence shows that it is possible to negotiate with fiction the terrain that is so difficult for their own characters.

Vietnamese Francophone novels give voice to the Vietnamese subjects of the colonial encounter. The process of articulating this voice has not been an easy one. In 1938, Raja Rao wrote: "The telling has not been easy. One has to convey in a language that is not one's own the spirit that is one's own. One has to convey the various shades and omissions of a certain thought-movement that looks maltreated in an alien language."[4] The notion of the "stranger" or "outsider" is an important element of this literature. Among Vietnamese Francophone writers, Nguyen Huu Chau and Pham Duy Khiem use French in an experimental form, with the resulting impression of breakdown and fissure in their novels. Ly Thu Ho, by contrast, writes in measured, contained prose. Vietnamese Francophone writers blend neither into traditional culture nor

Western culture. They are, however, inescapably Vietnamese and are formed by the Vietnamese experience. This underlying commonality is the thread that links their work and constitutes their originality. It provides the basis for this study. As Kim Lefèvre puts it: "Vietnam has shaped the core of my being."[5]

The broader issue of identity, in itself, is problematic in modern times. Stuart Hall suggests that, "identities are never unified, and, in late modern times, increasingly fragmented and fractured; never singular but [they] multiply constructed across different, often intersecting and antagonistic, discourses, practices and positions."[6] These shifting positions are of particular relevance to the Vietnamese, whose notion of identity has been forged by the country's long subjection to Chinese authority. As David Marr observes, "the historian of Vietnam is repeatedly struck by the degree to which the Vietnamese have tended to define themselves in terms of their neighbors."[7]

By "neighbors," read Vietnam's vast and powerful northern neighbor, China, "the Middle Kingdom, the ubiquitous Han."[8] Vietnam's efforts over the centuries, to retain its cultural autonomy in the face of overwhelming influence from Chinese cultural practices and beliefs, attests to a fierce desire for independence. The Vietnamese saw no contradiction in this resistance existing side by side with an assiduous borrowing of China's bureaucratic and economic model. Their perception of identity is strongly rooted in kin and land, and displays a hostile reaction, with strong xenophobic overtones, towards those who stand outside this invisible boundary. This obsession with the maintenance of an ethnic divide between themselves and others flared up again during the period of French colonization, and again during American involvement in the 1960s.[9] It will be interesting to observe how Vietnamese communities in the West deal with this rather vexed issue.

Post-colonial France now hosts a new generation of Vietnamese Francophone writers whose works have come into prominence in the 1990s and continue to emerge in the earlier years of the twenty-first century. The most prolific and successful of this "new" generation of writers is Linda Lê, who began publishing novels and short stories in the late 1980s and has a significant body of works to her name. She is representative of the post-colonial generation of Vietnamese who have settled overseas in such large numbers since the fall of Saigon. The post-1975 Vietnamese diaspora arising from a massive exodus of Vietnamese refugees in the late 1970s and 1980s following the reunification of Vietnam under a Socialist regime is a new phenomenon in Vietnamese history. Until then, Vietnamese students, intellectuals, political activists, and revolutionaries who went overseas represented a small minority. The difficulties and adjustments of exile and of cross-cultural negotiation that signified the site of struggle for Vietnamese Francophone writers are, half a century later, multiplied many times in the experience of the nearly two million Vietnamese who have settled in North America, Europe, Australia, and New Zealand since 1975. What form will this experience take? How will it translate into literature?

If the use of French was "both empowerment and subversion"[10] for the earlier generation of Vietnamese Francophone writers, what does its use designate for this new generation? Paradigms have surely changed. France is no longer the colonizing power and Vietnamese voluntarily choosing to settle in France have made a conscious decision to become part of French society. The works of contemporary Vietnamese Francophone writers reveals a fresh consciousness that is reacting to the pressures and challenges facing contemporary refugee and migrant communities. As French citizens, the use of French itself is no longer a clear tool of subversion, except inasmuch as it expresses a minority voice within French literary discourse. However, it no longer characterizes the voice of a small or embattled group of exiles, but the expressed vision of a well-established and thriving community.

These writings already differ from the earlier literature of the colonial and immediate post-colonial periods. The most dramatic change is clearly in the work of Linda Lê. Her violent allusions to death, cannibalism, self-destruction, and madness, for example in *Les Evangiles du crime* (The Gospels of Crime) (1992) and *Voix: Une crise* (Voices: A Crisis) (1999), are a far cry from the tempered novels of earlier female writers. Instead, they display an acute and anguished crisis of displacement, self-image, and identity. It is in some measure a testament to the violent trauma of the refugee experience for those who fled as "boat-people" and witnessed scenes of horror: the rape of loved ones; the drowning of family members; death by exposure; in extreme cases, cannibalism.

Lê however, is just one voice and that of a first-generation migrant. She left Vietnam as a fourteen-year old refugee,[11] at an age when she was not fully anchored in her own language and culture and where she found adjustment to a new culture a difficult and disturbing process. Lê, in Leakthina Chau-Pech Ollier's words, "is the embodiment of the *métèque* with the drifting identity . . . who has never found her voice and her place in her culture of origin and her native tongue, but does not yet quite have access to the new host culture. . . . She is thus condemned to remain midway between silence and an overflow of words."[12]

Other contemporary Vietnamese Francophone writers such as Kim Lefèvre and Phan Huy Duong belong to the earlier generation in that both were born in Vietnam during the colonial period and subsequently moved to France in the 1960s. Their work does not display the violent fissures in place and personality that characterize Linda Lê's. Phan Huy Duong's form of magical realism in short stories such as "Un Squelette d'un milliard de dollars" (A Billion-Dollar Skeleton) (1994) and "Vacance" (Vacancy) (1994) exposes a playful manipulation of the interaction between a Vietnamese consciousness and the French language.[13]

For other first or second-generation Vietnamese in France, the articulation of their particular vision as refugees or migrants will reveal the concerns of culture's new "in-betweens," to borrow Homi Bhabha's phrase.[14] The experience of the few writers in exile has been magnified to that of the many in the form of the numerous Vietnamese communities in the West. Like other diasporic communities, Vietnamese have had to adjust to the process of loss and mourning, as well as that of adapting to the new conditions. They are in the process of shaping a new identity for themselves, one that recognizes their cultural roots and also acknowledges the new country that they opted to belong to. This Vietnamese experience of exodus and exile, settlement and adjustment will provide the frame for new narratives of displacement and acculturation. It will also occasion reflection on and a new look at the travails and heartache described by earlier generations of Vietnamese Francophone writers.

Notes

Preface and Acknowledgements

1 See Jane Bradley Winston, *Postcolonial Duras: Cultural Memory in Postwar France* (New York: Palgrave, 2001) and Jack A. Yeager, "Colonialism and Power in Marguerite Duras' *The Lover*," in *Of Vietnam: Identities in Dialogue*, Jane Bradley Winston and Leakthina Chau-Pech Ollier, eds. (New York: Palgrave, 2001), 225.

2 In addition to Jack A. Yeager's work, the other dissertations are: Nguyen Hong Nhiem, "L'Echiquier et l'antinomie Je/Moi comme signe et substance du conflit Occident/Extrême-Orient dans les œuvres de Pham Van Ky." (Ph.D. dissertation, University of Massachusetts, 1982); Sharon Julie Lim-Hing, "Vietnamese Novels in French: Rewriting Self, Gender and Nation." (Ph.D. dissertation, Harvard University, 1993); and Karl Ashoka Britto, "Disorientation: Interculturality and Identity in Vietnamese Francophone Literature." (Ph.D. dissertation, Yale University, 1998).

3 Jack A. Yeager, *The Vietnamese Novel in French: A Literary Response to Colonialism* (Hanover: The University Press of New England, 1987), 2.

4 See Bernard Hue, Henri Copin, Pham Dan Binh, Patrick Laude, et Patrick Meadows, *Littératures de la péninsule indochinoise* (Paris: Editions Karthala, 1999) and Jean-Louis Joubert, ed., *Littératures francophones d'Asie et du Pacifique: Anthologie* (Paris: Editions Nathan, 1997).

5 In Vietnamese, the same letters can apply to different names depending on the tonal marks used and care has to be taken not to guess wrongly. There are, for example, three possibilities with "Nguyen" as a first name, which differ completely in their meaning.

6 Jane Bradley Winston, "Introduction: Projected Identities/Subversive Practices," in *Of Vietnam*, Winston and Ollier, eds., 1.

Introduction

1 Bill Ashcroft, Gareth Griffiths, and Helen Tiffin suggest that "A major feature of post-colonial literatures is the concern with place and displacement. It is here that the special post-colonial crisis of identity comes into being; the concern with the development or recovery of an effective identifying relationship between self and place." *The Empire Writes Back: Theory and Practice in Post-colonial Literatures* (London: Routledge, 1989), 8–9.

2 Dennis Walder, *Post-Colonial Literatures in English* (Oxford: Blackwell Publishers, 1998), 17.

3 Panivong Norindr, *Phantasmatic Indochina: French Colonial Ideology in Architecture, Film, and Literature* (Durham: Duke University Press, 1996), 1.

4 "Written records and chronicles document some two thousand years in the development of the Vietnamese ethnic group. Popular legends accord the Vietnamese an even longer history, four thousand years, claiming that civilization began in the Red River Delta with the creation of the kingdom of Van L[a]ng, later Au-Lac, by the first Hung kings. These popular beliefs may have some basis in fact, since archeological finds have led to speculation about a Southeast Asian "fertile crescent" similar to that of Southwest Asia." Yeager, *Vietnamese Novel*, 11.

5 "Poetry [was] according to old scholars the literary genre par excellence." Bui Xuan Bao, *Naissance et évolution du roman viêtnamien moderne 1925–1945* (Paris: Duong Moi La voie nouvelle, 1985), 4. Yeager notes: "On this subject Duong Dinh Khue declares: "Il faut...admettre que le roman en vers, très rare dans les autres littératures, a trouvé son terrain d'élection dans la littérature viêtnamienne, qu'il constituait presque un genre spécifiquement viêtnamien" (We must admit that verse romance, very rare in other literatures, found its chosen ground in Vietnamese literature and that it constituted almost a specifically Vietnamese genre)." Yeager, *Vietnamese Novel*, 30–1.

6 Yeager, *Vietnamese Novel*, 31.

7 "The Vietnamese intelligentsia had access to the works of these writers through the medium of Chinese translations." Ellen J. Hammer, *The Struggle for Indochina* (Stanford: Stanford University Press, 1954), 60. "Concerning the novel, let us mention the translation of *Gil Blas de Santillane* by Lesage, of *Manon Lescaut* by the Abbé Prevost, of *Les Trois Mousquetaires* by A. Dumas, of *La Peau de chagrin* by Balzac, of *Les Misérables* by Victor Hugo, of *Les Aventures de Télémaque* by Fenelon." Bui Xuan Bao, *Naissance*, 24.

8 Yeager, *Vietnamese Novel*, 33.

9 Ralph Smith, "Antecedents of the 'Viet-Cong,'" in Michael Leifer, ed., *Nationalism, Revolution and Evolution in South-East Asia* (Hull: Hull Monographs on SEA, 2, 1970), 3.

10 "After the French conquest, the name of Vietnam was practically forgotten by the rest of the world. . . . The French deliberately partitioned the territory into three separate regions giving each an arbitrarily chosen name and a different administrative status. These new regions were called: Annam, Tongking (in French spelling Tonkin) and Cochin China."

Hoang Van Chi, *From Colonialism to Communism: A Case History of North Vietnam* (London: Pall Mall Press, 1964), 10.

[11] See John C. Schafer and The Uyen, "The Novel Emerges in Cochinchina," *The Journal of Asian Studies*, 52 (4): 854 (1993).

[12] Schafer and The Uyen, "Novel Emerges," 857.

[13] Schafer and They Uyen, "Novel Emerges," 880.

[14] Cao Thi Nhu-Quynh and John C. Schafer, "From Verse Narrative to Novel: The Development of Prose Fiction in Vietnam," *The Journal of Asian Studies*, 47 (4): 756 (1988).

[15] The term "Annam" was the name given to Vietnam by China. It meant "Pacified South." The French used this term to signify the central region of Vietnam in French-administered Indochina, but often used the term "Annamite" to refer to all Vietnamese.

[16] Earlier examples of Vietnamese Francophone literature include a collection of poetry, *Mes Heures perdues* by Nguyen Van Xiem, and *Contes et légendes du pays d'Annam* by Le Van Phat, both of which appeared in 1913. Yeager, *Vietnamese Novel*, 46.

[17] Nguyen The Anh, "Vietnam," in Patricia Herbert and Anthony Milner, eds., *South-East Asia Languages and Literatures* (Arran, Scotland: Kiscadale Publications, 1989), 86.

[18] Nguyen Tran Huan, "La littérature viêtnamienne de langue française," *Culture française*, 22 (1): 10 (1973).

[19] Le Thanh Khoi, *Le Viet-Nam: Histoire et civilisation* (Paris: Les Editions de Minuit, 1955), 148–9. The first examinations took place in 1075.

[20] Nguyen Trieu Dan, *A Vietnamese Family Chronicle: Twelve Generations on the Banks of the Hat River* (Jefferson, N.C.: McFarland & Company, 1991), 162–3.

[21] The civil service examinations were suppressed in Tonkin in 1915 and Annam in 1918. Yeager, *Vietnamese Novel*, 27.

[22] "The Dong Kinh Nghia Thuc was inspired by the Keio Gijuke (later to become the prestigious Keio University), a tuition-free school that [Phan Chu] Trinh [one of the founders] had seen as the cradle of the Japanese drive for modernization. . . . Courses were developed in mathematics, science, geography, physical education, hygiene, political history and economics, French, and Chinese. But the primary emphasis was placed on popularizing the use of the romanized alphabet for Vietnamese in place of both Chinese and *nom*." Neil L. Jamieson, *Understanding Vietnam* (Berkeley: University of California Press, 1995), 58.

[23] Scott McConnell, *Leftward Journey: The Education of Vietnamese Students in France 1919–1939* (New Brunswick: Transaction Publishers, 1989), 54.

[24] R. B. Smith, "The Vietnamese Elite of French Cochinchina," *Modern Asian Studies* 6(4): 478 (1972).

[25] Joseph Buttinger, *Vietnam: A Political History* (London: André Deutsch, 1969), 121, 120.

[26] D. G. E. Hall, *A History of South-East Asia* (London: Macmillan, 1968), 761.

[27] Yeager, *Vietnamese Novel*, 46.

[28] Dennis J. Duncanson, *Government and Revolution in Vietnam* (London: Oxford University Press, 1968), 24.

[29] Bernard Clergerie, "Essai de prospective pour l'ancienne Indochine," *Esprit* 30: 729 (1962).

[30] Nguyen Tran Huan, "Des difficultés de l'édition française au Vietnam," *Culture française* 22 (4): 40, 42 (1973).

[31] Pham Van Ky studied at the Sorbonne and the Institut des Hautes Etudes Chinoises. Pham Duy Khiem was the first Vietnamese to study at the Ecole Normale Supérieure from which he received his *agrégation de grammaire* in 1935. Hoang Xuan Nhi received a doctorate in French literature from the Sorbonne. See the Appendix, Yeager, *Vietnamese Novel*, 165–86.

[32] Thuong Vuong-Riddick, "Le drame de l'occidentalisation dans quelques romans de Pham Van Ky," *Présence francophone*, 16: 145 (1970).

[33] Evelyne Accad, "L'Ecriture (comme) éclatement des frontières," *L'Esprit créateur* 33 (2): 127 (1993).

[34] Marc Laurent, "Cung Giu Nguyen—Ecrivain vietnamien de langue française," *Présence francophone* 5: 54 (1972).

[35] Pham Duy Khiem, "Réponse de M. Pham Duy Khiem," *Revue de la Méditerranée* 17 (4): 649 (1957).

[36] Nguyen Tien Lang, *Indochine la douce* (Hanoi: Editions Nam Ky, 1935), 45.

[37] Vuong-Riddick, "Le drame," 145.

[38] Yeager, *Vietnamese Novel*, 8.

[39] Julia Kristeva, *Strangers to Ourselves*, translated by Leon S. Roudiez (London: Harvester Wheatsheaf, 1991), 1.

Chapter 1: Francophone *Kieu*

[1] Xuan-Phuc and Xuan-Viet, "Introduction," in Nguyen Du, *Kim-Van-Kieu* translated from the Vietnamese by Xuan-Phuc and Xuan-Viet (Paris: Gallimard/ Unesco, 1961), 15.

[2] "A study in Hanoi has identified in it some fifty quotations from *The Book of Odes*, the Confucian anthology of verse; some fifty references to other Confucian classics; some sixty translations or adaptations of various Chinese poems; some seventy allusions to Chinese works of fiction; and

about twenty mentions of Buddhist or Taoist scriptures. Such erudition, if indiscriminately displayed in an imaginative work, runs the risk of boring or even offending. But in *Kieu* it fits so gracefully into the texture of the poem, it is so apposite to the purpose in each case, that it may elude the average reader while it surprises and delights the connoisseur". Huynh Sanh Thong, "Introduction" in Nguyen Du, *The Tale of Kieu: A Bilingual Edition*, translated by Huynh Sanh Thong (New Haven: Yale University Press, 1983), xxii.

3   "Reduced to its smallest unit, six-eight verse is a couplet with six syllables in the first line and eight syllables in the second; in contrast, most Chinese poetry has an odd number of syllables (five or seven) in each line. Many Vietnamese folk poems are simply six-eight couplets, shorter than Japanese *haiku*. But any number of couplets can be strung together into a continuous, unbroken whole without inducing monotony. By using end rhymes and internal rhymes at the sixth syllable of an eight-syllable line, one can make each line rhyme with the next and at the same time introduce a fresh rhyme in every other line." Huynh Sanh Thong, "Introduction," xix–xx.

4   Huynh Sanh Thong, "Introduction," xix.

5   Huynh Sanh Thong, "Introduction," xxi.

6   "Polygamy was an accepted institution...It lasted several centuries; it was officially abrogated on 2 January 1959 by law number 1-59." Tran Thi Tuyet, "La Femme viêtnamienne à travers la littérature populaire" Ph.D. dissertation (University of Brussels, 1974), 55.

7   Huynh Sanh Thong, "Introduction," xxxvi.

8   Alexander B. Woodside, "The Historical Background" in Nguyen Du, *The Tale of Kieu*, xv–xvi.

9   Woodside, "Background," xvi.

10   Huynh Sanh Thong, "Introduction," xl.

11   Nguyen Trieu Dan, *A Vietnamese Family Chronicle*, 142.

12   David Marr, *Vietnamese Tradition on Trial, 1920 –1945* (Berkeley: University of California Press, 1981), 191.

13   Nguyen Trieu Dan, *A Vietnamese Family Chronicle*, 122.

14   Ta Van Tai, "The Status of Women in Traditional Vietnam: A Comparison of the Code of the Lê Dynasty (1428–1788) with the Chinese Code." *Journal of Asian History* 15: 136 (1981).

15   The Three Submissions were to father, husband and son and The Four Virtues were "right occupation," "right speech," "right appearance," and "right conduct." See, for example, Cam Nguyen, "East, West, and Vietnamese Women," *Journal of Vietnamese Studies* 5: 46 (1992).

[16] Marr, *Vietnamese Tradition*, 195.

[17] Quoted in Xuan-Phuc and Xuan-Viet, "Introduction," in Nguyen Du, *Kim-Van-Kieu*, 26.

[18] As Kim Lefèvre's Vietnamese mother stressed: "A woman has only one treasure: her virginity." Kim Lefèvre, *Métisse Blanche* (Paris: Bernard Barrault, 1989), 125. In this autobiographical novel of her childhood and youth in Vietnam, Kim Lefèvre writes that her mixed blood meant that it was of even greater importance that she maintain her virginity. Her behavior had to be above reproach.

[19] Marr, *Vietnamese Tradition*, 195.

[20] Jean Chesneaux and Georges Boudarel, "Les Révolutionnaires vietnamiens face au *Kim Van Kieu*," in *Tradition et révolution au Vietnam*, sous la direction de Jean Chesneaux, Georges Boudarel, et Daniel Hemery (Paris: Editions Anthropos, 1971), 356.

[21] Pham Quynh, "Truyen Kieu," *Nam Phong* 30 (December 1919), 480–500. Reference from Marr, *Vietnamese Tradition*, 154. In the same footnote, Marr adds that "there is some evidence that Pham Quynh got the idea for the glorification of *Kieu* from a French article about the Persian masterpiece *Shah-Nama*, by Firdausi."

[22] Pham Quynh quoted in Huynh Sanh Thong, "Introduction," xxxix.

[23] See Jacques Baruch, *Notes sur le Poème Viêt-Namien Kim-Vân-Kiêu de Nguyên-Du* (Casteau: Chez l'auteur, 1961).

[24] Abel des Michels, *Kim Vân Kiêu Tân Truyên*, publié et traduit pour la première fois par Abel des Michels (Paris: E. Leroux, 1884), xi–xii.

[25] See Nguyen Van Vinh, *Traduction en français avec notes et commentaires du Kiêu de Nguyen Du* (Saigon: Les Editions Vinhbao-Hoanhson, 1952).

[26] Nguyen Du, *The Tale of Kieu: A Bilingual Edition*, translated by Huynh Sanh Thong (New Haven and London, 1983), 3. Further page references, referred to in parentheses in the text, will be to this edition.

[27] Huynh Sanh Thong, "Notes" in Nguyen Du, *The Tale*, 170.

[28] See Liu Wu-Chi, *An Introduction to Chinese Literature* (Bloomington: Indiana University Press, 1966), 173.

[29] Huynh Sanh Thong, "Introduction," xxxv.

[30] Huynh Sanh Thong, "Introduction," xxxv.

[31] Trinh Thuc Oanh et Marguerite Triaire, *En s'écartant des ancêtres* (Hanoi: Imprimerie d'Extrême-Orient, 1939), 7, 39, 35. Further page references, referred to in parentheses in the text, will be to this edition.

[32] Marr, *Vietnamese Tradition*, 193.

[33] Marr, *Vietnamese Tradition*, 193.

[34] This attitude is reflected in Chinese literature. In *Six Records of a Floating Life* (1809), the scholar Shen Fu mourns a talented and beloved wife: "Alas! Yün came to this world a woman, but she had the feelings and abilities of a man." Shen Fu, *Six Records of a Floating Life*, translated by Leonard Pratt and Chiang Su-hui (Harmondsworth: Penguin, 1983), 89.

[35] Cao Thi Nhu-Quynh and John C. Schafer, "From Verse Narrative to Novel: The Development of Prose Fiction in Vietnam," *The Journal of Asian Studies* 47 (4): 771 (1988).

[36] Cao Thi Nhu-Quynh and Schafer, "Verse Narrative," 756.

[37] Kumari Jayawardena, *Feminism and Nationalism in the Third World* (London: Zed Books Ltd, 1986), 186–7.

[38] It should be noted that To Tam also agrees to an arranged marriage, but insists on the union remaining unconsummated. See Cao Thi Nhu-Quynh and Schafer, "Verse Narrative," 763.

[39] Biographical note on Tran Van Tung by Yeager, *Vietnamese Novel*, 179.

[40] Lai Ming, *A History of Chinese Literature* (London: Cassell, 1964), 6.

[41] "Interestingly enough, the Chinese style at the time (second century B.C.) possessed such a rich, inexhaustible vocabulary and such an ornateness of usage that its nearest counterpart in English is to found in the euphuistic exaggerations and conceits of certain early Elizabethan writers in England some sixteen centuries later." Liu Wu-Chi, *Chinese Literature*, 53.

[42] Tran Van Tung, *Bach-Yên ou la fille au cœur fidèle* (Paris: J. Susse, 1946), 15–16. Further page references, referred to in parentheses in the text, will be to this edition.

[43] Cf. Xuan-Phuc and Xuan-Viet, "Notes," in Nguyen Du, *Kim-Van-Kieu*, 177.

[44] Ly Thu Ho, *Printemps inachevé* (Paris: J. Peyronnet et Cie, Editeurs, 1962), 55. Further page references, referred to in parentheses in the text, will be to this edition.

[45] This motif was a feature of Yüan drama (1234–1368) and was prevalent in Chinese novels and plays from the thirteenth century onwards. See Liu Wu-Chi, *Chinese Literature*, 173.

[46] Kim Lefèvre, *Retour à la saison des pluies* (Paris: Bernard Barrault, 1990), 80. Further page references, referred to in parentheses in the text, will be to this edition.

[47] As part of a new project on exile narratives by Vietnamese women, I have published two articles on Kim Lefèvre. See Nathalie Nguyen, "Writing and Memory in Kim Lefèvre's Autobiographical Narratives," *Intersections: Gender, History and Culture in the Asian Context*, Issue 5 (2001). http://wwwsshe.murdoch.edu.au/intersections/issue5/nathalie.html and Nathalie Nguyen, "'Métisse Blanche': Entretien avec Kim Lefèvre,"

Intersections: Gender, History and Culture in the Asian Context, Issue 5 (2001). http://wwwsshe.murdoch.edu.au/intersections/issue5/nguyen_interview.

Chapter 2: Patriarchal Constraints

1 "One of the most dramatic events of South Vietnamese literary history was the controversial appearance in the 1960s of five young women fiction writers in their twenties: Nguyen Thi Hoang, Nguyen Thi Thuy Vu, Nha Ca, Trung Duong and Tuy Hong. . . . [They] were dubbed 'Ngu Quai' (Five She-Devils). The five plunged headlong into both feminine and feminist writings. . . . While the first type of writing subtly informs of the reality of woman, the second type suggests or demands changes that could render that reality less oppressive and more equitable." Cong-Huyen Ton-Nu Nha-Trang, "Women Writers of South Vietnam (1954-1975)," *The Vietnam Forum* 9: 176–7 (1987).

2 Predecessors such as the eighteenth-century female poet Ho Xuan Huong, criticized political, social and sexual hypocrisy through the double-entendres of their verses. See Huu Ngoc and Françoise *Corrèze, Fleurs de pamplemoussier: Femmes et poésie au Vietnam* (Paris: L'Harmattan, 1984) and *Spring Essence: The Poetry of Ho Xuan Huong*, John Balaban, ed. and transl. (Washington: Copper Canyon Press, 2000).

   Ho Xuan Huong also distinguished herself from her male counterparts by rarely using Chinese literary or mythological allusions. She relied on her native language and native wit. Coming as she did from a scholarly background, her originality suggested considerable independence from the accepted literary mores of her time. In this respect, she resembles Japanese female writers of previous centuries. Japan was also heavily influenced by China. The greatest classics of Japanese literature from the Heian Period (*The Tale of Genji* and *The Pillow Book of Sei Shonagon*, eleventh century) were written by women in the vernacular, while men wrote in Chinese, the "scholarly language." See W. G. Aston, *A History of Japanese Literature* (Rutland, Vermont: Charles E. Tuttle Company, 1972).

3 Cam Nguyen, "Barriers to Communication between Vietnamese and Non-Vietnamese," in *Vietnamese Studies in a Multicultural World*, Nguyen Xuan Thu, ed. (Melbourne: Vietnamese Language and Culture Publications, 1994), 70–1.

4 Jayawardena, *Feminism*, 204–5.

5 The work of Christiane Rochefort and Annie Ernaux for example.

6   See also Nathalie Nguyen, "A Classical Heroine and Her Modern Manifestation: *The Tale of Kieu* and its Modern Parallels in *Printemps inachevé*," The French Review 73 (3): 454–62 (2000).

7   Ly Thu Ho, *Printemps inachevé* (Paris: J. Peyronnet et Cie, 1962), 11. Further page references, referred to in parentheses in the text, will be to this edition.

8   Casey Miller and Kate Swift, *Words and Women: New Language in New Times* (London: Victor Gollancz, 1977); quoted in Jane Mills, *Womanwords: A Vocabulary of Culture and Patriarchal Society* (London: Virago, 1991), 146.

9   Marr, *Vietnamese Tradition*, 193.

10 Susie Orbach has examined the ambivalence of the mother-daughter relationship. She is referring to Western society, but there are points of similarity between the mother-daughter relationship in both Eastern and Western societies: "The mother-daughter relationship is invariably an ambivalent one, for the mother who herself lives a circumscribed life in patriarchy, has the unenviable task of directing her daughter to take up the very same position that she has occupied. Explicitly as well as unconsciously she psychologically prepares her daughter to accept the strictures that await her in womanhood. She needs to do this so that her daughter is not cast as a misfit." Susie Orbach, *Hunger Strike: the Anorectic's Struggle as a Metaphor for our Age,* revised ed. (London: Penguin Books, 1993), 23.

11 Jean-Jacques Rousseau, *Emile or On Education,* translated by Allan Bloom (London: Penguin Books, 1991), 361.

12 See Lin Yutang, *The Wisdom of China and India* (New York: Random House, 1942), 867.

13 Liu Wu-Chi, *Chinese Literature,* 21.

14 Eva Figes, *Patriarchal Attitudes: Women in Society* (London: Faber and Faber, 1970), 86–7.

15 Susan Stanford Friedman, "Women's Autobiographical Selves: Theory and Practice," in *The Private Self: Theory and Practice of Women's Autobiographical Writings,* Shari Benstock, ed. (London: Routledge, 1988), 39.

16 African women writers record similar perceptions in relation to women in post-colonial Africa: "Writers stress the woman as scapegoat, called 'backward' when she is traditional, called 'western' or 'immoral' when in an attempt to better her life she is perceived as invading male domains." Barbara Christian, *Black Feminist Criticism* (New York: Pergamon Press, 1985), 147–8.

17 Germaine Greer, *The Female Eunuch,* 21st anniversary ed. (London: Paladin, 1991), 165.

18 Isabel Allende, "Isabel Allende", interview by Marie-Lise Gazarian Gautier, *Interviews with Latin American Writers* (Elmwood Park, IL: Dalkey Archive Press, 1989), 13.

19 "Between the ages of twelve and forty, European men outlived women well into the twentieth century...maternal mortality remained high: until the 1880s, motherhood was fatal for one woman out of every twenty." Bonnie S. Anderson and Judith P. Zinsser, *A History of Their Own: Women in Europe from Prehistory to the Present,* Volume II (London: Penguin Books, 1990), 241. These figures, applicable to nineteenth-century Europe, were probably similar in nineteenth-century Vietnam.

The issue of maternity is addressed by Simone de Beauvoir in *The Second Sex*: "It is in maternity that woman fulfils her physiological destiny, it is her natural 'calling,' since her whole organic structure is adapted for the perpetuation of the species. But we have seen already that human society is never abandoned wholly to nature." Simone de Beauvoir, *The Second Sex,* translated and edited by H. M. Parshley (London: Jonathan Cape, 1949), 467.

20 Ly Thu Ho, *Au Milieu du carrefour* (Paris: Editions Peyronnet, 1969), 59. Further page references, referred to in parentheses in the text, will be to this edition.

21 "If [Vietnamese women] wished to exercise power, it had to be via their men. This was reflected, for example, in the many folk sayings about wives slaving so that their husbands might become mandarins. If her husband were successful, a wife reaped some reflected glory . . . Perhaps the entire relationship was summed up in the adage, 'A man's property is his wife's work.' The same principle applied to mothers and sons. Vietnamese tradition abounded with mothers who made endless sacrifices for their sons." Marr, *Vietnamese Tradition,* 197–8.

22 As Mary Ellman writes: "By sexual correlation, all energy and enterprise is customarily assigned to male thought, and simple, accretive expectation to female thought." Mary Ellman, *Thinking About Women* (London: MacMillan, 1968), 13.

23 The same point is made by Tran Thi Tuyet: "We could cite numerous examples like those women with children, who could not take the place of their mobilized husbands and were forced to become bar-girls, prostitutes. . . . we would be wrong to believe that these practices are generalized the way an entire section of the Western media would like us

to believe. It is only a temporary phenomenon, common to many other countries at war." Tran Thi Tuyet, "La Femme viêtnamienne," 205.

²⁴ *Bà-Dâm* and *Mirages de Paris* are both set during the colonial period and involve foreign men falling in love with French women in the metropolis.

²⁵ Ly Thu Ho, *Le Mirage de la paix* (Paris: Les Muses du Parnasse, 1986), 119. Further page references, referred to in parentheses in the text, will be to this edition.

²⁶ Jack Yeager suggests that Thu-Thuy's and Huu-Lôc's union represents a "model for the peaceful reunification of North and South," a model that is later brought into question by Huu-Lôc's death in the final days of the war. See Jack A. Yeager, "La Politique "intimiste": la production romanesque des écrivaines vietnamiennes d'expression française," *Présence francophone* 43: 140–1 (1993).

²⁷ Jamieson, *Understanding Vietnam*, 27.

²⁸ Marcia K. Lieberman, "Some Day My Prince Will Come: Female Acculturation through the Fairy Tale," in *Don't Bet on the Prince: Contemporary Feminist Fairy Tales in North America and England*, Jack Zipes, ed. (Aldershot: Gower, 1986), 199–200.

²⁹ Tran Thi Tuyet, *La Femme*, 65.

³⁰ Jayawardena, *Feminism*, 257.

³¹ Carolyn G. Heilbrun, *Reinventing Womanhood* (London: Victor Gollancz, 1979), 72.

³² Jamieson, *Understanding Vietnam*, 295–6.

³³ Jamieson, *Understanding Vietnam*, 296.

³⁴ French, "Afterword," to Edith Wharton, *The Mother's Recompense* (London: Virago, 1986), 352.

³⁵ Trinh T. Minh-ha, *Woman, Native, Other: Writing Postcoloniality and Feminism* (Bloomington: Indiana University Press, 1989), 52.

³⁶ See, for example, Robert Gildea, *France since 1945* (Oxford: Oxford University Press, 1996), 120–6.

Chapter 3: Through Male Eyes

¹ See Lucy Nguyen Hong Nhiem, "Introduction" to Pham Van Ky, *Blood Brothers*, translated by Margaret Mauldon (New Haven: Council on Southeast Asia Studies, Yale Center for International and Area Studies, 1987), vii. Pham Van Ky began working on a doctorate under Marcel Mauss, but the advent of the Second World War and the death of his supervisor put an end to this. See the biographical information on Pham Van Ky in Yeager, *Vietnamese Novel*, 171–2.

2   See Lucy Nguyen Hong Nhiem, "Introduction," vii–viii.

3   Pham Van Ky, *Frères de sang* (Paris: Editions du Seuil, 1947), 27. Further page references, referred to in parentheses in the text, will be to this edition.

4   The Four Virtues are "(*tu duc*): labour (*cong*), physical appearance (*dung*), appropriate speech (*ngon*), and proper behaviour (*hanh*)." Marr, *Vietnamese Tradition*, 192.

5   Vuong-Riddick, "Le drame," 146.

6   "Articles 283–4, 288. He did not have the right to take their lives. Tran Thi Tuyet, "La Femme viêtnamienne," 176.

7   Ralph Smith, *Vietnam and the West* (London: Heinemann, 1968), 60.

8   "*li*: a measure of length, about one third of a mile." Lucy Nguyen Hong Nhiem, "Notes," to Pham Van Ky, *Blood Brothers*, 124.

9   "Polygamy was an accepted institution. . . . It was in any case recognized by custom...This custom has lasted several centuries; it was officially abrogated on January 2, 1959 under law number 1-59." Tran Thi Tuyet, "La Femme viêtnamienne," 55.

10   The word "sapèques" refers to low-value coin currency.

11   Marr, *Vietnamese Tradition*, 196.

12   "The Gia-Long Code decreed the death penalty for the adulterous woman caught in the act. . . . The husband, held up to ridicule, could, if he was vindictive, tie the two accomplices caught in the act on a raft which was then abandoned to drift down a river." Tran Thi Tuyet, "La Femme viêtnamienne," 56 and 58. This was an extreme example. Tran Thi Tuyet goes on to write: "But in general, people confined themselves to making satirical songs about the adulterous wife, or else, the affair was ended with the payment of a fine, by the husband or by the family of the unfaithful wife." Tran Thi Tuyet, "La Femme viêtnamienne," 58.

13   Virginia Thompson, *French Indo-China* (London: George Allen & Unwin Ltd, 1937), 34.

14   Thuong Vuong-Riddick, "Corps et acculturation selon Pham Van Ky," *Présence francophone*, 18: 169 (1979).

15   I am referring to Gayatri Chakravorty Spivak's "subaltern" woman: "there is no space where the subaltern (sexed) subject can speak." Gayatri Chakravorty Spivak, "Can the Subaltern Speak? Speculations on Widow Sacrifice," in *Marxism and the Interpretation of Culture*, Cary Nelson and Lawrence Grossberg, eds. (London: Macmillan, 1988) quoted in Robert Young, *White Mythologies: Writing History and the West* (London: Routledge, 1990), 164.

[16] This sense of alienation will be treated at greater depth in a later chapter.

[17] Marr, *Vietnamese Tradition,* 200.

[18] See Albert Memmi, *Le Racisme: Description, définition, traitement* (Paris: Gallimard, 1982), 47–8.

[19] "As long as he tolerates colonization, the only possible alternatives for the colonized are assimilation or petrifaction." Albert Memmi, *The Colonizer and the Colonized,* translated by Howard Greenfeld (London: Souvenir Press, 1974), 102.

[20] Yeager, *Vietnamese Novel,* 150, 152.

[21] Pham Van Ky, *Des Femmes assises çà et là* (Paris, 1964), 9. Further page references, referred to in parentheses in the text, will be to this edition.

[22] Nguyen Hong Nhiem, "L'Echiquier," 291.

[23] Nguyen Hong Nhiem, "L'Echiquier," 291.

[24] Yeager, *Vietnamese Novel,* 156.

[25] Susan Sontag, *Illness As Metaphor* (Harmondsworth: Penguin, 1983), 22 and 30.

[26] Yeager, *Vietnamese Novel,* 158.

[27] Lisa Lowe, "Literary Nomadics in Francophone Allegories of Postcolonialism: Pham Van Ky and Tahar Ben Jelloun," *Yale French Studies* 82: 51 (1993).

[28] Yeager, *Vietnamese Novel,* 151.

[29] Nguyen Hong Nhiem, "L'Echiquier," 271–2.

[30] I am indebted to Nigel Palmer for this information.

[31] J. Knight Bostock, *A Handbook on Old High German Literature,* second edition, revised by K. C. King and D. R. McLintock (Oxford: Clarendon Press, 1976), 27–8.

[32] "'When we come into the world,' wrote [the philosopher] Chuang Chou, 'it is because we have the occasion to be born; when we go, we simply follow what is natural.' So death is no occasion for sorrow as life is no cause for joy. Bearing this principle in mind, Chuang Chou refrained from wailing at his wife's death; instead, he sat on the ground, singing and beating time on a bowl." Liu Wu-Chi, *A Short History of Confucian Philosophy* (Harmondsworth: Penguin, 1955), 52.

[33] Sontag, *Illness,* 30.

[34] Van, the young and rebellious protagonist of Tran Van Tung's *Bach-Yên,* expresses himself with a similar impetus and violence. The Epilogue of *Bach-Yên* consists of a long and haunted letter from Van to his mother, recording his disillusionment with the West. They express a similar yearning and desperation:

Here rises the wind of Youth!
Here rises the sun of the Mind! Hope, like your nature,
blooms in all souls and in all hearts!
Here lights the dawn of impossible dreams!
Look! Mother, look at this sun!
Look! Look at this flame!
Look! Look at this light! !

    See Tran Van Tung, *Bach-Yên*, 229.

35 Trinh T. Minh-ha, *Woman, Native, Other*, 76.

Chapter 4: Colonial Love

1 The possibility of a relationship between French men and Vietnamese women are not touched on—partly because Vietnamese women seldom had the opportunity to study or to travel overseas. The Vietnamese protagonists in both *Bà-Dâm* and *Nam et Sylvie* are pursuing university studies in France. This indicates a degree of mobility, which, in the 1920s and 1930s, was easier for Vietnamese men than for Vietnamese women. Wealthy families sent sons, rather than daughters, to French universities. The examination of relationships between Vietnamese women and French men only appears in a much later work: Kim Lefèvre's *Retour à la saison des pluies* (see Chapter One). Even then, the liaisons between the Vietnamese mother and the French men are observed from a great distance. *Retour* neither portrays the progression of these relationships nor describes the French men involved. The incidents are episodes from the past. The other account of a relationship between a Vietnamese woman and a Westerner, this time an American, is the one between Xinh and John in Ly Thu Ho's *Au Milieu du carrefour* (see Chapter Two).

2 Alain Ruscio, *Amours coloniales: Aventures et fantasmes exotiques de Claire de Duras à Georges Simenon* (Bruxelles: Editions Complexe, 1996), 16.

3 Hugh Ridley, *Images of Imperial Rule* (London: Croom Helm, 1983), 80.

4 Alec G. Hargreaves, *The Colonial Experience in French Fiction: A Study of Pierre Loti, Ernest Psichari and Pierre Mille* (London: Macmillan Press, 1981), 29.

5 Milton Osborne, "From Conviction to Anxiety: Reassessing the French Self-Image in Viet-Nam," *Flinders University Asian Studies Lecture* 7: 10 (1976).

6 Osborne, "Conviction," 11.

7 Ruscio, *Amours*, 31.

8 Ridley, *Images*, 88–9.

⁹ Ruscio, *Amours*, 31.

¹⁰ Alain Ruscio, *Le Credo de l'homme blanc* (Bruxelles: Editions Complexe, 1996), 221.

¹¹ The *agrégation* is the most prestigious competitive examination for teachers in France.

¹² Truong Dinh Tri et Albert de Teneuille, *Bà-Dâm: Roman Franco-annamite* (Paris: Fasquelle, 1930), 7. Further page references, referred to in parentheses in the main text, will be to this edition.

¹³ Leela Gandhi, *Postcolonial Theory: A Critical Introduction* (New York: Columbia University Press, 1998), 14.

¹⁴ Jennifer Yee, "Colonial Virility and the *Femme Fatale*: Scenes from the Battle of the Sexes in French Indochina," *French Studies* 54 (4): 474 (2000).

¹⁵ Yee, "Colonial Virility," 474.

¹⁶ Jamieson, *Understanding Vietnam*, 97.

¹⁷ As related in Note 16 for the Introduction, the term "Annamite" referred to "Vietnamese" during the colonial period. *Bà-Dâm* reveals its colonial setting in using this vocabulary. Virginia Thompson's *French Indo-China* (published in 1937) also describes the Vietnamese as "Annamites."

¹⁸ Thompson, *Indo-China*, 300.

¹⁹ Yeager, *Vietnamese Novel*, 78.

²⁰ Frantz Fanon, *Black Skin White Masks*, translated by Charles Lam Markmann (London: MacGibbon & Kee, 1968), 63.

²¹ Memmi, *Colonizer*, 121.

²² Okakura Kakuzo, *The Book of Tea* (Rutland: Charles E. Tuttle Company, 1956), 5. Quoted in *Bà-Dâm*, 5.

²³ M. William Steele, "Okakura Kakuzo," *Kodansha Encyclopedia of Japan*, Volume 6 (Tokyo: Kodansha, 1983), 79.

²⁴ Amy Ling, *Between Worlds: Women Writers of Chinese Ancestry* (New York: Pergamon Press, 1990), 24. Ling describes the interesting case of a Eurasian writer in the United States, Winnifred Eaton (1875–1954), born of a Chinese mother and an English father. Her sister, Edith Maud Eaton (1865–1914), wrote under the Chinese pseudonym Sui Sin Far, but "Winnifred...decided to be the admired kind of 'Oriental.' Inventing a Japanese-sounding name, Otono Watanna, she also created an appropriate history, claiming Nagasaki as her birthplace and a Japanese noblewoman for her mother. . . . We do not know whose idea it was to go to such lengths to authenticate a Japanese identity, but apparently the plan worked. Many readers assumed that Otona Watanna possessed an

insider's knowledge of her subject and were charmed by her novels."
Ling, *Between Worlds*, 25.

25 Walter F. Langlois, André Malraux: *The Indochina Adventure* (London: Pall Mall Press, 1966), 55.

26 Langlois, *Malraux*, vii–viii.

27 Langlois, *Malraux*, 126.

28 Langlois, *Malraux*, 126. Langlois' emphasis.

29 Elizabeth Fallaize, *Malraux: La Voie royale* (London: Grant & Cutler Ltd, 1982), 18.

30 Langlois, *Malraux*, 56.

31 Langlois, *Malraux*, 122. Langlois' emphasis.

32 Thompson, *Indo-China*, 444.

33 Thompson, *Indo-China*, 445.

34 Osborne, "Conviction," 24–5.

35 Pham Duy Khiem, *Nam et Sylvie* (Paris: Librairie Plon, 1957), 7. Further page references, referred to in parentheses in the text, will be to this edition.

36 Scott McConnell writes that: "By 1930, radical Vietnamese students made the rejection of social interaction with the French a political imperative. When students who resided at the government-sponsored Indochina House of the *Cité Universitaire* held a dance and invited French girls, the other Vietnamese ripped down the posters and used the event to demonstrate their political and moral superiority." McConnell, *Leftward Journey*, 69. *Nam et Sylvie* makes no mention of this.

37 Karl Ashoka Britto, "History, Memory, and Narrative Nostalgia: Pham Duy Khiem's Nam et Sylvie," *Yale French Studies* 98: 137 (2000).

38 Edward W. Said, *Orientalism* (London: Routledge & Kegan Paul, 1978), 170, 184.

39 Gérard de Nerval, *Les Filles du Feu, Les Chimères* (Paris: Flammarion, 1965), 139.

40 Pham Dan Binh, "Ecrivains vietnamiens de langue française: Création et créativité," *Cahiers d'Etudes Vietnamiennes* 11: 13 (1994–1995).

41 Nerval, *Filles du Feu*, 138.

42 André Lebois gave a speech in honor of Pham Duy Khiem, who was then Vietnamese Ambassador to France, at the University of Toulouse in 1956, in which he implied that *Nam et Sylvie* was autobiographical. He identified Nam with the narrator of Pham Duy Khiem's autobiographical *La Place d'un homme: De Hanoï à la Courtine* (The Place of a Man: From Hanoi to La Courtine) published in 1954. André Lebois, "Le Viêt-Nam et

la Culture Française," *Revue de la Méditerranée,* 17 (4): 639–41 (1957). Pham Duy Khiem denied this link in his answer and went on to state: "There is the ordinary reality and the reality of dreams. Our task, my dear colleague, does it not consist in creating nostalgia and dreams, for others of course, but also for ourselves?" Pham Duy Khiem, "Réponse de M. Pham Duy Khiem," *Revue de la Méditerranée* 17 (4): 651 (1957).

[43] These are two separate sayings. The Vietnamese originals are: "Dong chu cong te" (We will cross the river together) and "Mot ngay nen nghia" (Even one day can create commitment and attachment).

[44] Memmi, *Colonizer,* 107.

[45] Yeager, *Vietnamese Novel,* 82.

[46] Alain Vircondelet, *Duras* (Paris: Editions François Bourin, 1991), 27.

[47] In Marguerite Duras' *Hiroshima mon amour* (Hiroshima My Love) published in 1960, she lays particular emphasis on the fact that the Japanese protagonist should look rather European: "He is a man of around forty. He is tall. His face is rather 'Westernized.'" She gives the following justification for this:

> A Japanese actor who has a marked Japanese look would risk making it seem that it is mostly because the hero is Japanese that the French woman is captivated by him. Thus we would fall again, whether we want to or not, into the trap of exoticism, and the involuntary racism which is necessarily inherent in all exoticism.
>
> The spectator must not stay: "Japanese men are so captivating" but "*This particular man* is so captivating."
>
> This *Franco-Japanese* film must *never* appear *Franco-Japanese* but *anti-Franco-Japanese.* That would be a victory.

Marguerite Duras, *Hiroshima mon amour* (Paris: Editions Gallimard, 1960), 136–7. Duras' emphasis.

[48] Lebois, "Viêt-Nam," 642.

[49] For example, Pierre Loti's descriptions of Japanese women in *Madame Chrysanthème,* the essay *Femmes Japonaises* (Japanese Women) in *L'Exilée* and *La Troisième Jeunesse de Madame Prune.*

[50] Madeleine Rebérioux, "Préface" in Ruscio, *Amours,* 6.

Chapter 5: Divided Loyalties

[1] They both fall under what Philippe Lejeune, in *Le Pacte autobiographique* (The Autobiographical Pact) categorizes as "romans autobiographiques" (autobiographical novels): "In the case of the fictitious name . . . given to a character who tells the story of his life, it can be that the reader has reason

to believe that the story lived by the character corresponds exactly to the author's . . . so that even with the reading of a narrative where the fictional aspect rings false (like when someone tells you: 'This happened to a very good friend I had . . .' and proceeds to tell you the story with a very personal conviction). . . . These texts would therefore enter into the category of 'autobiographical novels': I will so call all fictional texts in which the reader can have reason to suspect, based on similarities that he may guess, that the writer and the character are identical, when the author, on his part, has chosen to deny this or at least not affirm it)." Philippe Lejeune, *Le Pacte autobiographique* (Paris: Editions du Seuil, 1975), 24–5.

2 "In strict terms, autobiography is far from a new art in China but goes back to Ssu-ma Ch'ien in the second century B. C." *Anthology of Chinese Literature*, Cyril Birch, ed., Volume 2: From the 14th Century to the Present Day (New York: Grove Press, Inc., 1972), 259.

   Yeager notes that "The pretext of the *journal trouvé* (discovered diary) was a convention in eighteenth-century French novels, a device used to reinforce the illusion of a fiction's veracity. In his preface the narrator's friend (who found the diary, changed the names, and presented it for publication) places it in the tradition of *La Princesse de Clèves, Dominique, Les Liaisons dangereuses,* and *Madame Bovary,* preparing the reader for what turns out to be a thinly plotted *roman sentimental*." Yeager, *Vietnamese Novel,* 147.

3 "The hundred years from 1570 to 1670 witnessed a deep awareness of the human proclivity to evil, an urgent need to counter this proclivity, a readiness for self-disclosure, and a deep anguish over one's own wrongdoings, all to an extent and with an intensity never known before in Chinese history." Pei-yu Wu, "Self-Examination and Confession of Sins in Traditional China," *Harvard Journal of Asiatic Studies,* 39(6) (1979), quoted in Avrom Fleishman, *Figures of Autobiography* (Berkeley: University of California Press, 1983), 473.

   See, for example, Shen Fu, *Six Records of a Floating Life,* translated by Leonard Pratt and Chiang Su-hui (Harmondsworth: Penguin, 1983).

4 Nguyen The Anh, "Phan Boi Chau's *Memoirs* and the Autobiographical Genre in Modern Vietnamese Literature," Seminar Paper (Oxford: Nissan Institute of Japanese Studies, 1990), 1.

5 Nguyen The Anh, "*Memoirs,*" 2.

6 Nguyen The Anh, "*Memoirs,*" 2.

7 Nguyen The Anh, "*Memoirs,*" 2.

[8] Nguyen Huu Chau, *Les Reflets de nos jours* (Paris: René Julliard, 1955), 9. Further page references, referred to in parentheses in the text, will be to this edition.

[9] Yeager, *Vietnamese Novel*, 150.

[10] Fallaize, *Malraux*, 22.

[11] Fallaize, *Malraux*, 22.

[12] André Malraux, *La Tentation de l'Occident* (Paris: Librairie Bernard Grasset, 1926), 78.

[13] "he was alone with death, alone in a place without men, gently and simultaneously crushed by horror and the taste of blood." André Malraux, *La Condition humaine* (Paris: Librairie Gallimard, 1933), 15.

[14] "During this transitional period, the Vietnamese experienced the erosion and then disappearance of Vichyite French rule under Japanese occupation (July 1940–March 1945), the rise of two "independent" Vietnamese governments (The Empire of Viet-Nam in March 1945 and the Democratic Republic of Viet-Nam in late August 1945), the Allied occupation (1945–1946) and, finally, the first waves of Gaullist French reconquest." Chieu Ngieu Vu, "Political and Social Change in Viet-Nam Between 1940 and 1946." (Ph.D. dissertation, University of Wisconsin-Madison, 1984), xiv.

[15] Yeager, *Vietnamese Novel*, 148.

[16] Yeager, *Vietnamese Novel*, 150.

[17] Pham Duy Khiem, *La Place d'un homme: De Hanoi à la Courtine* (Paris: Librairie Plon, 1958), 1. Further page references, referred to in parentheses in the text, will be to this edition.

[18] Yeager, *Vietnamese Novel*, 177.

[19] "During World War I, France's demands upon her colonies fell most heavily upon Indochina . . . more than 43, 000 Indochinese soldiers and almost 49, 000 workers were sent to Europe." John T. McAlister, Jr., *Viet Nam: The Origins of Revolution* (London: Allen Lane, 1969), 67.

[20] Robert Young, *White Mythologies: Writing History and the West* (London: Routledge, 1990), 8. See Aimé Césaire, *Discours sur le colonialisme* 2eme édition (Paris: Présence Africaine, 1955), 12–3; and Frantz Fanon, *Les Damnés de la terre* (Paris: François Maspéro, 1968), 58.

[21] Yeager, *Vietnamese Novel*, 111.

[22] Jamieson, *Understanding Vietnam*, 172.

[23] Young, *Mythologies*, 147–8.

[24] "The relationship between academic performance and career possibility was muddied by the colonial situation. . . . Vietnamese still were barred

from the highest positions in the administration and judiciary of their country. Careers in politics and the press, though possible, existed only under the confining rules of ultimate French sovereignty." McConnell, *Leftward Journey*, 66.

25 "As Ly Binh Hue, a law student and editor of the moderate *Journal des Etudiants Annamites* put it in an 'open letter' to a compatriot...what was striking about French life was that one was treated with dignity, respect...He stressed that one found in France a completely different species of French man than was in the colony." McConnell, *Leftward Journey*, 59–60.

In Pham Duy Khiem's *Nam et Sylvie*, the protagonist Nam is cognizant of the fact that he enjoys greater freedom as an Vietnamese living in the metropolis than he would as a member of the colonized in his native land. The fate of Sao in Truong Dinh Tri and Albert de Teneuille's *Bà-Dâm* is indicative of this. While Sao's brilliance and academic qualifications are recognized and given credit in Paris, they are disregarded and ignored in French Indochina (see Chapter Four).

26 Accad, "L'Ecriture," 124–5.

27 This tradition persists in autobiographical accounts such as Doan Van Toai, *Le Goulag vietnamien* (Paris: Editions Robert Laffont, 1979), Lucien Trong, *Enfer rouge mon amour* (Paris: Seuil, 1980), and Tran Ti Vu, *Lost Years: My 1,632 days in Vietnamese Reeducation Camps* (Berkeley: Institute of Asian Studies, University of California, 1988).

Chapter 6: Strangers

1 Gerald Cannon Hickey, *Village in Vietnam* (New Haven: Yale University Press, 1964), 276.

2 "In Tongking, it was usual for villages to have thick bamboo hedges which provided an effective local defence against marauders, whereas in Cochinchina such defences are only rarely found." Smith, *Vietnam*, 58.

3 Hammer, *Struggle*, 62. "The life of the people was regulated, according to custom, within the confines of the village, the basic unit of Vietnamese society. . . . The imperial government had no direct contact with the individual but only with his village, which paid taxes and provided men to labor on public works and to serve in the army." Hammer, *Struggle*, 62.

4 Smith, *Vietnam*, 57.

5 "Orme[*sic*]-Paris. Summer–autumn 1946." Pham Van Ky, *Frères de sang* (Paris: Editions du Seuil, 1947). 205. Further page references, referred to in parentheses in the text, will be to this edition.

6 Vuong-Riddick, "Le drame," 144.
7 Nguyen Hong Nhiem, "L'Echiquier," 24.
8 "While in Vietnam, the state of war installs an ideological vice, perhaps as restrictive in the North as in the South, the Vietnamese writer overseas disposes of a much greater margin of maneuver and can also eventually offer himself the luxury of writing during those periods when this activity would have been impossible for those who have stayed in the country. Anyway in 1946, Pham Van Ky published the only Francophone work of that year, with the moreover significant title *L'Homme de nulle part* [The Man from Nowhere], followed the year after by *Frères de sang*." Vuong-Riddick, "Le drame," 144–5.
9 Yeager, *Vietnamese Novel*, 82–3.
10 See Yeager, *Vietnamese Novel*, 82–3; Vuong-Riddick, "Le drame," 143–8; Lucy Nguyen Hong Nhiem, Introduction," vii–xii.
11 Nguyen Hong Nhiem, "L'Echiquier," 83–4.
12 See Barbara G. Walker, *The Woman's Encyclopedia of Myths and Secrets* (San Francisco: Harper, 1983), 669–73.
13 Vuong-Riddick, "Corps et acculturation," 166.
14 Lucy Nguyen Hong Nhiem, "Introduction" to Pham Van Ky, *Blood Brothers*, ix.
15 Vuong-Riddick, "Le drame," 145.
16 Lucy Nguyen Hong Nhiem, "Notes," in *Blood Brothers*, 125.
17 Han-shan, *Cold Mountain* poems, in *Anthology of Chinese Literature*, Cyril Birch, ed. Volume 1: From Early Times to the Fourteenth Century (New York: Grove Press, Inc., 1972), 200.
18 Fanon, *Black Skin*, 189.
19 "White mourning" does exist in the West, but its manifestations are rare. François Mauriac makes a brief reference to this in his novel *Le Nœud de vipères*: "All was white on you, down to your knee-length boots: you were vowed to white, you told me, since the death of your two brothers. I did not know what 'vowed to white' signified. I have learnt, since then, to what extent, in your family, people had a taste for rather bizarre forms of devotion." François Mauriac, *Œuvres romanesques et théâtrales complètes*, *tome II* (Paris: Gallimard, 1979), 401.
20 Nguyen Hong Nhiem, "L'Echiquier," 68.
21 Nguyen Hong Nhiem, "L'Echiquier," 85.
22 Cung Giu Nguyen, *Le Fils de la baleine* (Québec: Editions Naaman, 1978), 22. Further page references, referred to in parentheses in the text, will be to this edition.

23 Yeager, *Vietnamese Novel*, 70.

24 Yeager, *Vietnamese Novel*, 68–9.

25 Smith, *Vietnam*, 57.

26 In the biblical story of Jonah, after "three days and three nights," the great "fish spewed Jonah out on to dry land," (Jonah 1:17 and Jonah 2:10).

27 C. G. Jung, *Symbols of Transformation: An analysis of the prelude to a case of schizophrenia*, translated by R. F. C. Hull, Volume 5 of *C. G. Jung: The Collected Works*, Sir Herbert Read, Michael Fordham and Gerhard Adler, eds. (London: Routledge & Kegan Paul, 1956), 210.

28 "We have . . . spoken about the fierce independence of the commune with respect to the central power and other communes. Another aspect of this tendency to isolationism is precisely that untractable hostility towards any intrusion into its internal life. Refugees (*dan ngu cu*) are treated like pariahs. They have to live on the edge on the village and prove their worth for at least three generations, before they are admitted to the village." Phan Thi Dac, *Situation de la personne au Viet-Nam* (Paris: Editions du Centre National de la Recherche Scientifique, 1966), 30.

29 Yeager, *Vietnamese Novel*, 97.

30 "In fact, the individual in Vietnam exists solely through his commune, the state does not know him." Phan Thi Dac, *Situation de la personne*, 25.

31 Marc Laurent, "Cung Giu Nguyen," 55.

32 This is unlike the situation described by Phan Thi Dac: "The commune, paradoxically, pays homage to the true 'independents' . . . who detach themselves from all relations and duties advocated by all, and live deliberately on the margins of the community. It is the case of those who . . . have retired radically from the 'noisy' and 'mediocre' world of men." Phan Thi Dac, *Situation de la personne*, 35. The old hermit in *Le Fils de la baleine* was not respected by the villagers.

33 Sung Yü, *The Wind*, in Birch, *Anthology*, 136–7.

34 Lucy Nguyen Hong Nhiem, "Introduction," xii.

Conclusion

1 Accad, "L'Ecriture," 121.

2 Interview conducted with Kim Lefèvre in Paris on 15 January 2001.

3 Elisabeth Mudimbe-Boyi, "Préface," *L'Esprit créateur* 33 (2): 7 (1993).

4 Raja Rao, Foreword to his novel *Kanthapura*, quoted in Bill Ashcroft, Gareth Griffiths, and Helen Tiffin, *The Empire Writes Back: Theory and Practice in Post-Colonial Literatures* (London: Routledge, 1989), 61.

5 Kim Lefèvre, *Métisse Blanche* (Paris: Bernard Barrault, 1989), 339.

6 Stuart Hall, "Introduction: Who Needs Identity?" in *Questions of Cultural Identity*, Stuart Hall and Paul du Gay, eds. (London: Sage Publications, 1996), 4.

7 David G. Marr, *Vietnamese Anticolonialism 1885-1925* (Berkeley: University of California, 1971), 7.

8 Marr, *Vietnamese Anticolonialism*, 8.

9 Jamieson, *Understanding Vietnam*, 339.

10 Mudimbe-Boyi, "Préface," 5.

11 Leakthina Chau-Pech Ollier, "Consuming Culture: Linda Lê's Autofiction" in *Of Vietnam*, Winston and Ollier, eds., 241.

12 Leakthina Chau-Pech Ollier, "Consuming Culture," 243.

13 See for example Phan Huy Duong's *Un Amour métèque: Nouvelles* (Paris: L'Harmattan, 1994).

14 Homi K. Bhabha, "Culture's In-Between" in *Questions of Cultural Identity*, Stuart Hall and Paul du Gay, eds. (London: Sage Publications, 1996), 54.

References

Accad, Evelyne
1993   "L'Ecriture (comme) éclatement des frontières." *L'Esprit créateur* 33 (2): 119–28.

Anderson, Bonnie S., and Judith P. Zinsser
1990   *A History of Their Own: Women in Europe from Prehistory to the Present.* 2 vols. London: Penguin.

Ashcroft, Bill, Gareth Griffiths, and Helen Tiffin
1989   *The Empire Writes Back: Theory and Practice in Post-Colonial Literatures.* London: Routledge.

Aston, W. G.
1972   *A History of Japanese Literature.* New edition. Rutland, Vermont: Charles E. Tuttle Company.

Baruch, Jacques
1961   *Notes sur le poème Viêt-Namien Kim-Vân-Kiêu de Nguyên-Du.* Casteau, Belgique: Chez l'auteur.

Beauvoir, Simone de
1953   *The Second Sex.* Translated and edited by H. M. Parshley. London: Jonathan Cape.

Benstock, Shari (editor)
1988   *The Private Self: Theory and Practice of Women's Autobiographical Writings.* London: Routledge.

Bhabha, Homi K.
1996   "Culture's In-Between." In *Questions of Cultural Identity.* Stuart Hall and Paul du Gay, eds. 53–60. London: Sage Publications.

Birch, Cyril (editor)
1965   *Anthology of Chinese Literature.* Vol. 1: From Early Times to the Fourteenth Century. New York: Grove Press, Inc.

1972   *Anthology of Chinese Literature.* Vol. 2: From the 14th century to the Present Day. New York: Grove Press, Inc.

Bostock, J. Knight
1976   *A Handbook on Old High German Literature.* 2nd edition. Revised by K. C. King and D. R. McLintock. Oxford: Clarendon Press.

Britto, Karl Ashoka
1998   "Disorientation: Interculturality and Identity in Vietnamese Francophone Literature." Ph.D. dissertation, Yale University.

2000   "History, Memory, and Narrative Nostalgia: Pham Duy Khiem's *Nam et Sylvie.*" *Yale French Studies* 98: 135–48.

Bui Xuan Bao
1985   *Naissance et évolution du roman vietnamien moderne 1925–1945.* Paris: Duong Moi La voie nouvelle. Originally published in Saigon: Tu Sach Nhan-Van Xa Hoi, 1972.

Buttinger, Joseph
1969   *Vietnam: A Political History.* London: André Deutsch.

Cao Thi Nhu-Quynh and John C. Schafer
1988   "From Verse Narrative to Novel: The Development of Prose Fiction in Vietnam." *The Journal of Asian Studies* 47 (4): 756–77.

Césaire, Aimé
1955   *Discours sur le colonialisme.* 2eme édition. Paris: Présence Africaine.

Chesneaux, Jean, Georges Boudarel, et Daniel Hemery (editors)
1971   *Tradition et révolution au Vietnam*. Paris: Editions Anthropos.

Chieu Ngu Vu
1984   "Political and Social Change in Viet-Nam between 1940 and 1946." Madison, Wis.: Ph.D. dissertation, University of Wisconsin-Madison.

Christian, Barbara
1985   *Black Feminist Criticism: Perspectives on Black Women Writers*. The Athene Series. New York: Pergamon Press.

Clergerie, Bernard
1962   "Essai de prospective pour l'ancienne Indochine." *Esprit* 30 (11): 723–36.

Cong Huyen Ton Nu Nha Trang
1987   "Women Writers of South Vietnam (1954-1975)." *The Vietnam Forum* 9: 149–221.

Cung Giu Nguyen
1978   *Le Fils de la baleine*. Sherbrooke, Québec: Editions Naaman. Originally published in Paris: Fayard, 1956.

Doan Van Toai
1979   *Le Goulag vietnamien*. Récit receuilli par Michel Voirol. Paris: Editions Robert Laffont.

Duncanson, Dennis J.
1968   *Government and Revolution in Vietnam*. London: Oxford University Press.

Durand, Maurice M., and Nguyen Tran Huan
1985   *An Introduction to Vietnamese Literature.* Translated by D. M. Hawke. New York: Columbia University Press. Originally published as *Introduction à la littérature vietnamienne* (Paris, Editions G.-P. Maisonneuve et Larose, 1969).

Duras, Marguerite
1960   *Hiroshima mon amour.* Paris: Editions Gallimard.

1984   *L'Amant.* Paris: Les Editions de Minuit.

Ellman, Mary
1968   *Thinking about Women.* London: MacMillan.

Fallaize, Elizabeth
1982   *Malraux: La Voie royale.* London: Grant & Cutler Ltd.

Fanon, Frantz
1968a   *Black Skin White Masks.* Translated by Charles Lam Markmann. London: MacGibbon & Kee.

1968b   *Les Damnés de la terre.* Paris: François Maspéro.

Figes, Eva
1978   *Patriarchal Attitudes: Women in Society.* London: Virago.

Fleishman, Avron
1983   *Figures of Autobiography: The Language of Self-Writing.* Berkeley: University of California Press.

French, Marilyn
1986   "Afterword." In *The Mother's Recompense.* Edith Wharton. 343–53. London: Virago.

Friedman, Susan Stanford
1988   "Women's Autobiographical Selves: Theory and Practice."
        In *The Private Self: Theory and Practice of Women's
        Autobiographical Writings.* Shari Benstock, ed. 34–62. London:
        Routledge.

Gandhi, Leela
1998   *Postcolonial Theory: A Critical Introduction.* New York:
        Columbia University Press.

Gazarian Gautier, Marie-Lise
1989   *Interviews with Latin American Writers.* Elmwood Park, IL:
        Dalkey Archive Press.

Gildea, Robert
1996   *France since 1945.* Oxford: Oxford University Press.

Greer, Germaine
1991   *The Female Eunuch.* 21st anniversary edition. London:
        Paladin.

Hall, D. G. E.
1968   *A History of South-East Asia.* 3rd edition. London: Macmillan.

Hall, Stuart
1996   "Introduction: Who Needs Identity?" In *Questions of Cultural
        Identity.* Stuart Hall and Paul du Gay, eds. 1–17. London:
        Sage Publications.

Hall, Stuart and Paul du Gay (editors)
1996   *Questions of Cultural Identity.* London: Sage Publications.

Hammer, Ellen J.
1954   *The Struggle for Indochina.* Stanford: Stanford University
        Press.

Hargreaves, Alec G.
1981   *The Colonial Experience in French Fiction: A Study of Pierre Loti, Ernest Psichari and Pierre Mille.* London: Macmillan Press.

Heilbrun, Carolyn G.
1979   *Reinventing Womanhood.* London: Victor Gollancz Ltd.

Hickey, Gerald Cannon
1964   *Village in Vietnam.* New Haven: Yale University Press.

Ho Xuan Huong
2000   *Spring Essence: The Poetry of Ho Xuan Huong.* Edited and translated by John Balaban. Washington: Copper Canyon Press.

Hoang Ngoc Thanh
1991   *Vietnam's Social and Political Development as Seen through the Modern Novel.* New York: Peter Lang.

Hoang Van Chi
1964   *From Colonialism to Communism: A Case History of North Vietnam.* London: Pall Mall Press.

Hue, B., Henri Copin, Pham Dan Binh, Patrick Laude, et Patrick Meadows
1999   *Littératures de la péninsule indochinoise.* Collection Universités francophones. Paris: Editions Karthala.

Huu Ngoc et Françoise Corrèze
1984   *Fleurs de pamplemoussier: Femmes et poésie au Vietnam.* Paris: Editions l'Harmattan.

Huynh Sanh Thong
1983   "Introduction." In *The Tale of Kieu.* Nguyen Du. Translated by Huynh Sanh Thong. xix–xl. New Haven: Yale University Press.

Jamieson, Neil L.
1995   *Understanding Vietnam*. Berkeley: University of California Press.

Jayawardena, Kumari
1986   *Feminism and Nationalism in the Third World*. London: Zed Books Ltd.

Joubert, Jean-Louis (editor)
1997   *Littératures francophones d'Asie et du Pacifique: Anthologie*. Paris: Editions Nathan.

Jung, C. G.
1956   *Symbols of Transformation: An analysis of the prelude to a case of schizophrenia*. Translated by R. F. C. Hull, Vol. 5 of *C. G. Jung: The Collected Works*. Edited by Sir Herbert Read, Michael Fordham and Gerhard Adler. London: Routledge & Kegan Paul.

Kristeva, Julia
1991   *Strangers to Ourselves*. Translated by Leon S. Roudiez. London: Harvester Wheatsheaf.

Lai Ming
1964   *A History of Chinese Literature*. London: Cassell.

Langlois, Walter C.
1966   *André Malraux: The Indochina Adventure*. London: Pall Mall Press.

Laurent, Marc
1972   "Cung Giu Nguyen: Ecrivain viêtnamien de langue française." *Présence francophone* 5: 53–9.

Le Thanh Khoi
1955   *Le Viêt-Nam: Histoire et civilisation.* Paris: Les Editions de Minuit.

Lê, Linda
1992   *Les Evangiles du crime.* Paris: Julliard.

1998   *Voix: Une crise.* Paris: Christian Bourgois.

Lebois, André
1957   "Le Viêt-Nam et la Culture Française." *Revue de la Mediterranée* 17 (4): 635–44.

Lefèvre, Kim
1989   *Métisse Blanche.* Paris: Editions Bernard Barrault.

1990   *Retour à la saison des pluies.* Paris: Editions Bernard Barrault.

Leifer, Michael (editor)
1970   *Nationalism, Revolution and Evolution in Southeast Asia.* Hull: Hull Monographs on SEA no. 2.

Lejeune, Philippe
1975   *Le Pacte autobiographique.* Paris: Editions du Seuil.

Les Editeurs Français Réunis
1969   *Anthologie de la poésie vietnamienne.* Paris: Les Editeurs Français Réunis.

Lieberman, Marcia K.
1986   "Some Day My Prince Will Come: Female Acculturation through the Fairy Tale." In *Don't Bet on the Prince: Contemporary Feminist Fairy Tales in North America and England.* Jack Zipes, ed. 186–200. Aldershot, U.K.: Gower.

Lim-Hing, Sharon Julie
1993   "Vietnamese Novels in French: Rewriting Self, Gender and Nation." Ph.D. dissertation, Harvard University.

Lin Yutang (editor)
1942   *The Wisdom of China and India.* New York: Random House.

Ling, Amy
1990   *Between Worlds: Women Writers of Chinese Ancestry.* The Athene Series. New York: Pergamon Press.

Liu Wu-Chi
1955   *A Short History of Confucian Philosophy.* Harmondsworth: Penguin.

1966   *An Introduction to Chinese Literature.* Bloomington: Indiana University Press.

Loti, Pierre
1905   *La Troisième Jeunesse de Madame Prune.* Paris: Calmann-Lévy.

1988   *Madame Chrysanthème* suivi de *Femmes Japonaises.* Pardès: Puiseaux.

Lowe, Lisa
1993   "Literary Nomadics in Francophone Allegories of Postcolonialism: Pham Van Ky and Tahar Ben Jelloun." *Yale French Studies* 82: 43–61.

Ly Thu Ho
1962   *Printemps inachevé.* Paris: J. Peyronnet et Cie, Editeurs.

1969   *Au milieu du carrefour.* Paris: Editions Peyronnet.

1986   *Le Mirage de la paix.* Paris: Les Muses du Parnasse.

Malraux, André
1926   *La Tentation de l'Occident.* Paris: Librairie Bernard Grasset.

1933   *La Condition humaine.* Paris: Librairie Gallimard.

Marr, David G.
1971   *Vietnamese Anticolonialism 1885–1925.* Berkeley: University of California Press.

1981   *Vietnamese Tradition on Trial, 1920–1945.* Berkeley: University of California Press.

Mauriac, François
1972   *Œuvres romanesques et théâtrales complètes.* Tome II. Paris: Gallimard.

McAlister, John T., Jr.
1969   *Viet Nam: The Origins of Revolution.* London: Allen Lane.

McConnell, Scott
1989   *Leftward Journey: The Education of Vietnamese Students in France 1919–1939.* New Brunswick: Transaction Publishers.

Memmi, Albert
1974   *The Colonizer and the Colonized.* Translated by Howard Greenfeld. London: Souvenir Press.

1982   *Le Racisme: Description, définition, traitement.* Paris: Gallimard.

Mills, Jane
1991   *Womanwords: A Vocabulary of Culture and Patriarchal Society.* London: Virago.

Mudimbe-Boyi, Elisabeth
1993   "Préface." *L'Esprit créateur* 33 (2): 5–7.

Mus, Paul, et John McAlister, Jr.
1972   *Les Viêtnamiens et leur révolution*. Paris: Editions du Seuil.

Nerval, Gérard de
1965   *Les Filles du Feu*. Paris: Flammarion.

Nguyen Du
1884   *Kim Vân Kiêu tân truyên*. Publié et traduit pour la première fois par Abel des Michels. Paris: E. Leroux.

1952   *Kim Vân Kiêu*. Traduction en français avec notes et commentaires du Kiêu de Nguyen Du par Nguyen Van Vinh. Saigon: Les Editions Vinhbao-Hoanhson.

1961   *Kim Vân Kiêu*. Traduit par Xuan-Phuc et Xuan-Viet. Paris: Gallimard/Unesco.

1983   *The Tale of Kiêu*. A bilingual edition translated by Huynh Sanh Thong. New Haven: Yale University Press.

Nguyen Hong Nhiem, Lucy
1982   "L'Echiquier et l'antinomie Je/Moi comme signe et substance du conflit Occident/Extrême-Orient dans les œuvres de Pham Van Ky." Massachusetts: Ph.D. dissertation, University of Massachusetts.

1987a   "Introduction." In *Blood Brothers*. Pham Van Ky. Translated by Margaret Mauldon. The Lac-Viet Series No. 7. vii–xii. New Haven: Council on Southeast Asia Studies, Yale Center for International and Area Studies.

1987b   "Notes." In *Blood Brothers*. Pham Van Ky. Translated by Margaret Mauldon. The Lac-Viet Series No. 7. 122–31. New Haven: Council on Southeast Asia Studies, Yale Center for International and Area Studies.

Nguyen Huu Chau
1955   *Les Reflets de nos jours*. Paris: René Julliard.

Nguyen The Anh
1989   "Vietnam." In *South-East Asia Languages and Literatures: A Select Guide*. Patricia Herbert and Anthony Milner, eds. 77–98. Arran, Scotland: Kiscadale Publications.

1990   "Phan Boi Chau's Memoirs and the Autobiographical Genre in Modern Vietnamese Literature." Paper presented at the Nissan Institute of Japanese Studies, Oxford, November 20: 1–10.

Nguyen Tien Lang
1935   *Indochine la douce*. Hanoi: Editions Nam Ky.

Nguyen Tran Huan
1973a   "La littérature vietnamienne de langue française." *Culture française* 22 (1): 6–23.

1973b   "Des difficultés de l'édition française au Vietnam." *Culture française* 22 (4): 40–43.

Nguyen Trieu Dan
1991   *A Vietnamese Family Chronicle: Twelve Generations on the Banks of the Hat River*. Jefferson, N.C.: McFarland & Company, Inc., Publishers.

Nguyen Xuan Thu (editor)
1994   *Vietnamese Studies in a Multicultural World*. Melbourne: Vietnamese Language and Culture Publications.

Nguyen, Cam
1985   "Women of the World: The Vietnamese." *Women at Work* March–May: 2–3.

1992 "East, West and Vietnamese women." *Journal of Vietnamese Studies* 5: 44–50.

1994 "Barriers to Communication between Vietnamese and Non-Vietnamese." In *Vietnamese Studies in a Multicultural World.* Nguyen Xuan Thu, ed. 65–72. Melbourne: Vietnamese Language and Culture Publications.

Nguyen, Nathalie
2000 "A Classical Heroine and her Modern Manifestation: *The Tale of Kieu* and Its Modern Parallels in *Printemps inachevé.*" *The French Review* 73 (3): 454–62.

2001a "Writing and Memory in Kim Lefèvre's Autobiographical Narratives." *Intersections: Gender, History and Culture in the Asian Context* Issue 5: 1–13. URL: http://wwwsshe.murdoch.edu.au/intersections/issue5/nathalie.html.

2001b "Métisse Blanche: Entretien avec Kim Lefèvre." *Intersections: Gender, History and Culture in the Asian Context* Issue 5: 1–8. URL: http://wwwsshe.murdoch.edu.au/intersections/issue5/nguyen_interview.html.

2001c "Across Colonial Borders: Patriarchal Constraints and Vietnamese Women in the Novels of Ly Thu Ho." In *Of Vietnam: Identities in Dialogue.* Jane Bradley Winston and Leakthina Chau-Pech Ollier, eds. 193–210. New York: Palgrave.

Norindr, Panivong
1996 *Phantasmatic Indochina: French Colonial Ideology in Architecture, Film, and Literature.* Durham: Duke University Press.

Okakura Kakuzo
1956   *The Book of Tea*. Rutland, Vermont: Charles E. Tuttle Company.

Ollier, Leakthina Chau-Pech
2001   "Consuming Culture: Linda Lê's Autofiction." In *Of Vietnam: Identities in Dialogue*. Jane Bradley Winston and Leakthina Chau-Pech Ollier, eds. 241–50. New York: Palgrave.

Orbach, Susie
1993   *Hunger Strike: The Anorectic's Struggle as a Metaphor for our Age*. Revised ed. London: Penguin Books.

Osborne, Milton
1976   "From Conviction to Anxiety: The French Self-Image in Viet-Nam." *Flinders Asian Studies Lecture* 7: 1–27. F1–F6.

Pham Danh Binh
1994–5 "Ecrivains vietnamiens de langue française: Création et créativité." *Cahiers d'Etudes Vietnamiennes* 11: 9–22.

Pham Duy Khiem
1957a   *Nam et Sylvie*. Paris: Librairie Plon.

1957b   "Réponse de M. Pham Duy Khiem." *Revue de la Méditerranée* 17 (4): 645–51

1958   *La Place d'un homme: De Hanoï à la Courtine*. Paris: Librairie Plon.

Pham Van Ky
1947   *Frères de sang*. Paris: Editions du Seuil.

1964   *Des Femmes assises çà et là*. Paris: Editions Gallimard.

1987 *Blood Brothers.* Translated by Margaret Mauldon. Introduction and Notes by Lucy Nguyen. The Lac-Viet Series No. 7. New Haven: Council on Southeast Asia Studies, Yale Center for International and Area Studies.

Phan Huy Duong
1994 *Un Amour métèque: Nouvelles.* Paris: L'Harmattan.

Phan Thi Dac
1966 *Situation de la personne au Viet-Nam.* Paris: Editions du Centre National de la Recherche Scientifique.

Rebérioux, Madeleine
1996 "Préface." In *Amours coloniales: Aventures et fantasmes exotiques de Claire de Duras à Georges Simenon.* Alain Ruscio. 5–7. Bruxelles: Editions Complexe.

Ridley, Hugh
1983 *Images of Imperial Rule.* London: Croom Helm.

Rousseau, Jean-Jacques
1991 *Emile or On Education.* Translated by Allan Bloom. London: Penguin.

Ruscio, Alain
1996 *Amours coloniales: Aventures et fantasmes exotiques de Claire de Duras à Georges Simenon.* Bruxelles: Editions Complexe.

1996 *Le Crédo de l'homme blanc.* Bruxelles: Editions Complexe.

Said, Edward W.
1978 *Orientalism: Western Conceptions of the Orient.* London: Routledge & Kegan Paul.

Shen Fu
1983   *Six Records of a Floating Life*. Translated by Leonard Pratt and Chiang Su-hui. Harmondsworth: Penguin.

Smith, Ralph
1968   *Viet-Nam and the West*. London: Heinemann.

1970   "Antecedents of the 'Viet-Cong.'" In *Nationalism, Revolution and Evolution in South-East Asia*. Edited by Michael Leifer. 1–15. Hull: Hull Monographs on Southeast Asia.

1972   "The Vietnamese Elite of French Cochinchina, 1943." *Modern Asian Studies* 6 (4): 459–82.

Socé, Ousmane
1948   *Mirages de Paris*. 2eme edition. Paris: Nouvelles Editions Latines.

Sontag, Susan
1983   *Illness as Metaphor*. Harmondsworth: Penguin.

Spivak, Gayatri Chakravorty
1988   "Can the Subaltern Speak? Speculations on Widow Sacrifice." In *Marxism and the Interpretation of Culture*. Edited by Cary Nelson and Lawrence Grossberg. 271–313. London: Macmillan.

Schafer, John C. and The Uyen
1993   "The Novel Emerges in Cochinchina." *The Journal of Asian Studies* 52 (4): 854–84.

Steele, M. William
1983   "Okakura Kakuzo." *Kodansha Encyclopedia of Japan*. Volume 6. Tokyo: Kodansha. 79.

Ta Van Tai
1981　"The status of women in traditional Vietnam: A comparison of the code of the Lê dynasty (1428–1788) with the Chinese codes." *Journal of Asian History* 15: 97–145.

Thompson, Virginia
1937　*French Indo-China.* London: George Allen & Unwin Ltd.

Tran Thi Tuyet
1974　"La Femme viêtnamienne à travers la littérature populaire." Brussels: Ph.D. dissertation, University of Brussels.

Tran Tri Vu
1988　*Lost Years: my 1,632 days in Vietnamese reeducation camps.* Berkeley: Institute of Asian Studies, University of California.

Tran Van Tung
1946　*Bach-Yên ou la fille au cœur fidèle.* Paris: J. Susse.

Trinh T. Minh-Ha
1989　*Woman, Native, Other: Writing Postcoloniality and Feminism.* Bloomington: Indiana University Press.

Trinh Thuc Oanh et Marguerite Triaire
1939　*En s'écartant des ancêtres.* Hanoi: Imprimerie d'Extrême-Orient.

Trong, Lucien
1980　*Enfer rouge mon amour.* Paris: Seuil.

Truong Dinh Tri et Albert de Teneuille
1930　*Bà-Dâm: Roman franco-annamite.* Paris: Fasquelle.

Vircondelet, Alain
1991　*Duras.* Paris: Editions François Bourin.

Vuong-Riddick, Thuong
1970   "Le drame de l'occidentalisation dans quelques romans de Pham Van Ky." *Présence francophone* 16: 141–52.

1979   "Corps et acculturation selon Pham Van Ky." *Présence francophone* 18: 165–76.

Walder, Dennis
1998   *Post-Colonial Literatures in English: History, Language, Theory.* Oxford: Blackwell Publishers.

Walker, Barbara G.
1983   *The Woman's Encyclopedia of Myths and Secrets.* San Francisco: Harper.

Winston, Jane Bradley
2001a   "Introduction: Projected Identities/ Subversive Practices." In *Of Vietnam: Identities in Dialogue.* Jane Bradley Winston and Leakthina Chau-Pech Ollier, eds. 1–15. New York: Palgrave.

2001b   *Postcolonial Duras: Cultural Memory in Postwar France.* New York: Palgrave.

Winston, Jane Bradley and Leakthina Chau-Pech Ollier (editors)
2001   *Of Vietnam: Identities in Dialogue.* New York: Palgrave.

Woodside, Alexander
1983   "The Historical Background." In *The Tale of Kieu.* Nguyen Du. Translated by Huynh Sanh Thong. xi–xviii. New Haven: Yale University Press.

Yeager, Jack A.
1987   *The Vietnamese Novel in French: A Literary Response to Colonialism.* Hanover: University Press of New England.

1993 "La Politique "intimiste": la production romanesque des écrivaines vietnamiennes d'expression française." *Présence francophone* 43: 131–47.

2001 "Colonialism and Power in Marguerite Duras' *The Lover*." In *Of Vietnam: Identities in Dialogue*. Jane Bradley Winston and Leakthina Chau-Pech Ollier, eds. 1–15. New York: Palgrave.

Yee, Jennifer
2000 "Colonial Virility and the *Femme Fatale*: Scenes from the Battle of the Sexes in French Indochina." *French Studies* 54 (4): 469–78.

Young, Robert
1990 *White Mythologies: Writing History and the West*. London: Routledge.

Zipes, Jack (editor)
1986 *Don't Bet on the Prince: Contemporary Feminist Fairy Tales in North America and England*. Aldershot, U.K.: Gower.

Index

women 200
Jayawardena, Kumari, 69, 190,
  191, 194
Jung, Carl G., 167, 205
Kim-Van-Kieu. See Tale of Kieu
Kristeva, Julia, 10, 187
Lai Ming, 190
Lament of a Royal Concubine, 31
Lament of a Soldier's Wife, 31
Langlois, Walter, 112, 199
Laurent, Marc, 172, 187, 205
Le Thanh Khoi, 186
Le Van Phat, 6, 186
Lê, Linda, 180–182, 206
Lebois, André, 127, 199, 200
Lefèvre, Kim, 8, 13, 39–43, 45,
  175, 177, 178, 180, 182, 189, 190,
  197, 205
Lejeune, Philippe, 200, 201
Lin Yutang, 192
Lieberman, Marcia K., 67, 194
Ling, Amy, 111, 198, 199
literary
  allusions, 19
  and historical allusions, 31
  device, 23
  differences between East and
    West, 2
  essays, 4
  form, 31
  genres, 3
  merits, 19
  norms, 2
  output, 1
  past, 31
  traditions, 31
  war, 4
*Littératures de la péninsule
  indochinoise*, viii, 184

*Littératures francophones d'Asie et
  du Pacifique*, viii, 184
Liu Wu-Chi, 189, 190, 192, 196
Loti, Pierre, 105, 125, 127, 197, 200
Lowe, Lisa, 95, 196
luc-bat, 13
Ly Thu Ho, 8, 9, 13, 35, 38, 39, 46–
  48, 50, 57, 58, 63, 64, 67, 71, 74,
  190, 192–194, 197
magical realism, 182
Maison d'Indochine, 5
malaise, 2, 102, 178
  cultural, 106, 177
male
  author, 12, 16
  colonial subject, 104, 120
  creator, 39
  military personnel, 68
  narrator, 9, 178
  protagonists, 10, 30, 71, 132,
    177
  writers, 71, 175–177
Malraux, André, 112, 133, 199,
  202
mandarinate, 4
mandarins, 4, 16, 24, 28, 30, 33,
  77, 87, 155
Marr, David G., 83, 87, 180, 188,
  189, 192, 193, 195, 196, 206
marriage
  arranged, 26, 30
  empty, 29
  end of the story, 67
  expectations of, 28
  forced, 30
  girls groomed for, 52
  inheritance and, 17
  male infidelity in, 52
  modern, 28
  platonic, 38, 39